GRANT ME *Serenity*

JANALEE CARD CHMEL

Janalee Card Chmel

PAROS PRESS
Denver

AFFILIATED PUBLISHERS
DENVER · MILWAUKEE · VANCOUVER B.C.

For information, contact Paros Press,
1551 Larimer Street, Suite 1301, Denver, CO 80202.
www.parospress.com

Publisher's Cataloging-in-Publication Data

Chmel, Janalee Card.
Grant me serenity / Janalee Card Chmel. -- 1st ed.
p. cm.
LCCN: 2001086002
ISBN: 0-9702093-0-4

1. Liver—Cancer—Patients—Family relationships.
2. Terminally ill—Family relationships. 3. Grief.
4. Terminal care. 5. Chmel, Sylvia. 6. Liver—Cancer—
Patients—Biography. I. Title.
RC280.L5c46 2001 616.99'436
QBI01-200061

Book Design by Scott Johnson

Printed in the United States of America
1 3 5 7 9 10 8 6 4 2

PART 1

Courage

PART 2

Wisdom

PART 3

Acceptance

PART 4

Serenity

Grant me Serenity

To accept the things I cannot change,

Courage to change the things I can, and

Wisdom to know the difference

This book is dedicated

to my mom and her extraordinary sunsets.

Jennifer, you gave me life again.

Judy, you carried my dreams in your heart when I lost hope.

Dave, my love, you give life and dreams meaning.

Dear Reader,

I'm sitting at my desk, pen to notepad, early on a wintry Thursday morning. A final proof of "Grant Me Serenity" sits with me, next to my coffee cup. Soon, it will be on a press. What an amazing process it's been.

Why did I write this book? I look at it now, all dressed up and looking professional, and I smile at its crude beginnings. On January 6, 1993 – the day after doctors found Mom's tumor – I began journaling. My fear was so overwhelming that the only way I could face it was to put it down. Get it out. I tried to carry my journal with me everywhere during Mom's illness. On the occasions when I didn't have it with me, I asked strangers, nurses, and friends for paper and a pen. Journaling helped me name and face my fears.

About three years after Mom died, I discovered that I still had fears and the need to put them down. I was reading "Motherless Daughters" by Hope Edelman and it was the first book I'd found that explored emotions and fears. So many other books explained grief in "phases" and told me I was "normal," when nothing in my life felt normal. "Motherless Daughters," instead gave me stories of other people in pain, and their stories allowed me to feel my own pain. Then, I could grow.

I decided to write my story for the same reasons that I kept a journal. I had to. The first three sections of the book gushed from my pen and I kept it all in coffee-stained notepads. The fourth section, though, was different. That section, "Serenity," is about my healing journey after Mom's death and I struggled to put words around my experience. Again, I look now at this tidy book, ready to go to the printer, and I nearly laugh out loud. It was a mess! But so was I, I suppose. Out of that mess came the words. And, ultimately, the words helped me to discover the lessons I had learned and will continue to learn.

So, this is my story, my journey. Mom's been gone more than seven years now, which simply feels impossible. I can feel her with me, though, as I sit here at my desk staring at the final proof of my book. And Mom's yakking it up in heaven (aka the Rocky Mountains) saying, "That's my daughter!" She's been with me all along.

Janalee
January 4, 2001

Courage

Chapter 1

The nightmare started with a death. Someone else's death, fortunately. Not my mother's. But it started with someone's death and that someone was in a long, black hearse followed by more than forty cars. I followed my mother to the doctor's office to learn if the big, black spot they found on her liver three days ago was cancer.

Mom drove that Nissan Stanza wagon I hated so much. Why she traded the Ford Ranger in for that thing, I never understood. She was a woman who belonged in a truck. The Ranger had represented her freedom.

"I never want to borrow someone else's truck to haul my stuff around," she had said.

Now she was in that wimpy, powder-blue wagon. Sure, it had

four-wheel drive, which she liked, but it looked so family. At 24, I hadn't lived at home for more than seven years and my brother was steaming around the world in the Navy. She opted for a wagon?

"Makes no sense," I said aloud in my own, wimpy Subaru hatchback. My excuse was financial. "Makes no sense."

That statement, so applicable to my current situation, dropped me back into reality.

I watched the caravan of mourners behind the hearse and I looked at the back of Mom's Nissan, hoping my little follow-the-leader routine was not a smaller version of the mourners' display.

Four days earlier, Mom had gone to the doctor with severe stomach pains. Every time she ate, her belly puffed up like an overfilled balloon. She'd had the pain for several weeks but assumed it was stress-related and thought maybe her hernia had returned. She ignored the pain and told only her sister, my Aunt Margie, who was out from San Diego for Mom's 50th birthday.

But when the pain became so intense that Mom's companion and lover of 10 years, Chuck, couldn't touch her without her screaming, she decided to go to the doctor.

That was a Monday. That night, I called to see how the appointment had gone. I expected her to say she received some pills and all would be fine.

"They need me to go back tomorrow for the results of some tests, babe," she said. "They couldn't figure anything out today."

"What do they think it is?" I asked, my voice ringing hollowly across my Denver apartment. Mom lived two hours south in a small town called Cañon City. I had just stepped out of a hot bath, the green silk pajamas Mom had given me a week earlier for Christmas clung to my wet skin. My hair dripped onto my shoulders, turning the pajamas a darker green. Brooke, my roommate, pushed her way past me into the bathroom.

"I mean, what did they test?"

"Oh, they ran all kinds of tests. I'm not sure. I'll know more tomorrow. It's best to wait until tomorrow."

Vagueness didn't suit Mom. She was the most straightforward

person I'd ever known — painfully so, sometimes. I didn't believe that she allowed tests to be performed on her without knowing their exact purpose.

"Mom?" I said simply. Then she said the three words that made me realize the news was bad. Very bad.

"Are you alone?"

"Mom, what is it? What's wrong?" Panic gripped me. I grabbed the phone base and walked into the hall, looking at Brooke in the bathroom. She stopped brushing her teeth and walked up to me. Her eyes mirrored my fear and I immediately saw in her my reflected terror.

"Are you alone? Is Brooke there, honey?"

"She's here!" I said furiously. "With me! What is it?"

No response.

"Say something!" I handed the phone to Brooke.

"I'm here, Sylvia," Brooke said.

I took the phone back.

"Mom, what is it? What is it!"

"Honey, they think they've found a tumor in my liver ..."

I lost all strength in my legs and sank down in the hallway. Mom talked to me about her day with the doctors, but we ended the conversation when there was simply nothing more to share. We had to wait until tomorrow. I began sobbing as soon as I hung up the phone.

"I'm so scared, Brooke," I said through tears.

Brooke didn't say anything, but curled up with me on the floor and rocked me in her arms. My knees were pulled tightly to my chest and tears soaked my pajamas. I rocked and rocked and rocked. My mind aborted the news, ejected it, but my body felt the aftershocks. For one brief moment, I felt that I could have stayed there in the hallway and rocked myself in that position until I died. Reality was rocking. Rocking.

The next four days were a small capsule of what the next seven months would be like. Doctors tested. We waited and hoped and prayed. We didn't sleep, tried to smile, and acted as though everything was normal.

After only four days, I thought I'd paid my dues, that we'd all coped valiantly, and that our reward would be a complete cure. Four days. If I had known then that the next seven months held only the same, I may never have stopped rocking. Luckily, I could only take one day at a time and I could not see what lay ahead. Hope is a lot easier to maintain with blinders on.

WEDNESDAY, JANUARY 6, 1993 — AT THE OFFICE

Last night, doctors found a tumor in Mom's liver. They did a CAT scan and said it's a tumor. I keep hoping that it's a cyst or something benign. I prayed all night long. When I tried to stop praying to get some sleep, I couldn't stop. I told myself that if I kept praying everything would be OK. I got up this morning early and got ready for work and came in just to keep my mind off things. Since that's impossible, I'm going to write about it even though I'm at work.

I can't even describe the feeling. Four months ago, my grandma, Daddy's mom, was diagnosed with a brain tumor so advanced that it was inoperable. I am so angry. Statistically alone, this should be impossible. My father is in remission from lymphoma. My grandmother has tumors all over her body. Now, my mother.

I found myself getting very angry at God. Then as I was praying, I began to question who I was praying to. For the first time since I was a child, I wondered what "God" is and how He works. I've always felt so strong with my faith and wondered how people could question, especially in times of greatest need. Now I know. Still, I kept begging. Please Please Please Please Please Please Please. Over and over, until it sounded like a demand. I try to think positively, knowing that Daddy thanks positive thinking for his life. But I can't help considering the worst — over and over. Even the worst seems impossible. It's like I can imagine it happening, and then my mind just says, "Nope," switching to something else like what I want for dinner.

I think, "Who can I turn to? Who will make this all

OK?" and instinctively I think of Mom. She's the one who's supposed to help me cope with things like this.

I find myself calling a lot of people for comfort and hanging up completely miserable. I feel like I'll eventually call somebody who can just solve it. Someone will say, "Oh, I'll be right there to fix that for you." Like a plumber.

I called Pat and Teri [good friends of Mom who were also nurses]. They said tumors don't usually start in the liver. They are the result of something else, which means whatever it is — cyst, tumor, benign growth — has spread to the liver. I hate the word "spread." That's what they kept saying about grandma. "Her tumors have spread to her back." "Her tumors have spread to her neck."

I also hate how well I know cancer terminology. As soon as the crisis hit, I knew who to call, what to say, questions to ask, the routine procedures for testing. The average person doesn't know the lingo quite so well. Shouldn't know the lingo so well.

If it is cancer, we'll fight, like we've always done. We're stronger now. We know what we're up against. We know how to battle this disease.

What if we can't? What if it's too advanced? I hate to think this way, but I can't help it. I can't even fathom my mother growing weak. She is the pillar of our family. She taught me to be strong.

No, it's impossible. It can't be. Mom simply can't be that sick. We just don't know what it is right now and I shouldn't jump to conclusions.

I talked to Aunt Margie this morning and she told me some things that Mom hadn't told me. Mom's trying to protect me. Apparently, they're sure it's a tumor and sure it's in the liver. They are doing upper and lower scopes to locate the source. Aunt Margie said that she had even asked Mom, "Are you accepting that it's cancer?" and Mom said, "I don't know."

I can't figure out how to act. I want to be at work because if I were home I'd be crying constantly and generally miserable.

At least here I can communicate with others, and get hugs when I need them. The only problem is when I cry. I don't want people to see me cry but I just keep doing it. I want to ignore everything and assume the best and go on with my day but it just won't work that way. I think of Mom drugged to the gills, having doctors probe her in the most sensitive areas. She's so wonderfully independent and strong. It will crush her spirit. I can't let it crush her spirit.

She cannot have cancer. She simply cannot. She is my mother, for God's sake, and she's only 50. Barely 50! We just had a surprise birthday party for her. My healthy-as-a-horse, 83-year-old grandmother was there partying with us.

I can't lose her. I need her as much as I did when I was 10 years old. Maybe more. She is now my best friend.

ABOUT 10 O'CLOCK on the morning after the phone call, Chuck called me at work. Mom had been dating him for several years and I adored him. They met when they both taught at a local high school. Chuck was an astronomer and one of the most brilliant men I'd ever known, balanced by a healthy dose of huggability. He was a large man, like a giant teddy bear. Only this bear could discuss quantum physics with the same enthusiasm as he shared his passion for Harleys and chocolate malts. Mom and Chuck owned matching black leather jackets and frequently rode his motorcycle (a "Harley wanna-be" or "Japanese Harley," as Mom called it) to a favorite hot springs in New Mexico, taking a detour to Walsenberg for that malt. Over malts, they discussed the books they were reading, Mom's dream log cabin, and Chuck's recent musings on the night skies. They played well together.

Chuck explained to me that during the lower scope, the doctors found a polyp in her colon. They removed it and were testing it for cancer. Chuck said the doctor didn't think it was cancerous. If it turned out benign, they would test her stomach the next morning. If it was malignant, they would schedule a biopsy of her liver. Chuckles, as I called him, also laid another bombshell on me. Apparently, the doctor had told Mom the day before that he definitely thought what they saw on her liver was cancerous. I silently hoped that the man was Pueblo's most inaccurate doctor.

WEDNESDAY, JANUARY 6 — 2:30 P.M.

... I hung up with Chuckles and went into Brooke's office for a hug. We shut the door so I could cry and I talked about what I had learned. I suddenly became terrified. Not a slow, dawning fear that you anticipate accompanies such trauma. But the kind of fear that I can only believe accompanies experiences like being a passenger on a crashing plane, or knowing you're about to be pushed off a cliff. Terrifying, gut-tossing, mind-altering fear. I stared out the window in Brooke's office, my fist clenched and my teeth biting hard on my fist. I am experiencing the scariest moment of my life.

I left the office since I was basically useless, and now I'm home. Jason called the instant I walked in the door. He sounds good ... well, better than me. I still remember that when we found out Daddy had cancer, Jason was the only one completely convinced from the very beginning that everything would be fine. He acted then the same way he's acting now. He will deal with it once we know what it is. I told him that I keep telling myself it's a cyst. He said he's not lying to himself. Jason believes it's cancer. We just need to figure out what kind and how to deal with it. He's right, of course, but I can't be that rational.

I think about all the times I joked, "Mom, when you die, can I have your ruby ring?" "Can I have the dining room table?" I know it's all jokes and I'd never take any of them back. It's just that I thought I'd never have to face these things.

My mother cannot have cancer. My father had cancer and his mother has cancer. That's enough, God. You've gotten my family with this. You've made us prove we can fight anything with our love. Get off it now. My mother cannot have cancer.

She's my MOTHER! She still provides my direction and is the voice of wisdom I seek on a daily basis.

If it is cancer, we're going to fight it again and beat it even better this time. We're going to scare Cancer so bad it won't even visit my grandchildren, or their grandchildren, or their grandchildren's grandchildren. We can fight this. We have in the past and we've proven we're too much for Cancer to best. We will kill this once and for all.

I think it's time for me to read "When Bad Things Happen To Good People" book. Why must I read that thing again? Why? There's a good question. Why. I ask it and I require answers but there are none to be found. Who can possibly answer that question?

THAT EVENING I finally spoke with Mom and things seemed to be looking up. The blood work they did the day before showed that her liver was working just fine! 100 percent! Hardly the result of a liver being attacked by cancer, I mused optimistically. Mom's spirits were much better and she said she felt better than she had in a long time. Apparently the polyp was not cancerous, just as the doctor thought. She was going to have the test on her stomach, pancreas, and gall bladder done the next day.

I was already sick of the diagnosis. I was impatient and wanted them to do the biopsy on her liver. I reasoned that if the liver wasn't cancerous, then we didn't have anything to worry about.

The next day, Wednesday, the doctors conducted the tests. I heard words I'd only heard on television. CAT Scan (or CT Scan), upper and lower GI, MRI, biopsy, blood work, and liver functions. I heard the phrases, thinking of my mother with tubes and needles sticking into and out of every orifice. Unfortunately, the doctors found nothing definitive, so they decided to do a biopsy of her liver tissue on Thursday. I drove down to be with her. Before that day, she had insisted that I not drive down until "necessary." When she asked me to come down, I knew — finally heard — that she was scared, too.

"Babe, I think I'll need you to drive me home Thursday," she said slowly. "They told me I'll be too weak to drive."

That fact alone must have frustrated Mom. She was proud of her independence, and had a strong do-it-yourself ethic. I think it was hard for her to accept that she'd need help doing something as simple as driving.

"I want to be with you, Mom," I said, "and if you're strong enough, you can drive us home."

Nothing prepared me for the moment I saw her after the biopsy on Thursday. I had never seen Mom in the hospital before. When I walked in, Chuck and Jane, a family friend for more than 15 years, were sitting next to her. Mom was lying on her back on one of those rolling carts with a white blanket pulled all the way up to her chin. Her hair was matted. Mascara smeared the pillow, so I knew she'd been crying. She looked tired, but alert. The drugs seemed to have worn off.

I walked right up to the bed and hugged her as best I could, and I hugged Chuck and Jane. Then, I stood next to her and grabbed her hand. A deep purple circle covered the back of her hand from a rough X-ray technician who had man-handled her IV. Her other hand had an IV needle inserted and taped to it, but no tube leading to it. She had a blood pressure cuff strapped to her arm and it automatically took her pressure every 15 minutes. The cuff was attached to a machine that tracked the latest systolic/diastolic readings and a countdown to the next reading. A narrow strip of paper a foot long hung from the machine next to her bed. A curtain hung around the area, but it was pulled open.

I took all these things in, perhaps in an effort to maintain reality. Seeing Mom in such a condition and location frightened me. I'd never seen this woman so weakened, so prodded by outside forces, so obviously not a person who could stand between me and all my demons as my protector. She was diminished, and her hero status was threatened in my childhood mind. Switching my attention to machines and structure allowed me to maintain my grip on reality.

Jane left a few minutes later. She'd had a long day. Mom briefly described the biopsy to me and Chuck but she looked at Chuck the whole time. I could tell she was trying to protect me from the facts.

"They took the tissue during yet another CAT scan," she said. "It helped them locate the unhealthy-looking tissue more precisely."

"Did they cut your stomach?" I asked.

She shook her head slowly, trying to decide how to describe the procedure. "No, not really. They numbed my tummy but the only cut was where they inserted a rod the size of a good-sized screwdriver. About like my pinky finger."

She held up her finger.

"They just stuck it in?" I asked, appalled.

"Yes," she said. "And it felt like that rod went right to where I've been hurting."

"Scary, I bet," Chuck said, reaching for her hand.

Mom nodded. "They did that three times."

"Was it painful?" Chuck asked.

She looked at Chuck with an expression that said, "Don't ask me that right now."

"Mom," I said. "You can tell me if it hurt."

She still didn't look at me, but she said, "It was the most uncomfortable thing I've been through so far."

The doctor said that, even under light sedation, Mom swung at him and tried to stand up on the table during the lower GI. I was proud of her.

After they released her, I drove us back to Cañon City. We were supposed to call the doctor the next morning to be sure our appointment was at 1:30. I hoped it would be earlier. I couldn't imagine waiting that long to get the results.

Once home, we finally talked. But she was very tired, so we kept it short.

"If this is all a false alarm, I will see it as God's warning for me to stop this," Mom said as she lit a cigarette. At the sight of her 30-year-old addiction, I became suddenly furious with her. I said nothing, though, and let it pass, realizing it was a small piece of the pie I'd have to eat in the next 24 hours.

"They know something's in there, right?" I asked. We were sipping coffee.

"Yes. There is definitely something in my liver. They're just trying to figure out what."

We paused.

"So tomorrow they'll tell us?"

She looked right at me and we froze our gaze on one another. Both of us seemed to be saying, "What if?"

All I'd been thinking the last three days was "What if?" This woman had been my mother and best friend all 24 years of my life. "What if" was all I could manage before I spun off into pleading denial.

At that moment, I realized the same was true for her. But it was her body. How must it feel to know you are carrying something foreign inside your stomach and that very thing might kill you? Like Rosemary's baby? Your own body feeds it, nurtures it, helps it grow — to your own demise. How could you sleep with that knowledge? That growth inside you? Your bed partner.

"How does it feel to know that's inside you, Mom? Are you scared?"

"Yes, Janalee, I'm scared. I think about it at night. But every morning since this started, I've woken up about 2 a.m., and I come out here to sit and talk to God. I feel like He wakes me up and says, 'Let's chat about this.' It has helped to calm me down."

My family always made a vast distinction between religion and spirituality. In my childhood, I may have entered a church two or three times, but I'm certain I had a better grasp on the value of a Higher Power than did most of my peers. I developed a mature trust in a Higher Power as a result of Mom's recovery from alcoholism. She got sober when I was nine. In order to attain her sobriety, she had to turn her life over to a Higher Power. That was a release she practiced throughout the rest of her life, ultimately developing a profound serenity.

Mom passed that gift of faith to Jason and me in many ways. Primarily, she allowed us to keep our sense of wonder over this world's most basic gifts — mountains, dirt, animals. We were allowed to be silly and to explore our external and internal worlds without retribution. Our curiosities about the unknown were supported unconditionally. With that kind of trust as a foundation, I learned to explore my faith and my beliefs. She even told me I was allowed to believe in things no one else did. At a time when most of my friends were fed religious edicts, my mom was saying things like:

"Your Higher Power may be that bucket over there, if it gives you strength and peace."

Luckily, Mother Nature provided my earliest sense of spirituality, and not a bucket. The mountains were a magical place for Mom, Jason, and me. I felt closer to God and, more important, to myself.

Since childhood, my Higher Power has lost its gender and has become more of an energy from which I draw strength, and for which I feel gratitude. I still call this energy "God." At the very least, people associate that word with some kind of faith, no matter how internal or external its development.

So, when Mom said she spent much of the night talking to God, I knew she was asking her Higher Power to work with her through this scary disease, just as she did with her alcoholism.

I ventured a question I hadn't dared ask before.

"Do you think it's cancer?"

Mom thought carefully and said, "I'm not sure. Sometimes I think it is and other times I'm sure it's not. I have too much to live for."

"Even if it's cancer, Mom, we'll beat it. Daddy did."

Daddy and Mom divorced when I was two, but remained good friends. They'd always been a team in my upbringing. Daddy moved to Missouri after the divorce, earned his Ph.D., and then moved east to New Jersey. He was always a presence, though, thanks to his constant calls and letters, and thanks to Mom's warm references to "your daddy." Both of them were determined that their separation did not have to mean a "broken" home.

"Yes, of course. We'll fight," Mom replied.

Thursday, January 7 — late at night

I'm scared to go to the doctor tomorrow. I may be the only one with her and if it's malignant, I don't know if I'll be able to control my reaction. I must. For her. All signs show she is very healthy — even her liver is functioning well, so even if it is cancer, we'll fight it, by God!

Something in me says it's not cancer, though. I hate to say that and jinx it. When Jason found out her upper GI was clean he said, "Fuckin' A! No shit!"

Another neat thing to come of this (talk about a silver lining-searcher), the people I work with have been wonderful. The assistant dean came to me and told me to do whatever I needed to get through. She offered her office to me for tears and phone calls. Brooke is always ready with a hug. Davi wrote me a simple, touching poem and framed it. Chris bought me flowers. Mark told me to take as much time as I needed. Jennifer offered to feed me! I am so loved, and with their strength, I have the power to fight anything.

Friday, January 8 — 10:10 a.m.

We both got up this morning around 6:30. She said she was having thoughts she "couldn't pray away."

We've been talking about all kinds of things — from my master's degree to hot springs in Ouray to cancer. She says my presence here helps, so I'm happy to be here. Aunt Margie and I have developed some questions for me to ask the doctor today. The appointment is at 1:30.

I keep trying to imagine my reactions to the doctor. I want to be able to control myself. I'm not sure if Chuck is going to be there, so it may be just me and Mom. If it's malignant — please, no, please — I must control myself and get the facts. What is the next step? How do we fight it? I will accept nothing. Anything they say will be checked through sources I've developed. I just can't even imagine how that one moment will affect me. I imagine silence, white lab coats, holding hands, manila files, holding our breath. How will it happen? Will he just tell us? Wait for us to ask? Lead up to it? Remind us to breathe? What will that one moment at 1:30 this afternoon be like?

Mom just took a shower and I took the opportunity to call Daddy and Aunt Margie. Daddy wasn't home, but Aunt Margie gave me some good advice: "You don't have to be perfect," and "Don't live in the future." I can't concentrate on what might happen; I must focus on what is happening.

Time to get ready to go.

WE DECIDED I would follow her to the doctor's office in Pueblo — an hour's drive east — and then after the appointment I would head back to Denver — a two-hour drive north. I would either get clothing and return to Mom's, should the news be bad, or stay up there and celebrate the end of a very long week.

I followed Mom's Nissan down Elizabeth Street, a grand tree-lined street near the center of town. It held fast to a conservative 35 miles-per-hour speed limit and a parkway split the four lanes down the center. If you were on the two southbound lanes, there was no turning around to go north for miles unless you turned off and took the winding side streets. The brownstone homes arched up from opposite sides of the road, their attics nodding at one another across the parkway, above the rows of trees.

When we came up behind the last car of the mourners' caravan, Mom moved to the left lane to try to pass it. But before we made much distance, an escorting police car blocked our path and we had to sit and watch the string of cars pass to our right. When the last one passed, we got back in line. Mom took a right off of Elizabeth and we zoomed up parallel side-streets to beat the caravan, but we ended up facing the mourners as they crawled past our perpendicular street. I sensed from Mom's darting head and her side-road searches that this event bothered her. It bothered me, too.

The mourner's faces looked vacant and resigned like those starving children on television. Headlights on, eyes glazed, the mourners passed in front of me not seeing me, but their pain sucked me in and consumed me. Had the person leading this procession, the person in the box in the back of the hearse, made a visit to the doctor just like me and Mom? How long ago? Years? Months? Was it someone's mother? Was that the daughter who just drove by me, stoic, pearls around her neck, hands tight on the steering wheel?

I snapped off my radio and watched Mom struggle. I felt like a disembodied spirit watching as things happened, unable to take control and stop the progressing panic I knew Mom must feel. I wanted to honk, to yell at the cops, to stop the caravan in the middle and let Mom through. I wanted to erase this scene. Instead, with my windows shut, I screamed at God.

It was the first angry, and probably the first honest conversation I'd ever had with God. And at that moment, reality hit. I was no longer rocking in the corner and sobbing. I was shouting, screaming at a reality I had not chosen and one which I believed I could not face. The hearse and the caravan of mourners had driven me straight into that black hole from which I'd been running. Over the past four days, I'd gripped tightly and held onto any sturdy thought that could keep me from being sucked into the abyss. Yet these perfect strangers, all dressed in black, had plucked my fingers one-by-one off of those safety branches, flinging me into reality.

Finally, our turn came and we took it gratefully, entering the parking lot of that horrible building. I looked up at its staunch face, believing it to be wholly evil and a container of only bad news.

When Mom approached me, I said, "That was pretty awful, wasn't it?"

She nodded. That's all we said — ever — about the hearse and the caravan.

Courage

Chapter 2

"Ms. Chmel to see Dr. Pratt," Mom said to the receptionist firmly and confidently.

I, on the other hand, was thinking, "Out of our way. Get the doctor in here. We are the most important people you will see all day."

Instead, we sat in the waiting room and, yet again, we waited. My heart raced and I doodled on a legal pad. The night before, Daddy had told me to take lots of notes and he had shared with me the story of the day he learned he had cancer. The doctor had called Daddy at his office on campus while he was grading papers. Across the top of a student's paper in red ink, Daddy wrote the doctor's diagnosis: "LYMPHOMA."

I stared at my legal pad and wrote the date on the top, "1/8." I hoped that would be the first and only entry.

"Ms. Chmel."

We were called and led to an examination room. We sat in the two side chairs and stared at a chart on the opposite wall. It was of the liver, pancreas and spleen. Mom pointed at areas she'd seen on her CT scans and we played with the blood pressure monitor the way we'd done when I was young at the doctor's office. Finally, Doctor Pratt entered. Mom's hand nervously jerked to the back of my neck, stroking my long, curly hair.

"Dr. Pratt, this is my daughter, Janalee," Mom said. I shook hands with the slight man who held the knowledge I sought. I searched his eyes for truth. I also noticed how strong Mom sounded.

"Sylvia," he said, "I'm afraid the news is bad. Your tumor is malignant. You have cancer."

The only recognizable reaction Mom had was to begin winding my hair strenuously around her finger. Within moments, pain from my roots shot through my neck and down my spine. It kept me present and in the moment, though, and for that I was grateful. Tears tried to come, but I swallowed hard and took a deep breath.

"The cancer is in the liver, but we don't believe it started there. Primary hepatoma is very rare. It is my belief that it started in the pancreas, here ..." He pointed at the chart. "But I was unable to see it with the scope. Therefore, I believe it started down here at the end and has metasticized to the liver."

I suddenly became angry. Who cares where it began! Let's just kill it and kill it now. Just tell us how to kill it. I'd heard the diagnosis. I immediately wanted the treatment.

"So, where is it in the liver?" I asked.

Dr. Pratt looked at me, glanced at Mom, and raised his hand to point at the chart. Then he dropped his hand and faced us full front, standing in front of the chart.

"It's everywhere."

Pain grabbed my brain, wrapped around my ears, and shot down my back. Mom had turned my hair into a rope that she was clinging to for life. I turned my thoughts to my pad of paper.

Primary hepatoma — no

pancreas

scope inconclusive

everywhere

I had made a list of questions to ask him and now none of them seemed appropriate. I couldn't speak. I stared at my notes, helpless.

My tears dripped quietly onto the note pad. Suddenly, Mom became herself.

She let go of my hair, grabbed my hand, and spoke.

"What's the next step?"

"I've taken the liberty to make an appointment for you with a surgeon," he said. "I'd like you to meet first with your primary physician, Dr. Roth. She will fill you in further before you meet the surgeon."

I took notes furiously. I could write facts and think facts. Linking those concepts with my mother's health terrified me. I could think about scopes or cells on a superficial level, like a student reading a textbook. When I imagined my own mother as "Figure A" in the text, illustrating all the ugliness of the various facts, I shuddered. So, like an efficient secretary, I took notes.

The whole time he spoke to us, Dr. Pratt remained distant physically and emotionally. He didn't respond, or even pause to acknowledge my tears or Mom's shock. He was protected by charts, an exam table, his stethoscope, his education.

I was proud of Mom when she forcefully stood up, stuck her hand out to him and said, "Thank you, doctor. I will go see Dr. Roth."

Dr. Pratt, surprised by her physical demand, hesitated before tentatively taking her hand.

"I wish you the best," he said.

I couldn't help but think he was lying or that he already pictured my mother as a corpse. As much as I wanted to, I could not follow Mom's lead and shake his hand. I hated him. He thought my mom would die. He obviously didn't know my mom.

"I need to sit down, Janalee." Mom sat down heavily in a chair in the hospital hallway.

"Mom, we've got to go see Dr. Roth!" I was panicky, as if a sprint to the next doctor would somehow speed the cure.

"I need to sit for a moment. Chuck should be here soon, too."

I sat down next to her.

"Mom? ..." It's all I could manage. She looked directly into my eyes, deeply, studying me as though I was a newborn first entering her life. Then she hugged me strongly.

Chuck walked in and smiled his comfortable, just-woke-up-from-a-nap smile. I ran to his arms. His tall, round body offered me peace and I suddenly believed everything would be OK.

"Bad, huh?" he said. His resonant voice came from his soul and the stars. It seemed all-powerful. It was so different from the doctor's. I just nodded my head against his chest. We sat on either side of her.

"Hey, lady," he said to Mom. "Got you a bad one?"

Mom held both our hands and looked at Chuck. They had a special way of listening to one another. They felt free to verbalize their mental explorations rather than waiting to speak when they were certain of their position. Unconditional listening, Mom called it. If she said something she didn't quite believe later, or felt she hadn't expressed herself right, she knew Chuck would open himself to her new thoughts, and vice versa.

"Janalee, tell me if I get this right," Mom began. "Dr. Pratt said I have cancer in my liver but they don't think it started there ..."

Facts. Again I was in my element. I ticked off my notes as she spoke, making sure she got everything.

"Dr. Pratt thinks it may have started in the spleen. No, the pancreas, but he didn't see it with the scope."

I interrupted, "That means it really could have started in the liver and it's not anywhere else!" This sudden nugget bolstered me. Fewer targets to fight, I thought.

"That could be true, but he said primary liver cancer is very rare," she continued. "He said it's all over my liver and we are supposed to go see Dr. Roth and then a surgeon."

"Today?" Chuck asked. "Do you have appointments?"

Mom nodded. "They're probably waiting but I needed some time to think."

The three of us sat there quietly for about five minutes. Then Mom, suddenly very determined, slapped her hands on her knees and said, "Let's go, folks!"

We drove to a different medical complex to see Dr. Roth. On the way over, Mom and I took her car. Chuck followed us. He had a class to teach later at the community college and might need his car.

Dr. Pratt had given Mom all of her scans and records to take with us. I pulled one of the scans out of the big green and white folder.

"What the heck is this?"

I looked at the images, altering all four edges of the scan to the top, but I couldn't make out the figures. The film was thick and made a loud crack when I shook it.

"Hold it this way, with this side to the top," Mom said, keeping one eye on the road. "OK, now imagine the camera shooting down this way, as if you're looking down on me from the top of my head. That's my spine, see?"

"OK."

"This is the outline of my body and that's the liver."

I stared at the dark figure and examined every pixel of the image. It was dark with varying sizes of white spots. I stared at the spots with the intensity of a child who believes she can move objects with her mind. I nearly grunted with the effort. Get off there! Get out of her! How did you get there?

Dr. Laura Roth had been Mom's doctor for 20 years. I assumed for some reason that she would be in the waiting room crying when we walked in, begging us to immediately come back to her private, plush office where healing tones would be spoken and gentle touches would be administered. I was wrong.

We sat in the waiting room with everyone else and we were later escorted to the exam room where we waited again. She swept in with a smile and leaned toward my mom, who was sitting on the exam table. Chuck and I took the only two side chairs. I wish we had been more unconventional to unsettle each doctor a little. I should have been sitting on the table with my shirt off, forcing Dr. Roth to step back and out of her "get through this" mode. She would have had to face us for one, brief moment as a human with a sense of humor and emotion.

"Hi, Sylvia," she said. "I guess we better talk about what's next."

Dr. Roth went through much of the same information that Pratt did and I dutifully took notes. Several times, she said, "I don't want to lie to you, Sylvia, this is very bad. You need to be aware of that."

Each time, Mom responded positively with "I am" or "I understand." When Mom offered Dr. Roth her charts, the doctor stepped back slightly and said, "I've seen them. You need to take them to the surgeon." She seemed to be afraid of the charts, glad to pass the buck. This surgeon was definitely getting slammed with bad duty.

When the appointment ended, Mom again shook the doctor's hand.

"I guess I'd better get out of work for a few days," she said. The doctor almost laughed.

"Sylvia! I don't think you do understand. I think you'd better try to get on permanent disability and do it fast. If you decide to fight this ..." (if!) " ... you will be unable to work for some time."

Seeing the horror on my mother's face, the doctor softened. "Of course, disability is reversible should this all work out."

No work. That was beyond my mother's realm of comprehension. Cancer may have been more believable to her. Mom had worked all her life, putting herself through graduate school, raising two children on her own, and attaining a level of respect via those accomplishments of which she was very proud.

We walked into the hall and ran into a friend of Mom's.

"Sylvia! How are you?" the short woman asked. Never has a question been so loaded. My nerves were pulled so tight an epileptic could have walked across them without a net. I wanted to pounce on this woman.

"Better than you!" Mom responded with her patented response, laughing.

"Here to see a doctor?" the woman asked. Idiot.

"No, I thought I'd come here and watch sick people all day," Mom said, again laughing.

We boarded the elevator and the woman waved us away, smiling, "You're sick, Sylvia. Just sick."

"You have no idea," Mom said, as the doors shut and the three of us burst out laughing.

Dr. Simmons' office was more stark than the others and when his nurse called Mom back, she told Chuck and me that we would have to wait while the doctor examined her. That took at least half an hour. I was certain that he was telling her things that I needed to record on my note pad. Things she shouldn't hear alone.

Finally, we were called back. Mom was dressed and sitting on the exam table. She sat up straight.

"Hi, babe," she said to me and winked. Suddenly I didn't trust her, either. How much would she share with me? From what would she try to protect me?

"Dr. Simmons, this is my daughter, Janalee, and this is Chuck."

The doctor was tall, thin, with a shiny head and narrow features. He nodded curtly at us and I decided to make him shake my hand. He took it with a wet-dishrag grip. He let go. Wimp.

"What's the news?" Chuck asked. I couldn't help myself from smiling at his casual attitude. He grounded me.

"I've been explaining to Sylvia that the situation is not good," he began. He pointed at the scans I'd examined in the car. "This is your mother's liver." He addressed me and ignored Chuck. "See the light spots? That's healthy tissue."

"What!" I said loudly. I'd assumed the few white spots were the cancerous tissue. It turned out those few beams of light coming through from the light board were the healthy tissue. The rest was all cancer. All.

Mom looked at me sympathetically. I bet she reacted much the same way. The doctor continued.

"To perform surgery to remove that left lobe would be foolhardy. Sylvia could die on the operating table, and it won't cure her. You've just got too much in there for removal of that lobe to even help. No surgeon would perform this procedure."

He puffed up at the word "surgeon" as though he'd just said "Jesus Christ."

"But we intend to get another opinion," I said curtly, trying to deflate his sails and inflate mine. Mom looked at me and winked.

"Well, of course, you may. But no surgeon will perform this," he said again, and that seemed to shut Mom's entire case for him. If he couldn't help her, no one could. Not any doctor, not any oncologist, not a surgeon, not a nutritionist, not anyone. She was dead to him and his eyes showed it.

"It seems 'hope' is a four-letter word to you folks," I mumbled.

He puffed up doubly and Mom jumped off the table. She grabbed her scans and files and stuck her hand out for him to shake.

"Thank you, doctor," Mom said, pumping his hand strongly.

"Of course," he said, grateful for the respect he thought she was giving him. He had no idea that she was taking back the respect he'd stripped from her.

After we left, Mom and Chuck went to a restaurant to get some coffee and to talk. I needed to find a friend; someone I could talk to.

I had grown up in Pueblo and I searched my brain for anyone who might provide comfort and a subjective hug.

"Jana! What are you doing all the way down here?" Jay's voice boomed throughout the convenience store. I knew how I must have looked by the sudden drop of his smile. "What's wrong?"

"Can we talk? It's Mom."

Jay and I had worked in a convenience store similar to this one for two summers. We'd also dated off and on. But since those summers had passed, we had established a strong friendship and he knew my mom well. I knew he would understand. Maybe he could even help. We went to the back room.

"What is it, Jana?" He sat on his desk. He had been promoted to manager. I sat in a side chair.

"Jay, Mom has cancer."

I expected him to leap from the desk, hold his head in anguish and scream, "No!" or at least something close to that. But he didn't. The only noticeable reaction was that his feet stopped swinging. He looked at the ground.

"Wow."

I started crying. For the first time that day, I allowed it to flow and gush from my body. It left me with the force of a nauseous stomach, coming from deep within and completely uncontrollable. I thought I might throw up.

"Lots of it, Jay. It's all over her liver. What will I do? I can't … She can't … this can't be happening."

Jay was still looking at the ground. He had not acknowledged my tears, nor had he looked at me. He had only spoken one word, "Wow." I looked at him and tried to catch his eye.

"Jay?"

He looked up and through me. It was as if he had left the room.

"I, I don't know what to say, Jana." He put one hand on my knee and then pulled it back again. "She'll be alright. Just be strong."

That was it? That was all he could offer? My heart fell. 'She'll be alright. Be strong.' It was so small. So full of nothing for me to latch onto. But then I looked at him and realized I had expected him to make it all better. I sought him as though he were some sort of carpenter who could take this damaged room of my life and refinish it. I just knew some outside force could and would make it all better, the way Mom's kisses could.

I left, grateful for the tears I felt safe to shed in front of him, and I drove to the restaurant to meet Mom and Chuck. They seemed calm.

"How is Jay?" Mom asked.

"Fine. Busy," I said. "What's our next move?"

"I want to see a doctor in Denver," Mom said. "I called Pat to see what she could do."

"How'd she react?" I asked.

"I think she took it hard. She's a nurse. She probably knows too much to be good for herself," Mom said.

"Janalee, I might as well tell you more about what the doctors have told me," she said. I was sitting next to her in the booth and she shifted to face me. I braced and mentally searched for my note pad. I'd left it in the car.

"On Tuesday, without a biopsy or any other studies, Dr. Roth told me that I probably had less than six months to live."

I was stunned. I said nothing and watched her eyes.

"Today, however," she continued, "I've been told that with the correct treatment, I may have a year to 18 months. That's good news, I guess."

Doctors were really ticking off dates as to how long she might live? They hadn't even done much testing. And they didn't know her. How can you determine how long someone might live if you don't know or understand their spirit? It couldn't be possible.

"Well, you don't believe them, do you?" I said. "I mean, how can they possibly know how much life is in you? They're not right." I began crying, pleading. "Mom, you're not going to die! You're not!"

"I am going to live, Janalee."

Chuck sat quietly. I felt safe sharing my fears with him.

"Mom, I'm so scared. I have so much hope, but how many times can you listen to what they're saying and remain upbeat? How can they say those things? It's like they think you're already dead."

Mom looked at Chuck and back to me.

"Janalee, this is not about dying. This is about living. This is about how we choose to live life today and every day. Three days ago, Dr. Roth told me I had six months to live. I now have a year to 18 months. You may only have two weeks, Janalee. We don't know and we will never know. But I do know this is not about dying. It is about living."

Instead of driving home to Denver that night, I went back to Cañon City with Mom. Chuck went back to his place in Pueblo. Mom had a lot of phone calls to make and wanted my help. We also had a long list of "to dos" and she'd need help with that. She had a lot of questions about her insurance and disability that we needed to figure out. But the most daunting were the phone calls we had to make to family and friends that night.

Sitting in the living room after a light meal — she couldn't eat much without severe pain — we stared at each other, the phone sitting between us like a pouncing cat. I imagined all of the reactions. How could we do this? How could she face this over and over? The phone looked like an evil enemy.

"I guess we'd better start calling everyone who loves me," Mom said, breathing in deeply. "And that begins with Jason."

She put her hand on the phone, but closed her eyes and sat very still. Tears came to her eyes and she lifted her face to the ceiling. A tear rolled down her cheek.

"Please give me the right words," she said.

Then she opened her eyes and picked up the phone confidently.

I left the room to give her some privacy. When I returned about 15 minutes later she was laughing with Jason and agreeing that, yes, she probably was too tough an old lady for cancer to stay inside her for very long. Then she handed me the phone.

"What do you think?" I asked. "Pretty scary, huh?"

"Geez, Jana, you're so dramatic," he responded. "This is a walk in the park for our family."

We proceeded to call the rest of the family. When we called Aunt Margie, she was prepared with all kinds of information about other steps we should take. She'd been busy talking to doctors, nurses, and nutritionists in San Diego. I took notes on my note pad.

Mom called Jane, the woman who had been with her all day during the biopsy. Jane was Mom's AA sponsor and was 75 years old. Mom considered Jane almost divine. We all pretty much worshipped Jane thanks to her role in Mom's alcoholism recovery. Jane took the news pretty hard. Her daughter and husband had both recently passed away. Still she agreed to call many of Mom's other friends so that we could relax.

Before I went to sleep, I called Daddy. As much as I was sick of the phone, I needed to talk to him. He lived in New Jersey where I had spent four years as an undergraduate, and I also worked there at a newspaper for a year after I graduated. In that time, Daddy had become more of a confidante and dear friend than a traditional father.

When I moved to New Jersey in 1986, Daddy was battling cancer, bald from the chemo, and very ill. I got off the plane and walked right by him, my very own father, the man who would be my sole lifeline through the next four years of college. I didn't recognize him.

From behind me, I heard, "What's the matter? Don't you recognize your old man doing his best impression of Yul Brynner?"

I turned to see none other than Yul Brynner wearing sunglasses and smiling. Daddy was as bald as my elbow. I was suddenly more nervous about my move from little Pueblo, Colorado to the big, bad east. Not only was Rutgers University more than half the size of my hometown, but my father was battling for his life.

Luckily, we had some time together before my classes started. I quickly learned what an asset his goofy wit and deep introspection would be to both his healing and my growing up. During his cancer battle, I once found him meditating on his bed. His eyes were closed and his bald head shined as though it were sending messages to the heavens. I immediately knew this man could beat cancer and be my daddy at the same time. At that moment, the peace I felt from him stirred me toward him in ways I'd never had the opportunity to feel from 2,000 miles. I was proud of him. Proud in more intimate ways; I was getting to know him.

He had also made it clear to me that life goes on. We went to the beach one day and he joked as he applied sunscreen to his head.

Then he said, "Let's take a picture to commemorate this moment!"

He sat down in the middle of his beach blanket and said, "Here's how I feel about my cancer," and he flipped the bird at me.

I took the shot and it sits in his office today, next to a more recent picture of him with a full head of hair, mustache, and beard.

"Daddy?" I said into the receiver.

"Honey, what time is it?" he asked.

"Oh! I'm so sorry! I had no idea. It's 1 a.m. your time."

"Don't be silly, I expected you to call," he said, already 100 percent alert. "Talk to me, princess."

"Oh, Daddy ..."

Once again, I lost it. My hand covered my face and I quieted my sobs. I didn't want Mom to hear. She was taking a bath and I wondered if she was crying.

"Bad is it?" He allowed space to fill the line and air whistled from Colorado to New Jersey at 4,000 miles an hour. My pain pushed it.

"Really bad," I gulped. "They said six months, then a year, then 18 months. But how can they know? Why do they say that? She's not going to ... to ... to die!"

When Daddy was diagnosed with cancer, he called Mom and asked that she tell Jason and me so that we would be looking someone in the eye rather than hearing it over the phone. Mom cried with us and answered all our questions.

"Janalee, there's a lot they don't know yet," he said. "She will probably see many more doctors and each will have a different prognosis. Just hang in there."

"OK, OK. Yeah. Right." I was trying to breathe.

"And how's my little girl?"

Whoa. That was from left field. Me? I considered my state as though I were taking an inventory of body parts. Two legs, two arms, ten fingers, ten toes. Yup, all must be OK. I couldn't look deeper than skin and joints. Everything I felt beneath terrified me. I took another breath, but it was shallow.

"Good. I'm fine, I guess. I don't even know."

More air whistled through the line.

"Daddy, I have no idea. I can't think about it. It's too scary. The what ifs are too scary," I said, and held my breath. "I couldn't live without her, Daddy."

"I know, honey. I know. It seems so impossible. It's very unfair."

I felt like a sponge soaked to the point of dripping and his gentle words squished out tears from every pore. I cried with my whole body, drawing my limbs in close and hemorrhaging tears. He was the first person that day to admit this was unfair, giving me freedom to do the same.

"Darling, I love you," he said, pausing to let me cry, giving me permission to hurt. "Please tell your mom that I'm here to talk. How is Jason?"

"He's trying to get leave from the Navy. I'm not sure how long he'll be able to stay, though. I can't wait to see him."

"I'm sure," Daddy said. "What can I do for you, Janalee?"

Left field shot again. All I wanted to do was scream, "Fix it! Make her better! Take it out! Pull it out of her gut and make it all better. Please, Daddy!" But that would only have pained him and frustrated me.

"You already have helped, Daddy, just by talking. Thank you."

"Call me any time. Give your mother my love and have that brother of yours call me."

Finally, the phone was silenced. The rest of the night was mine and Mom's. Would she sleep? Would I sleep? What would we do the next day? Saturday. No doctors. Apparently illness must take weekends, too. I wondered how much the cancer could grow in two days, and how long it would take us to fight it back to the size it was before the weekend. If she bumped her tummy, would it cause a growth spurt? Crazy thoughts spun through my mind. When the bathroom door opened, I jumped. Mom emerged, smiling, and I suddenly felt that all would be OK. She looked like a different person. She was in her men's pajamas, soft from years of wear, and I could smell the lavender from her bath. She sighed deeply.

"I feel so much better," she said. "I think I'll have a glass of milk and go to bed."

She sat down with her milk and a big chunk of a Hershey's chocolate bar, her normal evening routine. I made a cup of tea and joined her, but we sat quietly. What more could be said about this day?

Mom thought of something.

"I love you, honey." She winked at me. The moment when she twisted my hair seemed like months ago, though it happened just that afternoon. "Everything will work out for the best."

I did not trust that statement. Mom had always believed that cliché. Her faith and spirituality were very strong thanks entirely to AA and fifteen years of sobriety. But for me, there was only one way this could work out for the best: complete remission and a complete return to life of one week ago. I wanted that all back. I craved that normalcy already. Mom sensed my hesitancy and snuggled close to me on the couch, drawing me near.

"I don't want to be sick any more than you want me to be sick," she said. "I'm scared. Very scared. But I can only take this one day at a time. This day was horrible and I can only imagine that some worse ones are going to follow, but probably some good ones, too. I do know that we are going to fight this as a family. A team. And I need you."

She stopped talking and hugged me closer. I was being touched and tears again fell. I wondered if there was a well somewhere inside me drying up. I hoped so.

"Can we have an agreement?" she said.

I nodded.

"Let's make it a policy to be very open and honest with each other about everything we're thinking and feeling. You are safe to tell me anything and I will do the same with you. I really think that may be the only way to get through this."

I nodded again and I said, "We can just say, 'I need an honesty moment,' and no matter where we are, we'll sit down and listen to each other."

"You got it, kid."

"I like that idea, Mom."

I realized that there was much I wanted to tell her but was afraid. Could she handle the depth of my fears? Would she be mad that I had even considered that she might die? Should I burden her with my thoughts when she was contemplating her very life? And what about the trivial stuff I always discussed with her? Work, friendships, boyfriends, money. None of that even mattered when stacked up against this huge, towering barrier. But I believed she wanted me to tell her everything and I believed she would do the same. At that moment, there was only one thing I wanted.

"I need an honesty moment," I said.

She set down her milk and shifted a little. "OK. Yes?"

"Can I sit in your lap?"

I felt her pause mentally as she registered this request. Then she said very forcefully and carefully, "You will never, ever be too big for this lap."

I carefully slid up on her legs, avoiding pressure on her tummy. I wrapped my arms around her neck and I buried my face in her lavender-covered neck. This time, she rocked me while I cried. It was the most comfort I had received all day. Leave it to Mom.

Courage

CHAPTER 3

We arose Saturday at about the same time. I'd heard Mom up a couple of times during the night. Neither of us had slept much. When she wandered in the night, I assumed she was talking to God, so I left her alone and stopped my own praying so that hers had better access.

She put a pot of coffee on and went outside to find the paper. It had snowed the night before. I was struck by the absolute progress of the world. I smelled the coffee brewing and was amazed that Mom even thought to perform that task. Her life was in the balance and she put on a pot of coffee. The fact that the rest of the world still revolved and moved not only surprised me, but pissed me off. How could this tiny town even gather the energy to produce a newspaper when my mother had cancer? And how could God have the time to create a snow storm in the middle of the night when Mom was probably talking to him? All these normal occurrences were a slap in the face. Something also told me that my definition of normal would never be the same.

"Coffee?" Mom asked, and the normal routines within the completely abnormal situation began.

"What do we need to do today?" I asked after we'd read the paper and had some breakfast. Mom's appetite was, as the doctors predicted, poor because of the pain.

"Oh, I don't know," she said. "There's not much we can do given the fact that it's Saturday."

We had made a list of places we needed to call or visit, including her employer, health insurance, and disability personnel. But those people, as well as the doctors, were unreachable today. We decided to go to the bookstore and find any information on cancer and nutrition that was available. I offered to shovel the driveway first.

I bundled up and went outside. I pushed the heavy snow off one side of the driveway and then the other. As I warmed up, I moved faster and realized that I had the strength to shovel snow off the very road all the way around the block. My energy was unprecedented. I felt like I could shovel the snow off every block in town before nightfall. Instead, I went next door to Mom's neighbors and proceeded to shovel their large driveway. They were an older couple and I thought they'd appreciate the gesture. Plus, I needed it. I didn't want to stop moving. What if it caught up with me? Right there in the snow. What if I slowed down and let the darkness rush up from behind and tackle me? The evil laughs taunting me, "What good does this do? Think you can shovel away her cancer? Think again!" I couldn't stop. I had to keep moving, pushing the thoughts away like the snow. When I finished, I went to their front door to tell the neighbors what I'd done and to see if they needed anything else.

"Hi, Mr. Wolfers," I said. "I've shoveled your drive and …"

"Oh, look at you! Look at what you've done! You didn't have to do that. I'm laid up with a cold but I have a snow-blower and would have done your drive for you. Look at what you've done!"

His sincerity caught me off-guard, and all my defenses collapsed. I needed to tell this kind, old man about my terror and I nearly stumbled over myself, saying, "Mr. Wolfers, my mom has cancer. We just found out and I think she may get pretty sick before she gets better. I'll be down here a lot but would you mind shoveling her drive when it needs it? I know she'd appreciate it. I'd really appreciate it."

He stood silently for a moment.

"I'm so sorry. She seemed like such a wonderful lady. I mean she is a wonderful … Of course I will help her out in any way I can. We both will. Please give her our best."

I nodded and walked away with my shovel, sniffing from the cold workout. I didn't tell Mom that Mr. Wolfers knew about her cancer. I wasn't sure she'd want them to know yet. But the next morning when the newspaper was sitting on her front porch and the driveway was freshly shoveled, I think she knew.

After shoveling, I made some calls to my old world in Denver.

"Brooke? Hi, it's Jana."

"Jana! Where are you? How is your mom?"

I rattled off details like a grocery list. It took less than five minutes. When I was done, my spirits were about eight notches lower and Brooke was in shock.

"Oh, my God, Jana. Oh my God."

In one night, I had forgotten how hard that news hits. I was already on to the "what's next" phase and I had run over Brooke with hard, difficult news.

"I'm sorry, Brooke. I guess I handled that poorly. Are you OK? Maybe I should have asked you if you were alone. Are you? Is Bill there?"

"No. I'm going over to his place in an hour. God, Jana, how are you? You sound good, but how can you?"

"I don't know," I said, glad to hear that at least I sounded sane. "I think I'm in shock. It seems like so long ago that we got the news. It does sound bad, but being with her makes it less scary. She looks so good, Brooke. We're going to fight this. You have to see her to feel better."

I asked if anyone called for me.

"Jared called," Brooke said, a smile and devious laugh in her voice.

"Great timing," I said. Jared was an ex-boyfriend.

"Call him!" Brooke exclaimed. "You could use something fun to look forward to. Not to mention the fact that he's hot!"

"The last thing I'm good for right now is a first date with an old beau," I said. "Poor guy would never survive. I'd either be bitchy all night or take him to bed, which would not be a good move right now."

"Yeah, not for you, anyway," Brooke said. We both laughed.

"Well, I guess I'd better start calling everyone to let them know what's up," I continued. There was a long pause. We both imagined those conversations. It was more than I could bear.

"Brooke, can I ask a favor?"

"Sure, anything."

"I can't face telling people this information over and over. Would you please tell them? It's just too much right now."

"Of course. No problem at all. I may not get all the facts right, but ..." she stopped suddenly.

"But you couldn't make it much worse, right?"

"Well, right," she said. "Sorry."

"That's OK. I know how it sounds."

I listed the people I'd like her to call and then we talked a little more about random things.

"Jason's coming to town as soon as the Navy lets him off," I said.

"Your handsome, stud of a brother is going to be in town?" Brooke said, snickering. "Being the generous friend I am, I'd like to offer him the use of my bed!"

"I'm assuming you'd be at Bill's?" I said.

"Oh, just let me get my hands on that baby brother of yours!" she said.

"Hands off! He's too sweet and innocent for you!"

"Yeah, right. A sweet, innocent Navy man. Especially with the way he looks."

When we hung up, I felt better. Maybe the fact that the world kept turning was good. I took a shower, which helped to pick me up even more. The day looked better as I accomplished mundane tasks. The basics never changed: feed me, clean me up, and all looks better.

Chuckles arrived at one o'clock and we went to the town's only bookstore. I bought "Gray's Anatomy" because it had information about all the organs the doctors mentioned the day before and it was thick. The sheer bulk made me feel like I was battling cancer simply by holding it.

SATURDAY, JANUARY 9 — 9:20 P.M., MOM'S HOUSE

The way I see it, there's an angel in deep shit in Heaven right now. I believe there is a "Cancer Department" in Heaven and the angels working there are to dole out cancer to those who either, 1) are needed in Heaven or, 2) need to experience a miracle through recovery. However, because my family has both, 1) experienced the miracle of recovery through my father and is, 2) losing my grandmother to cancer and Heaven, we have been wrongfully given this dose of cancer to deal with.

I believe God has heard the many, many complaints registered concerning the Cancer Department via our prayers and has been alerted. He went to the Cancer Department and demanded that they put an order through to the "Healing Department" STAT! So, I figure we've got yet another miracle headed our direction.

Daddy is headed for Rome Monday and he said he's going to talk to the Pope, so I figure that ought to speed things up sufficiently.

All joking aside, we had a very good day. It doesn't take this family long to "circle the wagons" and "get our ducks in a row."

Chuck showed up and we went to a bookstore. We each bought our own copies of Bernie Siegal's "Love, Medicine and Miracles." I also bought "Gray's Anatomy" and a medical dictionary. I want to have quick access to any terms, parts and locations doctors may bring up. I also bought myself an inspirational desk calendar. I believe positive thinking, honesty, and courage will win this battle.

We also went to a couple of nutrition stores. Mom's considering going on a macrobiotic diet. She is having a lot of trouble eating and we've heard only good things about such diets. I'm going to try to find a cookbook at the Tattered Cover bookstore in Denver tomorrow. We bought her a rice cooker today, too, because there's a lot of rice in such diets.

Her attitude is very positive. Chuck has been suggesting that the two of them go on a macrobiotic diet for a long time and she always said, "Go ahead." Now she's considering it seriously. She joked, "My mind has suddenly been opened wide. I guess maybe I didn't know everything."

So much has changed so drastically in our lives over the past five days. It's hard to believe. We're even changing our diets, which to some may seem rather secondary. I imagine people saying, "You're fighting liver cancer with rice?" But that's not it at all. We are becoming healthier; physically, mentally, emotionally, spiritually, intellectually — fundamentally. We are also pursuing medicine with a vengeance, but there must be a balance.

Mom and I had some good "alone" time today without Chuck and that felt good, too. We needed Mom and Jana time. We are being very honest with each other about our fears and needs. Tomorrow, I'm heading back to Denver to get some work done, but also to see some people who can give me a reality check. I told Mom I needed people to sit down with me to talk about everything. I feel like I'm handling things well, but I need a hug from someone other than Mom. I need to be able to cry in front of someone who won't get scared.

I've been very hesitant to cry in front of Mom because I don't want her to think I'm having doubts. I honestly believe we have a miracle in the works here, but I'm damn scared of the process.

I want to wrap this up with a list of good things that have already occurred because of Mom's cancer, including things we have become more thankful for:

- *I'm getting closer to Chuck*
- *We are already laughing in the face of unbelievable odds*
- *Mom has a garden to grow her organic vegetables in*
- *I live in Colorado instead of New Jersey*
- *Living healthier*
- *Mom's going to quit smoking when it's all over, or maybe sooner*
- *It's proving to me — all of us — just exactly what we're capable of*

It's been a good day

DESPITE THE TRAUMATIC news we were getting on a daily basis, it was easy to keep our sense of humor. We had always been a family that was used to laughing in the face of difficulty. We shared many silly, and even gross inside jokes, which developed out of experiences only a family could find humorous.

Shortly into Mom's diagnosis, we discovered a nuance surrounding her meals. She couldn't eat much because it hurt so badly, but when she burped, she experienced immeasurable relief.

One day after lunch, Mom leaned back in her chair and said, "Here one comes!"

I knew exactly what she meant and I held my breath hoping she could burp long and deeply. She did. I watched my mom burp like I'd only seen frat boys do in belching contests. She really ripped one out.

Then, she relaxed down in her chair and surprised me again by saying, "That was orgasmic."

I nearly fell out of my chair. Then she inhaled again suddenly, and another one came rolling out of her gut.

I screamed laughter, and said, "Mom! You're experiencing multiple burps!"

She started laughing and said, "I am just far too easy."

SUNDAY, JANUARY 10 — A LETTER WRITTEN TO EVERYONE ON MOM'S SIDE OF THE FAMILY

Dear Family,

Do you hear it!????! It's a Battle Cry! It's filled with LOVE, PASSION, FEAR, HONESTY, SPIRITUALITY, and INTELLECT.

We have a fight ahead of us and what family is better equipped for this type of battle than ours! If we can plan the kind of 50th birthday party we did, we can certainly circle the wagons and strategically, lovingly conquer this weak villain: cancer.

If you are like me, you need information. I bought

> *"Gray's Anatomy" and "The New American Medical Dictionary." I'm forwarding some things to you that I found particularly informative. It's easier for me to picture the cancer being destroyed if I can picture the organs.*
>
> *I don't know if this will work for you, but I do know we all like to be as informed as possible, so I thought I'd send this along.*
>
> *PS: Mom and I have decided that this is all a plot by AT&T.*

BEGINNING THE NEXT Monday, Mom and I ran from doctor to doctor in Pueblo. Meanwhile, Pat and Teri combed Denver for a doctor with as much gusto as we possessed.

Only days into this experience, I was feeling quite a bit of anger toward doctors and the entire medical industry. Surely some of it came from a "kill the messenger" reflex, but much also stemmed from a feeling that we were not being treated by humans, but by droids. Some of the doctors possessed egos-run-wild while others acted like "Teflon Doctor! I feel nothing!" Many times, I tried to put myself in their shoes and imagine what it must be like to tell people that they have cancer on a daily basis. I can see how they might become jaded and distanced. However, oncologists choose their specialty knowing they will face very sick people every single day. They have a responsibility to carry their duties with compassion as well as knowledge. Too often in our experience, the physicians thought the knowledge was enough.

We sought a doctor with a sense of hope. "Hope?" I can hear them saying. "Bah!" But, yes, we sought a doctor who knew how to hope. Hope indicates a will to try even when knowledge presents no cure. Hope believes in a patient's individuality. Hope allows you to say, "Don't give up" instead of, "Prepare to die." Hope sees the patient's children as a reason to live, rather than as orphans. Hope says, "I don't know everything about you, but if you're a fighter, I'll fight with you."

During Mom's illness, I read several of Bernie Siegal's books and was lucky enough to hear him speak in Denver. He is first a man and second a doctor. Hope, individuality, and miracles are all part of his physician's bag. When I read and heard his words, I knew we could and should expect more from the doctors with whom we worked — and we would work with doctors, not for them, around them, or despite them.

So, when Pat and Teri said they'd found a Denver doctor Mom should see, I was pessimistic. Teri said she asked all her fellow oncological nurses which doctor they'd send their family to and every one of them said, "Dr. O'Rourke." She made an appointment for us to see him January 12. I was excited at the chance to get a fresh opinion, but I still thought someone could take it all away and make it all better.

In the meantime, Jason finagled his way into a leave from the Navy. He had to lie and tell the Red Cross that Mom was on her death bed, but he made it. I picked him up at the airport in Denver.

"Broski!" I yelled upon seeing him.

"Shithead!" he said, equally loud.

"Dork face!"

"Nerd nose!"

"Godzilla breath!"

"Shithead!" he repeated.

"I win! You lose!" I said. We hugged.

Jason had not been in the information loop since we found out it was cancer because the Navy has strict phone rules. He knew nothing about what the doctors had recommended, or more accurately stated, how little they had recommended. I'm sure Jason thought we'd received all sorts of treatment options. I planned to take him out for dinner and lay it all on him as gently as I could. I wasn't sure how he'd react. For all of his bravado, Jason is an extremely sensitive man. I credit it to being raised by a single woman, and having a sister. As children, I'd protected him on the playground because he was more prone to tears than his boy counterparts. I imagine now that I was probably the source of some of those tears; what guy wants his big sister finishing fights for him? As we grew up, I was the worry wart, the straight-A nerd, and the perfect daughter. He was funny, a trouble-maker, and a true challenge to Mom's parenting skills. Mom's philosophy raising Jason walked the line between setting strong boundaries, and knowing when to "let kids be kids."

Case in point: Because we grew up in rural farm country, every boy had at least one BB gun, and usually the teens had shotguns. Jason got his first BB gun after we moved to Ashley Lane, where we owned an acre with two large corrals and three barns. They weren't barns in the sense of hay lofts and owls' nests, but we called them barns because they looked like larger versions of the garden shed and calling them sheds would have been too disappointing.

Jason used to sit on one of the barn roofs for hours pumping that BB gun and shooting at stray birds. He cast his blue eyes around the yard looking for prey. He shot at anything that flew by and when he got bored, he shot at the ant piles in the corral. Sometimes, when the bird activity was particularly slow, he found other targets to sacrifice. He thought clothes pins were the ultimate target. They were small and already perched in a row on the clothes line. I think Mom bought more than six bags of clothes pins one summer. Just as soon as she'd get them all clipped nicely to the string, she'd turn around and find dead pins all over the back yard. After the third time, her light came on.

Mom had this attribute any kid would love their mom to possess; an indicator light. You could always tell when she was getting angry because she had a birthmark on the center of her forehead that was unnoticeable until her blood pressure went up. It was like a dial on a furnace.

As always, Jason was long gone by the time she discovered the clips in the grass, so he missed the process of Mom's light glowing bright and then slowly diminishing to embers.

"Jason," she said later that night when he'd returned. "I put those clothes pins there for a reason and it's not because I want you to become a good shot."

"But there weren't any birds," Jason said. He seemed to think this a perfectly rational explanation.

"I understand that, Jason, but my clothes pins are not targets and I'm getting tired of finding them all over the backyard."

"I'll pick them up."

"That's not the point, Jason," she said. I watched her light. "I want you to stop shooting them. Pick another target."

Then she clarified that statement, saying, "Outside our property."

Jason glanced at me and she clarified it again. "Not your sister."

"Can I still sit on the barn?" he asked.

"You may sit on the barn, just don't aim the gun in this direction. Aim over Sarlo's field. He ought to have a conniption fit over that one."

Old Man Sarlo was our neighbor. His corn fields neighbored our land and he sat on his back porch and watched his crop like a buzzard. If a leaf moved, KA-BOOM! He shot. He knew all the local boys ran through his corn and he shot many butts full of rock salt. It was a game between the boys and Sarlo. The boys knew that if they ran through the field, he'd shoot at them. Sarlo knew they ran through just to see if he could hit them. If he had ever quit shooting, they probably would have stopped running.

Obviously, Mom thought it might keep Sarlo extra busy if another person was shooting at the corn field. Jason liked the idea and decided it would be a lot more fun than stationary clothes pins. Problem solved.

Sometimes, though, Mom encouraged Jason in seemingly unmotherly ways. Once, she saw a profile on television about an Oklahoman who was making a mint by shooting jeans with a shotgun. At the time, ripped, shredded, and generally unwearable jeans were "in" and this man was selling the jeans at a huge profit.

"Jason," she said playfully, "I think you should tell your friends that they can bring you their jeans and you'll shoot 'em full of holes for 10 bucks a pair."

She winked at me as if to say, "This ought to be interesting."

Jason thought he was in heaven: make money shooting other people's clothes with his mother's consent. What else could a 14-year-old desire? Mom's suggestion had one minor flaw, though. Jason, being the business brain that he was, decided that to make it marketable, he would have to endorse the product himself. So, once

Mom was gone, he took a pair of his own jeans out to the corral, shotgun crooked through his arm. He went in silence, like a man with a man's job to do.

I sat inside, determined not to be an accomplice, and I heard the shots — many, many shots. When he returned, the jeans were held together by threads. He had focused most of his attention on the backside.

"Cool, huh?" he said. A crazy grin appeared and his eyes were wide.

"Jason, I think you might have overdone it a little," I said, giggling. It was too much to bear. He shot his jeans!

He offered to put my jeans out of their misery, but I declined. I was never cool.

When Mom came home, Jason told her he wanted to show her something. Immediately, her parental antennae went up. She glanced at me for a good or bad sign and I merely shrugged. I felt sorry for her, but she brought it on herself.

When he came waltzing out with the jeans on, her eyes popped out and her head almost fell off her neck.

"Jason Paul! What have you done? Are those gun shots?"

"Yeah, Mom, it's great! Just like you said!"

Jason was no dummy. Throwing in "just like you said" cleared him; he was untouchable.

"But Jason," Mom said, "I said other people's jeans. Not your jeans. Which ones were those? Are those the Levis I just bought?"

He nodded brightly.

"Turn around." She wanted to assess the entire situation. "Jason, I can see your underwear."

"That's the best part, Mom."

He turned around and gleamed at her, truly thrilled with his new attire. Mom was stuck and she laughed despite herself.

Unfortunately for him, Jason only made about $70 before people decided they could shoot their own jeans.

Jason's playful, optimistic demeanor had not diminished one ounce as he grew older. I expected him to react to the news about Mom buoyantly. "Big deal. She'll be fine." But then I thought about the waiting rooms, the exams, scopes, and biopsies. I remembered the doctors' grim faces, their grimmer news, and the moment I saw the spots on the CT scan for the first time. I heard tapes in my head of doctors saying, "foolhardy to operate," "six months," and "18 months." I almost cried before I started. I was about to break his heart.

After we ordered, I said, "So, ready?"

"For what?" he said cheerily.

"Jason, the news is very bad."

"Jana, listen, she's going to be fine."

"I know, Jason, but I think you'd better hear everything before you see her tomorrow."

"Why? Does she look bad?"

"No, actually, she looks great and says she feels great. Except for when she eats." I paused. "I just think you'd better hear everything. Besides, I need you to know. I need to talk to you about it."

He nodded and visibly braced himself. I could see his little-boy face appear before me and he gritted his teeth. He used to look like that when he got grounded. If only this were that easy. I dove in with the most brutal information in my bag of baddies. He needed it straight.

"Jason, when doctors first found the tumor, they told Mom she had six months to live."

"What?" He immediately teared up. "What!"

I kept going.

"Since then, they've changed that to 18 months."

I paused to let that sink in. He looked around the restaurant like he had no idea where he was. I began crying quietly, seeing all of my own fears in him. Everything I'd had a week to digest, he was suddenly enduring over one meal.

"What?" he asked again, weakly. His whole body collapsed.

I told the full story, from the first day to that day, leaving nothing out. Our food arrived and neither of us ate. When Jason could control his tears no longer, we left and I finished the story in the car. He grew very quiet and responded little, but he didn't ask me to stop. When we got back to my place, Brooke had made the hide-a-bed for Jason.

"I don't know if I can handle the doctor's appointment tomorrow," Jason said as I sat on the bed next to him.

"Jason, it's entirely different when you're around her," I said. "You feel like there's nothing she can't do and you know she'll live. You will handle it fine because you have to. Something in you just kicks in and you run on a strength you didn't know you had."

We hugged tightly and went to bed.

At 5:30 the next morning, our cousin, Jennifer, called. The phone's ring sent me leaping out of bed.

"Jana, Grandma died last night," Jennifer said, and she started sobbing.

I said nothing. I couldn't even think. Daddy's mom had been fighting brain cancer for months. I had heard stories from Aunt Chris about Grandma's weight loss, hair loss, and her vacant stares. We'd all been praying that she would find peace soon. However, of course, none of us wanted her to die. We never stopped hoping. I guess I was relieved for Grandma, but I know what was going through Jennifer's mind and, of course, scary things occurred to me, too.

Jennifer said, "I figured you'd want to hear it from me since your dad's in Europe. Jana, I'm so sorry about what you're going through." She kept crying.

I finally told her that I'd be fine but I should call her later. I couldn't listen to her cry. She gave me her work phone number which I immediately forgot. I didn't have a pen near the phone and didn't feel like hunting for one in the dark. I promised I'd call her back. It took a lot of courage and strength on her part to call and I guessed that she volunteered for the job.

After I got off the phone, I wandered over to where Jason was sleeping.

He said, "Do you think you've got that phone's ringer turned up high enough? Geez!"

I looked at him and found that I couldn't quite get my arms around the news. Grandma died. Mom has cancer. Could this be happening, really? The early hour and the state-of-mind I'd been in for a week limited my ability to process the news. When I told Jason, my expression was one of confusion, not pain.

"Jason," I said, "Grandma died."

He just said, "Good."

I sat on his bed and we tried to think of things to say, but he covered it. He said, "Let's go to sleep. I have to cuss God out."

I went back to bed but I couldn't sleep, so I went back to the living room and crawled in with him.

"I can't understand why God would need both of them," I said.

"I was just thinking the same thing."

"At least Grandma's up there fighting for us."

He said, "Yeah," and we both giggled.

I imagined Grandma sailing through the Pearly Gates straight up to the Big Guy and tap dancing all over his world until he agreed to cure Mom. Grandma had tapped until she got cancer.

I said, "Either things really suck in Heaven right now and He needs two incredible people to help Him out, or He screwed up."

Jason agreed.

We tried to sleep, but it just amounted to us holding onto each other.

TUESDAY, JANUARY 12, — IN MY APARTMENT BEFORE THE APPOINTMENT

Today marks one week since this all began. Last night, after we heard about Grandma, I just prayed that God would give us hope today. I don't think I can take one more doctor dooming us. I just need hope. I didn't even ask for a miracle last night. I just asked for hope.

ON TUESDAY, JASON and I met Mom and Chuck at Dr. O'Rourke's office. Before they arrived, Jason and I were sitting in the waiting room where a woman sat in a hospital robe with her husband. About 10 minutes after we arrived, a nurse came out, smiled, and shook her head. Apparently, at that moment, the woman learned she did not have cancer. She jumped up, screamed, hugged her husband and the nurse, and then walked back into the doctor's office to change.

I looked at Jason and said, "I'm having the most terrible thoughts right now."

He said, "Me, too."

I thought, 'Why can't this woman have cancer and my mom be the one jumping around happily?'

As the woman and her husband walked out, Jason leaned over to me and whispered, "You hold her down, I'll get her liver." We had a good laugh.

When Mom arrived, Jason jumped up and held her tightly for a long time. He cried.

"I'm not handling this too well, am I?" he asked.

"You are just fine, Jason. Just fine," she said, and she hugged him tighter.

"Sylvia … uh … Schmel?" the nurse said. "Would you like to join me now?"

The nurse smiled pleasantly, embarrassed by her inability to pronounce our name.

Chuck, Jason, and I sat around and talked. A little later, the doctor himself came to call us all back to his office and he must have listened very well to Mom because he knew all of our names, knew that Jason had flown in the night before, knew that I worked at the University of Denver, and knew that Chuck was her beau. He walked us back to an office — not an examination room — and we waited for Mom. She was changing back into her clothes.

When she arrived, Dr. O'Rourke began discussing his thoughts.

"I recommend against surgery," he said, quickly adding, "But we aren't closing any doors."

Whoa! I suddenly wanted to listen to this man who seemed willing to risk.

"I'm not completely satisfied that the cancer started in the pancreas," he continued. "Perhaps it is primary hepatoma — a rare occurrence when cancer actually starts in the liver. The biopsy shows that the cells in the left lobe of your liver, Sylvia, are different than cells in the right lobe. I'm wondering if perhaps the left lobe, which is entirely cancerous tumor, is the only cancer in your body, and the spots on the right lobe are cysts or broken blood vessels."

He paused again, and added, "This is only a possibility. I don't want to instill false hope, but I also want you to know I'm not giving up if you aren't."

At that moment, I think the man grew a halo. He suggested an MRI be done that day, as well as a "tumor marker" blood test. Both would help locate the primary source for the cancer. He said that if it was primary hepatoma and if the right lobe was cancer, we may be able to control the cancer in the right lobe and remove the left lobe. The liver is one of the few organs that regenerates if part of it is removed. Mom could live with only one lobe of her liver. Dr. O'Rourke said he was going to speak to a chemotherapist about his plan.

Mom said, "Doctor, I've listened to your suggestions carefully and I'd like to aggressively pursue your recommendations."

An MRI was scheduled for 1:40 p.m. and blood was taken for the tumor markers immediately.

Hope! Finally, a doctor who recognized in us a determination to fight.

However, within days, we learned that the right lobe was also cancerous. We had to wait even longer for the tumor marker results and Dr. O'Rourke's treatment recommendations. The waiting was hard but it felt good to know a doctor was working with us, which angered me further at the Pueblo doctors. Why were they so willing to concede defeat? They hardly had the strength to shake Mom's hand, let alone fight for her life. They were far too willing to accept the death of a woman seeking their help. They were far too willing to tell a strong, fighting family to give up. They did not know us or her and, worse yet, chose not to.

At the end of that long day, Tuesday, Jason went to Cañon City with Mom. I worked Wednesday and drove to Cañon that evening.

On Thursday, Mom woke up and announced, "I'm tired of having cancer. I need to do something other than have cancer. Let's go to Cripple Creek."

The little town of Cripple Creek was one of Colorado's earliest, and most prosperous mining towns. Its population rivaled Denver's during the gold boom. Later, it relaxed into a quiet little town where wild burros, descendants of those brave animals that trekked with prospectors, roamed the streets looking for handouts of carrots and sugar.

Years earlier, Mom had taken us up for one of the nation's oldest melodrama productions. Every year since the 1800s, a small theater in the basement of the Imperial Hotel produced an authentic melodrama. When I was about nine, Mom brought us up one summer evening, committing a good sum of her small teacher's salary to this entertainment. Jason and I couldn't believe we were allowed to boo and hiss at the villain! Sanctioned yelling in a theater! After the show, we had wandered through the town's window-front stores, and stumbled across another childhood joy: a store called "The Brass Ass." Ass! The bad word was part of the name of the store which left it fair game for kids to say freely. We delightfully pelted out the name repeatedly until Mom said, "Enough!"

Unfortunately, in the early 1990s, the town had voted to legalize gambling. The rush to Cripple Creek was renewed, but the results turned out to be less than charming. The burros all but disappeared, the quaint shops turned into cheap T-shirt stores, and every nook and cranny offered a one-armed bandit.

Still, it was better than sitting around thinking about cancer, and it had been quite a while since the three of us had been together. The trip offered opportunities to regroup on familiar, beautiful terrain. We drove up to Cripple Creek on Phantom Canyon road, a mountain road where we used to take quick, weekend camping trips. As we drove, we remembered our favorite camping spots.

"Remember the time I almost threw Jana in the fire?" Jason said proudly. He was driving us in the Nissan Wagon.

"Do I remember?" Mom said. "I almost threw you in the creek!"

"I remember how you used to wash the dishes, Mom," I said.

"Yeah!" Jason yelled out. "You just threw them in the creek! That cast-iron skillet sizzled and sank to the bottom."

Mom smiled. "And what kind of soap did we use?"

"Ivory!" we both said.

"Because it floats and you can set it down on top of the water while you're washing up," I said.

"Oh, I did teach you two the benefits of fine living, didn't I?" Mom laughed.

In Cripple Creek, we located the Brass Ass, which now offered slot machines. We found the Imperial Hotel where they still produced the melodrama in the basement, but the hotel itself had been upgraded and modernized. We had lunch in the hotel and then decided to test Lady Luck. Before we drove up to Cripple Creek, a friend of mine from work, Jennifer, said we should all start buying lottery tickets because our luck had to turn around. However, we all lost money that day. We were on a roll.

The next day, Friday, Jason had to go back to the Navy. His good-bye with Mom was short and positive; typical Jason. He gave her a strong hug with tears in his eyes.

"I get out for good in June," he said to Mom. "I wish I could be here to help you, but you're going to be fine. I'll see you soon."

Mom didn't cry but hugged him proudly.

"I love you, Jason."

"I love you, too, Mom."

I drove Jason back to Denver and took him to the airport. He confided that he didn't want to leave, but that he was certain Mom would be OK.

"I'll be back in June, Jana, and she'll be on the road to recovery. You'll see."

"I hope so," I said. "I'm going to miss you."

"Love you, nerd nose," he said.

"Love you, too, dork face."

I had planned to go back to work for a half day after that, but realized I had scheduled an appointment with a counselor in DU's Employee Assistance Program.

I walked into David's office carting Bernie Siegal's "Love, Medicine, and Miracles." Dr. Siegal writes about how to help the mind and body communicate for better health. He's an evolved physician who believes that we can cause our own illnesses through negative messages or experiences. The idea is that we can also avoid illness and even cure ourselves by changing our self-perceptions, attitudes, and stress levels.

"Excellent book," David said when I walked in, and he gave me a hug.

This was my first visit with him since Mom's diagnosis. I had visited him when Grandma was diagnosed. When I told him about Mom's cancer, he sounded astonished.

I set the Siegal book down and he said, "So, is that book helping you with your stomach?"

I looked at him in confusion. Stress had always manifested itself in my gut. David and I had talked a lot about the reasons for the pain during previous visits. However, it had never occurred to me that I might read Siegal's book to help my health. I was reading it purely to figure out a solution to Mom's health. I bought it as an assignment and a mission which I tackled just as I tackled everything else since her diagnosis.

"Well, my stomach is killing me almost all the time," I said. "But I'm reading this to help Mom."

"What about you?"

David had this annoying habit of making me talk about myself. I found it difficult to switch gears from my constant attention to Mom, to an hour focused entirely on me. The idea that this book might help my health was a brand new concept, and as I relaxed into the hour, I liked the idea a lot.

"Maybe I will re-read this with my health in mind. It never even dawned on me, David," I said. "I'm no good to Mom if I'm not 100 percent healthy."

David smiled. "Don't try to get healthy for your Mom, Janalee. Get healthy for you. You've been suffering from stomach pains for over five years. Siegal is a good way to figure out what you're doing to yourself. This is a life lesson. Not a way to better help your mom."

After discussing Siegal, I began talking about what I've learned since Mom's diagnosis. I told him I was proud of myself.

"I feel like I really am helping her," I said. "I'm not just a daughter any more. I'm her friend. She really does need me. In a way, that feels good, and in a way it scares me. But I'm glad I seem to be coping alright and really helping to find solutions."

David responded by saying that the whole experience, regardless of the outcome, would give me a new perspective on life and help me to know myself better. I had a strange reaction to that: I became very angry.

After a long pause during which I tried to understand the source of my anger, I said, "David, for several years, many of my closest friends have told me that I know myself better than most people our age. When people say that, I've always believed it's because of the good and bad experiences I've had. Mom's alcoholism and recovery, Daddy's cancer, Mom's divorces, my grandma's cancer. I think that they all made me a stronger person.

"David, I don't want to know myself any better if this is the cost. And anyone who tries to tell me that this is worth the self-discovery can just get out of my life. This is most certainly not worth it. I'd trade it all, I'd be the most shallow person on earth, if I could have Mom's health back."

I was crying and David handed me a box of tissue.

"Unfortunately, that's not an option," I continued. "I can't just turn away from this and say, 'No thanks.' And so-called personal strength is no reward."

David was the only person to whom I could share such anger and not feel guilty. I needed that outlet. With everyone else, I focused primarily on the facts of Mom's illness and what we were doing to cure her. I rarely talked about my deepest fears.

TUESDAY, JANUARY 19

The last two weeks have taught me a lot about myself, my family and, of course, my mother. One thing that continually occurs to me is honesty. We have always tried to be honest with each other, but it has now become absolutely crucial.

The honesty is difficult, though, when I am facing my

deepest darkest fears. I've not yet breached the thoughts, "Have you thought about dying, Mom?" or "I've tried to imagine life without you, Mom." I can't. I can't imagine where that conversation would lead and, quite simply, I really don't believe she's going to die, so why even ponder it at this point? My Aunt Margie and I discussed this yesterday as I took her from Stapleton Airport to Colorado Springs to meet up with Mom. Aunt Margie feels the same way as I do. Are we in a state of denial if we don't talk about Mom's death simply because we honestly believe she's going to live? No! Like Mom said, this is not about dying, it's about living. Sure, we're going to treat her cancer with the best medicine and intellect we can. But we're also going to live. We are going to change some of the ways we've lived and even improve on what was already a damned good life. We are not — Mom is not — dying! That is honesty in its most healthy application.

"I'M GOING TO bring something up that I've wanted to talk to you about for many months now, but this seems as appropriate a time as any other," Mom said.

We were sitting at the heavy oak dining table over the morning's first cup of coffee. She wore her robe and I was in old shorts and a T-shirt, which I'd slept in. Her words did more to wake me than the caffeine.

"You need to know that I wanted to bring this up a while ago and it isn't necessarily the present situation that makes me suggest this," she continued.

I recoiled. She had obviously been considering how to approach me for some time. She watched me as I took a deep breath and she let me brace myself.

"Janalee, if anything happens to me ..."

"Mom!"

"Janalee, I must ask you this. We must be realistic. I must be prepared and this task is very important to me."

I began crying and she moved to the chair next to me. She took my hand and I breathed deeply to stop crying.

"You know I've kept journals ever since I got sober, right?" she asked.

I knew exactly what was coming. She wanted the journals destroyed. Mom had kept journals for over 15 years. After the first three years of her sobriety, she read parts of those journals and decided that she wanted the thoughts and "hateful emotions" gone forever, so she burned them. After that, she saved all of the journals. I'm sure her second marriage and divorce with Rex were chronicled in them. I know she wrote about her big decision to quit her high school librarian position to become a middle school assistant principal. She definitely wrote about her decision to become CEO at the treatment center where she got sober. And I remember that she did a lot of writing before she finally quit that place to once again do something she truly loved — librarianship. Mom had become the librarian at the women's prison in Cañon City only nine months before this fiasco, finally feeling she'd found the career she'd be with for the rest of her life. She wrote about all of those things, as well as about people who made important impacts on her life.

I promised to respect her wishes because if anybody found the things I had written over the years, people I loved dearly would get hurt.

Later that day, she laid another one on me. We drove to her bank and put my name on her checking account. She said that if the treatments made her too ill to pay her bills, someone would have to do it. Practical. She was being practical and yet every move she made while in this mode terrified me. Being practical or realistic didn't mean we weren't fighting, but that line was so easily blurred in my mind. If I really believed she was going to live, I wouldn't think about matters involving her death. Vicious circle. I frequently experienced guilt, which is an entirely wasted emotion. Of course, I'd fulfill her requests, but I hoped that by agreeing, I didn't indicate my fight was gone.

Over the next couple of days, she showed me how she organized her finances and I paid some of her bills. This was the first moment I realized that our roles may reverse. What if she did become too weak to pay her bills? Not only could I not visualize that depth of weakness on her tough body, but I couldn't fathom the idea that I would have to care for her, down to her most basic needs. I imagine that she hated the idea more than I. I wished that I could just be her little girl and let her take care of me forever. The way it's supposed to be.

Courage

CHAPTER 4

One evening this week when Mom was curled up under a blanket in her recliner, I walked up to her and stood looking at her. She asked, "What are you thinking?" I said, "Do I still fit?"

"Of course you still fit," she said, and pulled me into her lap, beneath her loving arms.

I said, "Mom, we're being honest, right?" She said, "Yes."

I dug my face further into her neck and said, "I want to tell you this, and we shared moments like this before you had cancer so I don't want you to think I'm saying this because I'm predicting bad things. But I want to say it," I paused, wondering if I sounded like I predicted doom, but I decided to go on. "I've always learned from you. And even today, in the situation you face now, I continue to learn from you. Your strength inspires many people and by watching you the last few days I realize how much of it comes from your unique faith and relationship with God. It makes so many other things seem insignificant."

I explained that there were many characteristics she possessed that I admired, but it was only through these tough circumstances that I learned everything she was and everything she stood for was a result of her absolute faith in her Higher Power. That's how she had maintained an inner peace through the trauma, showing us all that when you believe in yourself and your Higher Power, good will come. We both cried and hugged.

And I definitely still fit.

About this time, I started realizing that cancer diagnosis is not a clean science. I don't know why I thought it should be. Perhaps I wanted it to be easy so that treatment could begin immediately and aggressively. Two weeks into the discovery that Mom had cancer, we were still hunting for the type of cancer, let alone a treatment. I began to feel like a rat in a maze. Scurry down one blind alley only to discover a dead end. Turn around, retrace my steps, and scurry down another dark path only to run into another wall. I kept expecting some doctor to finally say, "This is what it is and this is what we should do." But that never happened. Never. I'm still not sure that any of the doctors were convinced of any single diagnosis. We ultimately learned that they thought it was primary liver cancer, but I don't think they knew if it spread from there.

Two weeks into the ordeal, though, I still sought definitive knowledge. I wanted a plan! I could pursue a plan with gusto: this day-to-day, wait-and-see game made me dread every morning. What would we learn? What would be discovered? Would one theory dissolve in the face of new information?

I became panicky. Every day that passed felt like lost opportunity and lost ground to the cancer. I could almost hear the cancer growing in Mom's belly and I truly imagined that every day we didn't do something, we lost a day of Mom's life. Her distended belly occupied my mind continuously. I stared at it wondering if the cancer was moving to new ground, multiplying as we ran from doctor to doctor. My impatience multiplied like the cancer cells, and my imagination ran as rampant as I imagined the cancer did inside her body.

I longed for a treatment. I couldn't understand why nothing had been done. Just poking, prodding, and picture-taking. No action. No fights. I wanted to stick my own hands inside her belly and pull out the cancer. I wanted medicine inside her, doctors inside her, good cells inside her instead of bad. I was obsessed.

I also expected that once they did discover the source and type of cancer, the treatment would start and it would be smooth sailing from there. No new discoveries, just fighting with treatment. Little did I know that the diagnosis was just the beginning.

FRIDAY, JANUARY 22 — 8:30 A.M.

I'm at work and it's Friday. Mom is on her way up here for more tests. We got really good news on Wednesday evening. The cancer is primary liver cancer, meaning it didn't start somewhere else and move to her liver. It also hasn't metastasized from her liver anywhere else. That means all they have to treat is the liver! And and and!!! She may not have to go through chemotherapy! I had just taken that as a given, but the doctors seem to believe a different type of treatment would be more effective. Dr. O'Rourke took Mom's case to the Tumor Board at the hospital and got the opinions of at least five other doctors. They decided to try to shrink the left lobe of her liver by cutting the blood off to it. They will clot the left hepatic artery and maybe they can eventually remove the left lobe. Then, they are going to pinpoint the cancerous tissue in the right lobe and kill it. They will insert a catheter through an artery in her groin and poison the cancer sites with a certain type of alcohol. We all found that fairly ironic. I mean, 16 years ago she was pouring alcohol onto her liver and now they're going to treat her liver with alcohol! Friends have said, "Haven't you had enough of that, Sylvia?" Pat said, "Well, if they're going to do that, they'd better do it right! I've got a bottle of Stoli's from Russia that I've been saving for a special occasion. I'll donate it to this cause."

Anyway, Mom is coming up to Denver today to have tests done on her blood. They need to see how well her blood clots. They will also conduct some other tests and hopefully she can have the procedure done next week. Once they cut off the blood to the left and poison the right, we wait 2-4 weeks and then do some more MRI and CT scans. If the left has shrunk and the right is responding to the alcohol, they may be able to surgically remove the left lobe and then treat the right! HOPE HOPE HOPE! It can make all the difference in the world.

TUESDAY, JANUARY 26 — 8:30 A.M.

Friday was not a good day and the weekend carried that feeling through. We learned Friday that Mom cannot do the alcohol treatment on the right lobe. They tried to locate the spots with the ultrasound but realized they could not pinpoint them as precisely as they needed to. They also did an angiogram, which basically lets doctors know how blood travels throughout your body. The doctors needed to know how the blood enters and exits her liver to see if they can cut off the supply to the left lobe. We should get the results either today or tomorrow. If they can't cut the blood off and they can't pinpoint the sites in the right lobe, all the good news we got last Wednesday is null. Well, except for the fact that it's primary liver cancer.

When we got the news about the ultrasound, Mom said, "They keep ruling things out. I want them to rule something in." She asked the doctor, "Am I wasting time by not starting chemo right away?" He said, "You can't start the treatment without knowing which kind is the best for you."

Ruling out out out out out out. Let's get going!

We're all getting so tired of waiting. Three weeks ago, it was much easier to wait because there was so much to concentrate on — finding a doctor, how to change her diet, who should come out to be with her, books to read about cancer, books to read about diet, books to read about attitude. Now we want to start treatment! The doctor said, "An hour or a day won't make a difference with this type of cancer." Well, it's been three weeks! Three Weeks! That's almost a month!

Friday left us all feeling depressed and not ready to face yet another weekend of waiting for results. I have this irrational belief that if I let my spirits get down, less positive energy will be contributed to Mom's health and somehow she won't get well as quickly. So, whenever I get scared, I get angry with myself for not being "up." It's a lot of pressure. Also, when I describe the situation to people I find myself trying to be as upbeat as possible because I consider every person a potential "positive energy convert." I don't want people to get the impression that we are fighting a losing battle because we aren't. I want them to think, "There's a family that will beat this cancer."

WEDNESDAY, JANUARY 27

Nobody can tell us we should quit fighting. Nobody should tell us to quit fighting. Why quit fighting for your life if somebody's telling you you're going to die? That seems the perfect time to start fighting hard for your life — hard.

We got yet more bad news yesterday. The doctor said the angiogram turned up more cancer in the right lobe of the liver.

liver, live, vile, rile, vie, IV, lie

I just saw that "live" is part of liver and decided to see what else I could find.

Anyway, they also said the blood does not travel well through her liver and that chemotherapy would be toxic to her system. It would kill her. Where does that leave us? That's what we're trying to find out. A transplant, maybe. We're not giving up. I must admit, though, that I'm very down. And I am extremely angry. Why can't we just finally know exactly what we're dealing with and treat it?! No more surprises.

I called Mom from the office yesterday to see if the doctor had made an appointment for her to start treatment. She said, "Honey, it's bad news again. Do you have someone there with you?" I got angry and said, "Just tell me, Mom." She said, "Is somebody there?" I said, "I'm at work. There are all kinds of people here. What." She told me the doctor did not recom-

mend chemo. Basically, that rules out both chemo and surgery. At my desk, I suddenly felt like I was in a time warp or that all the air had been vacuum-sealed out of my office. There wasn't even enough air for me to blink. Mom said Aunt Margie was reacting the same way I did after we met the doctors in Pueblo. Aunt Margie was flaming angry and crying scared. Mom said she was, once again, in shock. The doctor said he was trying to contact a doctor in Washington who frequently dealt with this type of cancer and that he would call Mom by 6:30 p.m. So we all got off the phone to allow him to get through.

I immediately started breathing very heavily because I didn't want to cry at work. I threw everything into my bag, told one person I'd gotten bad news — she tried to hug me and I backed away, knowing I'd break down — and I ran outside. As I was walking toward my car, I heard, "Hey you!" It was the dean of the school where I work. I turned and looked at him, stopped in my tracks and started bawling. My bag fell off my shoulder and he came up and put his arms around me. He talked to me until Brooke arrived from a meeting and I asked her to take me to Pat and Teri's. Brooke took me to Pat's and I stayed there waiting for a call from Mom until 9:15.

The waiting is becoming more and more unbearable. As soon as the hands hit 6:30, Pat and I began "waiting" which involves so much more than planting yourself in front of a TV. I kept moving from the fireplace to the couch to the floor. I'd look at Pat, thinking she was watching TV, and she'd be staring off. She grabbed a bowl of carrots out of the fridge and before we knew it, they were gone. She made jokes that seemed extraordinarily funny, primarily because we needed to laugh. We ripped apart commercials. She played the piano. And when the phone rang, we both sucked air and hoped that it would be Mom, that it wouldn't be Mom, that it would be Mom, that it wouldn't be Mom. We wanted to know more, but we didn't want more bad news.

When Mom finally called, she sounded better. After 6:30

when the doctor hadn't called, she and Chuck went for a drive. She said, "We walked under the stars and I played with the curls on the back of his neck and I knew I could not leave this place. I ain't goin' nowhere, Janalee." She also said, "I feel healthy. I feel healthier than I did three weeks ago. None of these people who are telling me I'm going to die have experienced what it's like to live in this body. If they had, they'd know their diagnosis is inaccurate."

So, we fight on. The Denver doctor is supposed to call Mom today to let her know what the Washington doctor said, but we don't expect anything new. In the meantime, I bought Mom a magazine called "Organic Gardening." I think I'm going to get her one of those small, indoor garden boxes so she can play in the dirt. She always found that very therapeutic.

Oh! One thing I didn't mention that I tend to find very encouraging, though a doctor may try to poo-poo this as well. Her tumor is getting softer. It used to be very hard. She described it as a basketball under her skin. Now it is very soft. We've been killing cancer cells with our hope! I honestly believe that. I have this mental image of those nasty, evil, weak cells screaming, "I'm melting! I'm melting! Oh, what a world, what a world."

We've got them right where we want them, just like The Wizard of Oz. Cornered in the liver. Nowhere else to go. We're going to dowse those babies with laughter, hope, love, faith and joy.

Ding Dong The Cancer's Dead!

THURSDAY, FEBRUARY 17

It's been a long time since I wrote and I think my emotions show it. The last couple of weeks have been very trying and I've been doing a supreme job of getting Mom everything she needs to be as comfortable as she can possibly be, but I haven't taken much time out for myself.

I have to write about Waiting. I've waited for guys to call and ask me out. I've waited for mail. I've waited for grades. I've waited for letters of acceptance. I've waited for pregnancy test results, which I thought was the most excruciating 10 minutes of my life. But nothing compares to waiting for cancer treatment suggestions from doctors.

For 10 minutes, I sat and stared at that pregnancy stick. Would it be blue? Pink? Would I be relieved? Would I have more decisions to make? Watching the clock as the second hand slowly circled the face. Trying to occupy myself by cleaning the bathroom, never leaving the vicinity of the test. Cocking my head one way and then another to look at the stick from different angles. Reading the instructions over and over to make sure I had conducted the test correctly. Thinking of people I'd have to call if the news was bad.

Waiting for cancer treatment suggestions from doctors takes you beyond the second hand into minutes, hours, days, months of the worst kind of waiting. Multiply the stress of waiting 10 minutes for a pregnancy test times 4,000,000 and that equals two minutes of the waiting we've endured over the past month and a half. Month and a half!

During the first couple of weeks, there was so much to do that we never felt like we were waiting. We had to find doctors, get tests done, read about different cancer clinics, find other people with the same cancer, change her diet, go food shopping, figure out how to get her on disability. There wasn't a free moment. But now we're past the tests and we're trying to adjust to the facts, but we still have to wait for a "plan of attack." I only feel so powerful, only so effective, when all I do is change her diet from meat to rice.

I should write a brief synopsis of what's happened. We got the bad news about the alcohol treatments on Friday, Jan. 22. Then, the day of my last entry the doctors here in Denver said, "There's nothing we can do." Once again, we all headed down to the bottom of this amazing roller-coaster we're on. I was here in Denver and Aunt Margie and Mom were in Cañon City. We were angry, scared, confused, hurt. You name it. But by the end of the evening we had regrouped and re-circled the wagons. We refused to give up simply because doctors were giving up.

Dr. Grady, a colleague of O'Rourke's, had told Mom there was nothing he could do but he would make a couple more phone calls. We waited all day that day and heard nothing. I went down to Cañon City Wednesday night and on Thursday, Grady called and said that he had located a treatment being done at a hospital in Texas. He said it offered "zero chance for a cure" but it might extend her life a couple of years. He scheduled an appointment for us with Dr. Marks in Denver for Friday afternoon. Marks is a chemotherapist who can tell us more about the Texas treatment.

Friday, we went to Denver to see Marks who I really liked. He said, "I know you've been told that the chance for a cure is one in many million, but that's what we're going for here, isn't it? We're in this for the long haul, aren't we?" He was the first doctor to speak beyond statistics. Hope! From a doctor! Go figure! He, too, said Mom looked way too good for what she was going through. He felt her liver and "mapped out" the organ on her stomach with a ball point pen. I was amazed when Mom showed me his marks later in the bathroom at the hospital. It covered her entire, bloated stomach. That's what really drove the whole, awful idea of liver cancer home to me. The lines started right below her breasts, ran around her sides so far that she had to turn to show me part of her back, and down to right above her pubic hair line. A small section on her lower left abdomen was liver-free.

Finally, we had been given information about a possible treatment. But a huge decision remained. Should it be done at MD Anderson in Texas where they did approximately six such procedures a year, or in Denver where it had never been done before?

SINCE THAT MOMENT January fifth when we'd discovered the tumor, every minute of our lives had been consumed with hunting for a treatment. Every single day had revealed new information or new bodily glitches that made the situation seem hopeless. Doors slammed closed just when we seemed to get our foot into them. We'd functioned purely on hope in a situation that was presented to us as hopeless on a daily basis for weeks.

Given that desperate context, we took this treatment news as a starving man takes food. We were hollow, dwindling, and ravenous. The mere mention of a possible treatment sustained us. However, this was no simple treatment. There was a reason only a few hospitals in the country performed it. In concept, chemo would be trapped in one lobe of the liver to kill cancer cells, while the other lobe functioned to the best of its ability. Then, if there was any positive response, they could go in and do the other lobe later. The concept sounded good, but in practice it was rife with potential dangers.

Doctor Marks told us as we sat in his office that Mom would be under full anesthesia. Then they would insert a long, skinny tube into her femoral artery, beginning at her groin. They'd push this tube all the way up to her liver where they'd assure no blood supplies could exit the lobe, and then they'd fill it full of chemo. They said the one benefit of this treatment would be that she wouldn't lose her hair because the chemo was trapped. However, all the stops along the way presented life-threatening possibilities.

Mom sat quietly throughout his explanation. I took notes and Aunt Margie asked questions like a dog on the scent. Chuck listened patiently. I tried to separate the doctor's clinical description from my mom's body, but I couldn't. As usual, this disease and its treatments upset me most when I considered their physical impacts. I knew that emotionally and spiritually, Mom could grow and even thrive through this. I feared seeing her weaken physically.

With this information, we finally faced our first treatment decision. We left the doctor's office excited and nervous, much the same as I feel before public speaking. I anticipated good results but I dreaded the process, and my nerves were like antennae outside my body, picking up every energy vibration.

The four of us went to dinner in Denver and tried to talk about it. The tension felt like a first date, not knowing who should speak first and how to bring it up.

"How's your soup?" Mom asked.

"Good," I said. "Yours?"

"So far so good."

Long pause.

Eventually, we got around to the topic at hand.

"I think you should go to Texas," Aunt Margie stated, and Chuck nodded his head in agreement.

Whether I was unaccustomed to telling Mom what to do, or if I had the opposite opinion, I didn't know. I wanted to hear Mom's thoughts.

Chuck and Aunt Margie made strong arguments for going to Texas. The only drawback, they said, seemed to be that she'd have to wait a few weeks before treatment. Mom wavered.

"But Sylvia," Aunt Margie said, growing more adamant, "you cannot trust just anybody to do this. Why go to doctors who've never done this before?"

"I trust these doctors," Mom said. "And I'm learning that's not something to take for granted. Also, it's here. I like the idea of being able to go home within a week. In Texas, I could be in the hospital much longer. I don't think I could take that."

"We're talking about your life here, Sylvia!" Aunt Margie said.

Mom's face hardened and her eyes lowered slightly. "Yes, we are talking about MY life," she said.

Our nerves and impatience were overpowering us. We were all desperate and we all thought we could think clearly enough to make this decision. As Mom always said, "Our copers were shot." We lacked the powers of logic and balance.

"Mom," I said, as we all picked at our food. "I'm really not sure what I think you should do, but I want to know what you would do if it were me receiving the treatment."

Mom looked at me and said, "There will be no more delay." We exchanged a long look and she nodded her head. "I have not made a decision yet," she said, "but my gut reaction to your question is that if this were you, I would not allow another delay in your treatment. I would have it done in Denver."

She went on to tell a story about my brother when he was a newborn.

"He was born without tear ducts, so when he cried, his little eyes filled up and spilled over. When he slept, his lids would stick together. The poor guy was miserable. The doctor said he needed surgery to give him tear ducts, so being the good mother, I went ahead with it. I can still see his little six-month-old body as the doctors took him away in their lab coats."

She looked down at her food and shook her head.

"But within a few weeks, the ducts closed, and I was faced with the same dilemma. You have to understand how much this upset him."

We listened to Mom's story earnestly. She had stopped eating, probably from pain, and she had placed her palms flat on the table. Her elbows hung at her side.

"I decided that we had to do it again. The doctors said so. But again, the ducts closed. When I took Jason in that third time, he started screaming and crying at the sight of white lab coats."

Tears formed in Mom's eyes and rolled down her face. She didn't move to wipe them away.

"This mother instinctively knew her baby could not go through that trauma one more time," she remembered. "I said, 'There will be no more surgery on that child.'"

She said she took Jason to a doctor in Denver who told her that if she did nothing, Jason would eventually grow his own tear ducts, and he did. Her nurturing instincts were right on the mark.

After that story, we all knew Mom had taken the power of this decision squarely into her corner.

Mom said she wanted to take the weekend to make her decision. In the meantime, Aunt Margie returned to California on the agreement that if Mom needed her or if Aunt Margie needed to see Mom, she would return in an instant. I stayed in Denver and Chuck went to Pueblo. This was Mom's ultimate decision and she made it clear that she would decide by herself in her own time. Of course, Aunt Margie and I talked frequently even though we didn't agree on what we thought Mom should do. However, we did agree that no matter what Mom decided, we were her most avid, strongest allies.

I did call Mom once over the weekend to remind her of some advice she had given me one year earlier.

I was unsure whether I should remain in Colorado and break up with my boyfriend, or move with him to California. I kept thinking that some golden, brilliant moment would hit me and suddenly I would know exactly what to do. Mom said, "Janalee, the moment of absolute certainty never arises. You must use all the information you have at the time and do what you believe is right. After that, you can never look back with regret because you made the best decision you could based on the information you had."

I reminded her of her own advice and she seemed to appreciate it. Monday she called her doctors and told them that she wanted the treatment done in Denver. They scheduled her to check into the hospital Tuesday afternoon. The procedure was scheduled for Wednesday morning, February 3. Chuck drove her to Denver on Monday afternoon and they stayed in a hotel near the hospital that night. I planned to meet them on Tuesday and then wait out the procedure at the hospital on Wednesday.

THURSDAY, FEBRUARY 17

The procedure went wonderfully! They said they got "excellent" coverage of the lobe with the chemo and part of the reason was because the chemo was made of an oil base. We had starved the liver of any fatty oils, tissues, etc., with the macrobiotic diet. The doctors said the liver "felt like it needed" the chemo and soaked it up. On Thursday they did another CT scan and the tumor had already shrunk! It was softer, too.

There was one complication. Mom retained a lot of water.

Twenty pounds of water! None of us could believe it. They measured her waist and it measured 82 inches! She blew up. Nurses kept saying, "When are you going to deliver that thing?" Due to that, she had to stay in the hospital almost a week. Mom was going nuts. Her elbows were scaly from propping herself up in bed all the time. Her butt was scaly from sitting on sheets all day long. She had a catheter so that she wouldn't have to get up to urinate. She couldn't eat any solid food. She was attached to an IV "tree" and had at least three tubes running into her arm at once. She was miserable.

I had a very difficult time watching her and being with her that week, though you wouldn't have guessed it from the amount of time I spent with her. I actually stayed the night with her twice. I told her it was because I wanted to be with her in case anything happened. She had gotten nauseous the night of the treatment and would have puked all over herself if I hadn't been there to grab the bucket. But, beyond that, I also didn't trust myself to drive home.

Toward the end of the week, I helped her get out of bed and we walked up and down the hall. This remarkable woman had defeated alcoholism; she had changed careers when most people were looking toward their retirement; she went through two divorces; she had taught me to believe in my own strength. This woman was wearing a backless hospital gown, hanging on a pole for support with bottles dangling off of it in four directions, tubes poking into her arms, water retention so high her eyelids were thick. She was also missing a tooth — during the procedure, one of her teeth fell out as they intubated her. I have trouble believing it's the same person sometimes. If I could forget her past vitality, this would be a lot easier.

EVERYTHING CHANGED AFTER that treatment. We no longer had to search for treatments, we prayed for results. Yet another shift in focus.

FRIDAY, FEBRUARY 19 — A LETTER

Dear Lori,

Well, I figure that since you quit calling, you probably gave up on me. I hope you forgive me. I really miss you, Lori, and I want you to know I appreciated every one of your messages. I was just so completely wiped out last month that picking up the phone after a day with doctors was about the last thing I wanted to do.

Here's the scoop. I'll make it as brief as possible, since getting mired in details gets very depressing.

Mom's got liver cancer, one of the rarest types of cancer in this country. It equals 1/2 of 1 percent of all cancers diagnosed in this country. That's been one of the most difficult obstacles to overcome because doctors so rarely see this type of cancer and treatments are still basically at the "experimental" stage. They found the tumor Jan. 5, diagnosed it as cancer Jan. 8, and on Jan. 11 two doctors told us they offered "no hope for recovery." I cannot even describe the mental trauma of sitting in a doctor's office and hearing them tell me that I'm going to lose my mother within "six to 18 months." I have since found that I have to take such information with a grain of salt. We have heard such diagnoses from several doctors who then back-track, suggest a treatment, back-track again saying there's "no hope", back-track again ... you get the picture. I have learned that if I let doctors "give" Mom the amount of time left in her life, we will inevitably live up to their expectations. We have refused to give up when we're told to. We have refused to live life as though she's dying. We have refused to allow doctors to bury her with statistics. We fight everything.

Finally, they located a treatment being done at a hospital in Texas. They performed it here and her tumor responded immediately! I'm talking one day! They did a CT scan the very next day and it was already smaller, and it was softer to the touch. The doctors were as elated as doctors can get. The treatment does involve chemo, though, so she is very weak and in a lot of pain. Luckily it is not systemic. It is localized to the left lobe of her liver, so she shouldn't notice much hair loss. But the pain is apparently excruciating.

So, now we wait a couple of weeks while the chemo fights cancer cells in her liver. We all have our own ways of imagining that battle. I tend to think of the Tasmanian Devil whirling around inside the lobe, wiping out cells as he travels, stopping occasionally to pant and look around, and then whirling around again. We have lots of jokes about "killing cancer cells." Every time she gets a good laugh, that's good for about 2,000 cancer cells. Every time the pain really hits her, we say a whole colony of cells just bit the dust. But everything is cancer cancer cancer cancer. My life has been forever altered by this experience.

The hardest part for me has been seeing Mom weaken. She's been through several CT scans, MRIs, given vials and vials of blood, had IVs hanging out of her, unable to walk, unable to urinate without a catheter ... The list goes on. She's pretty mobile now and unattached to any machines or tubes, but when she was in the hospital, I ached for her. This powerful, incredible woman was at the mercy of doctors, nurses, cancer, and chemo. If someone had told me two months ago that I'd be going through this, I would have told them that I would never have made it this far. It's amazing what you're capable of when you are needed. My brother and my aunt are in San Diego. I am the only family member in Colorado, which makes me feel like I should do everything for her, but I have to keep my sanity, too. It is so hard keeping a balance.

I hope things are going well with you, Lori. I hope you understand my silence. It doesn't mean I'm not thinking about you. I just can't bear to pick up the phone and talk about it after living it all day.

IN THE TWO weeks following the treatment, my family was forced to do more of what we don't do well — wait. And during this period, we had to switch gears slightly. Finally, after almost two months of testing, prodding, and poking, a treatment had been performed. During January, we hunted for a treatment as though all feeling of crisis would stop once it was performed. To us, finding a treatment had meant saving Mom's life, plain and simple. But now a new gremlin haunted our dreams. It crept in with dripping saliva and hoarse voice, whispering, "What if it doesn't work?"

As much as I wanted to have faith in the procedure and believe we were fighting a winning battle, echoes of the doctors' words kept me up nights. No cure, buy time, add time, extend life.

Obviously, the fear I felt stemmed from the idea that Mom could die. Prior to the treatment, however, I defined my fear in short-term concepts. What if this doctor can't help? What if this test gives us bad news? What's the next step? When I focused on doctor appointments, treatment options, statistics, and test results I could ignore the big picture. Once the treatment was over and I had to sit and wait for results, I realized my powerlessness. The questions changed from "what if she can't eat today?" to "what if Mom dies?"

When I found myself thinking about Mom's death, I felt guilty and admitted my thoughts to no one. How could I tell Aunt Margie when she seemed so convinced that Mom would live? And Jason showed anger at even the slightest hint of Mom's demise. I decided he was in complete denial and, at this stage, why ruin it for him? I ached for such comfort. I longed to be able to muffle my brain when it screamed "Cancer!" The doctors' predictions repeated in my head like an annoying song. I wanted to put it all down, like a piece of food too big to finish at one time — just set it aside until it looked appetizing again. But I couldn't find such comfort and I couldn't admit my thoughts to anyone for fear of being a traitor.

During one of the weekends after the treatment, I was down in Cañon City taking care of Mom. She did alright on her own, but I wanted to be with her and she needed help with the house and shopping. On Saturday night, we were in the living room talking. I offered to give her a foot massage since she was still pretty swollen from water retention. She laid back on the couch and I sat down near her feet. We wandered back into our own thoughts and were quiet. This was the moment I discovered my fixation — obsession — with the purely physical aspects of her battle.

Mom's eyes were shut and I stared at her belly. I continued rubbing her feet and as time passed, I imagined myself pulling the cancer out of her toes. I rubbed and rubbed and stared and stared. I started to feel panicky. How can that much cancer be sitting right there — right there! — and be so untouchable? We can orbit the moon, make robots as life-like as humans, give people organs made of plastic, yet we can't find a cure for cancer? We can't see distant galaxies, yet we know they're there. We can see this cancer, we can touch it, watch it grow, watch it kill. I can place my hands on Mom's belly where only centimeters beneath grows death and I can do nothing!

"Honey?"

I looked up at Mom who watched me closely. She looked relaxed as she lay on the couch, one hand over her head, thrown on the armrest like an Egyptian queen.

"Are you OK?" she asked.

I burst angrily.

"It's right there! It's right inside you and I can't get at it. I can't pull it out, punch it out, cut it out. It's right there and we can't do anything about it. If it were a car speeding at us, we could jump out of the way or we could at least point at the driver and say, 'It's your fault.' With this, we have to just sit here and wait."

Mom's silence told me that she felt the same way.

WEDNESDAY, MARCH 10

I've been having awful dreams again. Last night I dreamt that I felt Mom's stomach, and it felt like there were hundreds of little marbles under her skin, rolling around. Two nights ago, I had awful dreams about me. I was in a lot of pain and I was getting my period, but it was more like what I imagine a miscarriage or hemorrhaging must be like. There was blood everywhere and I was crawling around in it trying to get help.

The past month has been very difficult, though not as bad

on a daily basis as January. Mom has gotten weaker and her spirits have occasionally plummeted. When she gets weak, she gets very weak, very fast. Apparently her thyroid gland just shuts off at random moments and it forces her to fight for every breath. It literally changes the way she looks and acts in one split second. No matter how easy it can be to laugh or joke about her silly, skinny legs or her snaggle-toothed grin, something always yanks you back with "This is cancer, stupid."

Two weekends ago, I was visiting her and we had a great Saturday — it felt a little like old times. But Sunday was bad. She woke up with "weird pain" and about 9:30 a.m. she started throwing up in the bathroom sink. I was on the phone when I heard her gagging and I hung up and ran to help her. There was nothing I could do but sit on the tub and rub her back as she puked. Her whole body convulsed, she shook her head in frustration and spit out what she could. It was the first time she'd gotten nauseous since the hospital.

For an hour afterward, it was all I could do to look at her. I cleaned the bathroom, cleaned the kitchen, and tried to get a grip. I couldn't look at her for fear of bursting into tears. Finally, she came to me and said, "You're very traumatized, aren't you?" We went into the living room to talk. We discussed how difficult it is to see someone you love go through an illness. She said she had suffered through my common illnesses and couldn't imagine how it must feel to watch my own mother fight a life-threatening disease. We ended up curling up on the couch with me sobbing in her arms. It was very good for both of us. She needed to feel needed — like a Mom again. I needed to sob in my mommy's arms.

AFTER THE TREATMENT, Mom's routine changed entirely. In fact, the word routine implies a predictability that we quickly learned had been a luxury. We used to be able to plan her naps, her pill popping and her meals. This time, we were slaves to a body that lacked all control. I learned how complex our systems must be as I watched Mom's randomly shut down on her.

"Could you eat?" I asked. She had been awake for about 10 minutes. It was around two in the afternoon.

"Let's try it," she said, winking at me. We commonly discussed her body as though it was a third person.

I prepared a simple lunch of soup and crackers, putting less than half a cup of soup in a bowl. Even that was optimistic. I put her pills in a little cup and brought it all out to her, with a glass of water. I handed her the water first and put a couple of pills in her other hand. Then I sat on the couch next to her recliner. She sat still, holding both hands up in front of her as though she was getting ready to throw the pills in her mouth and take a drink. Instead, she just sat there. She stared straight ahead and didn't say anything. Then I noticed her eyelids drooping and her neck relaxed. Just as her arms dropped, I grabbed the water, saving her lap from a sudden dowsing. She was out, sound asleep, and I was again alone in the living room, looking at another uneaten meal.

I found the pills on her blanket and took everything back to the kitchen, fighting back the fear. What could possibly be next?

I tried to act as though the energy loss was all part of some plan I'd anticipated. Time to switch from daughter to caretaker? OK! Right away! Can do! But one incident forced Mom and me to admit we weren't entirely prepared for, nor pleased with, this new glitch in her health.

I prepared to leave one afternoon after spending a few days with her. When I went outside to load up my car, I discovered I had a flat tire. It was a Sunday so buying a new tire was out and my spare was in no condition for the 130-mile trip home. Mom said we could get some flat-fixing goo at Wal-Mart, so we took off in her car. By now, she was continually wearing sweat-suits because her belly was too distended for jeans. She looked cute and peppy, even though her legs and face were scrawny. But she seemed strong enough for a short trip.

Once we got to Wal-Mart, we headed for the automotive section. We had barely made it past greeting cards when she grabbed my arm and said she had to sit down. Frantically, I searched for a chair or stool, but found none. We moved very slowly, holding up the busy, get-out-of-my-way shoppers. Finally, she said, "I have got to sit NOW!" We found a large box of detergent waiting to be shelved and she collapsed onto it, out of breath. I kneeled next to her, watching her struggle for breath, knowing she needed to lie flat. What could I do?

She, however, was on to other things.

"Go find the stuff for your tire. I'll catch my breath here and wait for you."

I argued that I should get her home but she insisted.

So, I ran to the automotive section and returned to find her leaning over her knees, looking at the ground, working for breath. I will never forget that image. She appeared helpless. Other shoppers may have assumed she was drunk or very old. I wanted to protect her from their gaze, shelter her dignity so that she didn't have to fight to keep that, too, as she fought to breathe.

We finally made it out to her car and she was silent for the ride home. The goo worked on my tire and she sat on the porch as I loaded everything into my car. Before I left, she told me that she'd always been proud of the fact that she could help me when I needed it most, but that day she felt not only useless, but burdensome. She said she was frustrated.

In the blink of an eye that day, our roles had reversed and neither of us wanted nor accepted the switch gracefully.

WEDNESDAY, MARCH 10

Mom has a CT scan tomorrow to determine if the chemo has done any good. I'm a nervous wreck. I cried at work today for the first time in weeks and realized what a luxury it had been to not have to deal with doctors every day, hospitals for weeks at a time, uncertainty every minute. I honestly don't think we'll learn too much tomorrow because the doctors won't be able to prescribe the next treatment so quickly. But I do believe we will learn how well the liver has responded to the chemo. I asked Mom what her gut reaction is; does she think it's gotten smaller? She said she thinks the left lobe is smaller, but that there's something "funny" going on in the right lobe.

She said she doesn't feel like she's living in the same body anymore. Every day is different, with new pains, new aches, and new healing (I hope). She's sick and tired of being so unpredictable. Going grocery shopping is something she has to do between 10 a.m. and noon, so that she can nap from 1 to 3. Sometimes she can't move out of her chair due to pain, even when her energy level is high. She recently broke out in a rash thanks to the pain medication. The pain used to be in her left lobe but it recently switched to the right.

I find that I want to be with her every second, and then when I am, fear and anger hit me with the force of a sledgehammer right between my eyes, blinding me, knocking me to my knees.

I wish Jason was here. Aunt Margie is coming back this Tuesday. I want her to see Mom and tell me she looks OK. I've gotten too used to how thin she is to be a good judge. I miss Jason so much. He gets back in June. I need to see him so badly.

Daddy has arranged for me to fly to NJ the beginning of April for a long weekend. I'm both excited and anxious. What if Mom is in the hospital being treated that week? I won't want to leave. I'd be nuts. But I can't run my life as though something might be happening to Mom. Something is always going to be happening to Mom.

That's another thing I'm having a lot of difficulty with. When I returned the Sunday after seeing Mom on the box in Wal-Mart, I talked to Brooke about some of my reactions. I wondered — and wonder — if life will ever be "normal" again. I long for a day that I don't have to think about cancer, questioning if Mom is OK, can she take care of herself, does she have everything she needs, how are her spirits, should I be with her. I want to feel like things that I do on a daily basis aren't just "going through the motions" in order to avoid thinking about cancer. I want to not go see Mom on a weekend without thinking, "I may regret not having that time with her in six months." I want to be able to date without thinking, "This pour soul has no idea what he may be getting himself into," and then ending it in some ridiculous way. I want people at work to stop asking about her, but I want them to be there for me when I need them. I want to stop, once and for all, thinking that "maybe this is just a bad dream."

But tomorrow she has the CT scan and there's no avoiding that. I'm taking the day off to meet her and Chuck at the hospital. I thought I might work a half-day and meet them at 11:30, but I was pretty worthless today. Tomorrow I'll probably be worse. I'm so anxious. I wish I could completely relax for one day, but that sounds so self-pitying. I wish I could take all the cancer out of her.

Courage

CHAPTER 5

Spring was Mom's season. Every year, she geared up for it by spreading her seed catalogs all over the dining room table and mapping out her garden. Carrots, corn, broccoli, beans, tomatoes, even brussel sprouts, horseradish, and gourds. One year, she told us that she would show us how to grow the biggest pumpkins ever. As the pumpkin vines grew and spread out across her plot of dirt, she told us to select three pumpkins for nurturing. We picked off every other bud the vines put out. We did this all summer, forcing the vines to focus all their attention on the three chosen ones. She showed us how to rotate our prize pumpkins to prevent flat sides, and so they would be an even orange. Come autumn, the pumpkins were so huge we couldn't turn them. We took a picture of Jason sitting next to one just to prove its height and circumference. Jason was dwarfed, sitting proudly on his knees, one hand on the orange boulder as though he had been the vine attached to it all summer.

Mom picked her seeds and flowers carefully. No average plants would do. When they arrived in the mail in the big brown cardboard box, we all gathered around to pull out the treasures. We counted the order to make sure everything arrived and then we sat down with a pencil and paper and mapped out the garden-to-be. On the table, we lined up the seed packets in rows just as they'd be in the garden. Corn all bunched closely together in short rows so the stalks could pollinate each other. Carrots in two long rows, planted at different times so we could have carrots all summer. Beans received two rows and the tomatoes were clustered like a group of gossipy old women. Beyond those veggies, we planned mounds for the cucumbers, mounds for the gourds, and mounds for the pumpkins. The back fence was lined with Russian Olive trees, providing shade for anything that needed it. One year, Mom planted irises back there, to give herself a colorful backdrop for the hours she spent in the garden daily.

This was both hobby and therapy for Mom. Jason and I might be cooped up inside watching TV and she would come running in, giggling with a handful of beans. Beans hung out of her mouth, carrots stuck out of her pocket.

"Here! First beans from my garden!" she said.

We'd grab some and she'd turn off the TV and show us which rows needed weeding. At first, we moaned and groaned but shortly we would start telling each other silly stories. Sometimes we lost ourselves in our own thoughts.

Then, there was the manure tea. Mom read a lot of gardening magazines and one year she happened upon a recipe — literally a recipe — for a concoction called manure tea. Supposedly it was the best fertilizer a garden could receive and since we had plenty of the main ingredient — manure — Mom set to work. The only problem was the size of Mom's garden. The recipe specified portions in terms of cups. The brew was mixed in a small bucket. Undaunted, Mom ran right out and bought a trough! A huge trough meant for watering several large livestock. Into that large, metal tub, she ran the hose and filled it full of well water. The crystal clear base needed to sit in the sun for several days to warm up. On the third day, when Mom had baked beneath the sun in her garden for several hours, I watched as she jumped into the warm water with her clothes on! She yelled, "Yaaah Hoooo!" and sat down quickly. I was swinging in our tire swing in the backyard and watched this spectacle with embarrassment and shock. She threw her arms up on the edge of the trough and cocked her head back against the frame as though she were in a porcelain tub. She smiled.

"Mom?"

"Yes, honey?" she said without looking at me. She may as well have been reading a book in her recliner.

I didn't say anything else.

The next day, she started up our little tractor, tug-tugged into the donkey corral, and filled the scoop full of poop. Then she rolled over to the trough, which had yesterday been her bath, and dumped. She did that once more, sufficiently topping off the trough, and then stirred it gently with a shovel.

It baked for two weeks. The tea became a source of wonder for Jason and me. The top formed a thick, brown, mottled crust and little pebbles bounced off of it when tossed lightly. At first, the flies were thick, but as soon as the crust formed, the smell and the flies departed. We asked Mom why it had to bake so long and she said the sun was turning it into God's plant food and it would make everything grow healthier. Even though I knew the tea would nurture the earth which would in turn help the carrots taste better, I couldn't fathom eating anything this stuff touched.

Finally, after two weeks, Mom broke the seal. We all gathered around the trough and Mom found a heavy rock. We backed up a safe distance and Mom granny-styled the rock into the air. Hitting the crust evenly, it fell straight to the bottom creating a hole only where it hit. That was one thick crust. It didn't even crack around the edges of the hole. And if smell had a color, a pustulant green-brown would have risen out of that hole like snot running from a kid's nose. You couldn't get within 20 feet of it without catching a disgusting whiff. Mom was exuberant. We watched from our safe places as she walked boldly up with a bucket, broke through more of the crust with the bottom of the bucket and ladled out the first, warm plant refreshment. We were immediately curious and ran up to see what had happened below the surface. The liquid was brown but there were very few floaters and even those looked harmless. The manure had mostly dissolved, creating an intense brown syrup. Mom said it was black gold.

Like the weeding, all chores were shared around the house. Before Mom bought our home on Ashley Lane, she sat both of us down for a long talk about the new responsibilities we'd have. Only an acre, Ashley Lane included three small corrals, four shed-like barns, an unattached garage, a large garden, both front and back yards, and a three-bedroom house. With the land came a horse named Missy, which we could ride bare-back. Mom made it clear that though this new homestead seemed a child's playground, it would require a lot of work. I was only ten and Jason was nine. He and I traded mowing duty on the front and back yards because the front yard was bigger. All three of us traded kitchen duty, helped with the garden, and, most importantly, cared for the animals.

Ours was not a normal acre with normal animals. Whereas most people raise animals for a purpose (except for cats and dogs) we had a farm of useless livestock. Instead of cows, we had donkeys. Rather than sheep, we had goats. Tyrone, the rooster, crowed all hours of the day except dawn and could be seen hauling tailfeather over to the neighbor's hen house at least twice a day. For some odd reason, he always returned to our land though we housed no hens. Ashley Lane was like a sports bar to Tyrone, offering time away from the clucking women. We had one rabbit, two cats, and two dogs. We did raise one animal for food, a pig cleverly named Miss Piggy, but, of course, we let her run around the back yard as we ate dinner at the picnic table, rode her, fed her food scraps and talked to her like a good friend. We attached ourselves to her, but, surprisingly, still enjoyed her salty ribs.

I remember winters most. When it came to the animals, love made all the difference. Every morning before we got ready for school, Jason and I would run, sandy-eyed, out to the barns and silently perform our duties in the pre-dawn darkness. Crack the ice on the water, portion out the hay, pour the oats, and clean the pens, all in the pre-dawn freeze. If I hadn't loved those awkward beasts, I might not have cared enough to remove the cracked ice, or to touch them gently as I offered oats, or to talk to them as I shoveled shit. I didn't enjoy the winter work, but I did it dutifully out of love.

These were our seasonal rituals. This thawing, nurturing, development and growth is what we expected of spring.

Courage

CHAPTER 6

Three months into the ordeal and I was still trying to convince myself that it could somehow be organized and filed into my life. I could be daughter, employee, and wonder-caretaker simultaneously. At the very least, I could pull out the appropriate roles at the appropriate times like files in a cabinet. I performed each documented role flawlessly and then re-filed that action for a later date, and moved smoothly into the next. I believed organization would keep the process running smoothly and in my pre-cancer world, a smooth process typically led to success.

When time arrived for the second treatment, I opened up the caretaker file, dusted off the "how to remain calm in the face of unknown" file, and the file titled, "show no one your fear." I read up, studied, internalized, and went into battle.

We entered the hospital the second time like veterans entering a familiar fox-hole. We brought family pictures, our own blankets, a radio, and magazines. We walked onto the cancer floor and greeted familiar nurses. I asked about the young boy with leukemia who'd been in the room next door and happily learned that he'd made it through his latest treatment.

Mom and Chuck situated her room and I went down to the hospital cafeteria to get a bowl of raisins, which I liked having in the room for snacks. By now, nurses had shown me the back staircases and staff entrances to various elevators, so I made my way like a regular through the secret mazes of the hospital. Part of me was glad to feel more comfortable this time around, but the other half was bitter at the natural feel of such an unnatural setting.

The morning of Mom's treatment, a nurse came into the room to check Mom's vitals and casually told me I could accompany her through the prep work and procedure room if I wanted. She said Mom would be alert until then and I could keep her company. It sounded so easy. Mom and I looked at each other, shrugged, and said, "OK!" I still wish I had said no. The nurse should have been more descriptive of the coming events.

First, I followed Mom's gurney to a room where they were going to insert an epidural. The doctor told me where to stand if I wanted to watch. It all felt so intimate — sharing the room with the doctors, watching Mom as she bravely prepared for uncertain treatment. I felt mature and proud of the fact that all these people trusted me to be there. However, as I watched the needles and tubes, and viewed Mom's face and watery eyes, I quickly lost my grasp of the caretaker role and slipped into the shaky daughter mode. As the caretaker, I was safe thanks to emotional distance. As the daughter, I was unprotected.

Mom rolled over on her side and I watched as the doctors cleaned up her lower back and pressed a long needle into her skin. Mom grabbed the rail of the gurney and inhaled sharply. Her eyes squinted shut and a little gasp escaped her throat. Silent tears ran sideways off her face. I quickly lost my stability. Suddenly, the room was too big. I wanted to put both hands on the walls, one on each side, to stay vertical. The walls wilted, rippled into fun-house mirrors, expanding, yawning, heating, and freezing. The floor lifted me up then collapsed below me.

I told Mom I had to go to the bathroom and a nurse directed me to a door. Inside the very small bathroom, I grabbed the walls, kept my eyes on the floor, and breathed. I felt nauseous and chilled, then weightless and hot. I thought that if I kept breathing I might not fall, but breathing, which is supposed to be instinctive, required more thought than a college prep exam.

Finally, I realized that if I didn't pull it together they might take her to the procedure room without me and I wanted to be there with her. I imagined her fear building as time passed before they put her under. I wanted to hold her hand.

I looked up at the mirror, keeping my hands on the walls and watched myself breathe. Slowly, I stood up taller and let myself trust my legs again. I noticed tears and quickly grabbed toilet paper to wipe them away. No tears. Strength. I spoke out loud to myself. "She needs you. Be strong." I said the Serenity Prayer for the umpteenth time in three months, choosing the refrain I needed most at that moment.

God, grant me
Serenity to accept the things I cannot change
Courage to change the things I can, and
Wisdom to know the difference

Serenity, wisdom. They sounded so cerebral and manufactured. I needed courage of the purely physical variety. The kind that stops the bile churning. The bones in my legs felt like they'd been shattered into a thousand pieces. I didn't need the stuff made of conscious thought, but of some deeper, baser substance.

When I exited the bathroom, we proceeded to the room where Mom would spend the next four hours under doctors, lights, and scalpels.

I had anticipated a hospital room like in the movies. Fairly small, intimate, a few machines with green lines running across their screens, and a couple of nurses to assist the doctor. I physically jerked when I followed Mom's gurney into a room the size of a small movie theater. The ceiling echoed at least 12 feet above my head and the walls felt football fields away. And it was cold. Very cold. I grabbed Mom's hand.

As I took in my surroundings, I saw another TV room attached, looking out on the main room through windows. At least five people in white lab coats sat in front of uncountable TV screens. Multitudes of cameras, TV screens, and incomprehensible machines hung from the ceiling and walls of the main room. All focused specifically into the center of the room where they wheeled Mom and left us to wait — no explanations or welcomes. Mom was just a prop in their huge techno-production. Cameras were trained on us, eyes saw through us, and lab coats brushed past us, stirring the cold air around us.

I began shaking. Mom felt my hand move and looked up at me from her white encasing.

"I want you to leave, Janalee."

"No, Mom. I want to be with you until they start."

"No, you shouldn't be seeing this," she answered. "I love you and will see you when it's over. Nurse?"

She told the nurse to take me back to her hospital room.

The next thing I remember is the doctor's voice speaking my name. I don't remember the walk to her room nor making any decision to sleep in her bed. My mind must have shut my body down completely. Opening my eyes to the doctor's voice hurt every joint in my body. I felt like I'd just fallen a long distance and broken every bone, ruptured every organ. Opening my eyelids made my entire body awaken with a scream. I had not been sleeping. I'd been unconscious.

"Miss Chmel? Miss Chmel!"

From a vast distance — galaxies — I heard my name. As soon as he saw my eyelids creak open, he began.

"Your mother came through the procedure well, but there's been a complication. I need you to follow me."

Immediately alert. Following the doctor. Watching his footsteps in front of me. Silent. Not wanting to ask. Not wanting to know.

We entered a recovery room where Mom was lying on a gurney unconscious. Three men, including the doctor I knew, stood around her. She had white stuff all over her lips, they looked chapped and raw. Her face was mushy-looking, like someone had stretched her skin two feet and let it go, and it hadn't bounced back yet.

"Miss Chmel, this is Dr. Case, a specialist in arterial clotting. He will explain. We must be brief as time is of the essence."

"Miss Chmel, your mother underwent the procedure and everything went well. However, in the last half hour, she has developed a clot in her right leg. We cannot find a pulse in her foot. Her right leg has not received blood ..."

I listened, dazed, as the doctor explained that they would have to remove Mom's leg if they did not go back in to loosen the clot.

" ... and because she is not alert, we need a family member to approve the procedure. Keep in mind, Miss Chmel, that we may have to remove your mother's leg."

Then, offering nothing further, he stopped and all three stared at me. I stared back with the same blank gaze they gave me. Did they get it? Did they understand what they were asking me to do? I thought, "Mom makes those kinds of decisions for me! Not vice versa! I'm only 24."

I thought of Daddy, Aunt Margie, Grandma, Chuck. I looked at the doctors dumbfounded. Then, in an effort to speed my thoughts, the doctor removed the thin sheet from over Mom's right leg. I gasped. Her leg looked like a pillar of purple, mottled marble. I reached out instinctively to touch it and felt hard, cold skin, furthering my impression that her leg was turning to stone.

"Miss Chmel?"

I hesitated, then, "I can't! This is my mother! How can I ..."

"Really, we must do this. We just need your signature here."

Across Mom's body from the other side of the gurney, the doctor handed me a clip-board with a one-page sheet. Just then, Mom awoke. Everyone stirred, stepped back, and then forward again. The doctors seemed to forget I was there. They accosted Mom in her dream-like state, explaining the situation, and they got her to sign the form. Her scrawl looked more like her heart monitor line than her loopy, direct signature. Then they wheeled her away.

I retreated back to her room where I found Pat seated on Mom's bed. I started hyperventilating. The harder I tried to explain my day to Pat, the worse I got. I found myself staring off into space, suddenly crying and then, just as suddenly, frozen stiff. I paced the room and picked up items from the window sill, only to leave them on the bedside table on the other side of the room. I stopped and tried to breathe, and then started shaking uncontrollably. Finally, Pat grabbed me, and hugged me. I sobbed. After several minutes, my breathing calmed and I again fell asleep.

SATURDAY, APRIL 10

Dear Chris,

I'm at Mom's and I want to call you but she's sleeping and I don't want to wake her or have her hear what I need to say. I don't even know where to begin. She left the hospital Tuesday evening and it is now Saturday. I arrived last night. I have to be strong when I'm around her. A lot of people say, "Maybe she'd like you to show her you're scared." But there's no way she needs that right now, and there's no time for it. When she's awake, all the time is taken up feeding her, bathing her, taking care of her wounds ... maybe I should back up and tell you what led me to the brink of hysteria I'm feeling right now. I need to cry so badly, but I don't think I'd be able to stop and she might call for me.

Since she came back from the hospital, we've been very worried about the high ammonium level in her blood. It means her liver is not functioning correctly. For a couple of days she was an orange color, and it doesn't take a genius to say, "liver." But the results of the high ammonium are even more startling. She slurs like she's completely drunk. Sometimes she has to say a word several times before we understand her. When the problem was at its worst, she couldn't focus, she couldn't hold a glass of water without falling asleep and spilling it on herself. She would forget she was speaking and just fall asleep in the middle of a thought. Sometimes she'd say something from out of nowhere and have no idea what she was talking about.

When she checked out of the hospital four days ago, her ammonium level was at 90. Normal is 20. She's now down to 29, which is an amazing plummet! Now she slurs sometimes and shakes quite a bit, but the sudden sleeping fits have subsided. She still sleeps a lot, but she's in more control of when it happens.

Aunt Margie told me to be prepared because she is very weak. I had no idea, though, Chris. I had been home about an hour and Mom said she needed to go to the bathroom. I thought, "OK, go ahead." She used to be slow, but we all waited for her because she has been adamant about doing things on her own (go figure). Well, instead, Aunt Margie got up from her chair, walked over to Mom's chair, removed the blanket from Mom's lap, bent over, and hugged her. Mom hugged her back and Aunt Margie began to pull Mom out of the chair. You know how little Aunt Margie is. They struggled for a bit and finally they were both standing up, hugging. Mom was breathing heavily. Aunt Margie then offered her left arm like a crutch. They then proceeded to walk very slowly to the bathroom. Aunt Margie had to lower Mom onto the toilet, then go back in when Mom was done and lift her up. They got Mom into her pajamas, a task of such magnitude I can't even describe it, and then brought her back to the living room to sit and catch her breath before she took her next round of pills to go to bed.

The next wave of shock hit me when I realized she's wearing diapers — Attends. The recliner and the couch are both covered with this blue plastic stuff because her diarrhea is so bad that she can't predict when it's going to hit, so the plastic makes her feel more secure. Up to last night, there had been no messes.

Next shock: I went into the bathroom to wash up and the whole shower stall is rigged up for somebody who's 98 years old. Chuck installed grab bars on the wall and they bought one of those chairs that hangs off the side of the tub so she can sit when she showers. She can't bathe because of the wound from the blood clot surgery. Then, I went into her room to pull down her bed and, besides the blue plastic on her bed, there was a portable commode sitting in the room.

All of it hits with the force of a sledgehammer to the side of the head. Mom's very sick. Up until Tuesday, I had functioned on pure hope. Now she even looks sick and she's so weak she needs help to sit down. How do I continue to hope?

Today, Aunt Margie took off to run some errands and all of a sudden, Mom needed to go to the bathroom badly. I yanked the covers off of her, closed the recliner, hugged her, pulled her up, and supported her as we walked as quickly as we could to the bathroom. The whole time she was saying, "Oh, Jana, I'm not wearing a diaper. I'm not wearing a diaper." I kept saying, "It's OK. It's OK." We got to the bathroom, but not before she had messed her pants and pooped all over the bathroom rug and the toilet. She was humiliated and I was devastated. I helped her remove her pants as she sat on the toilet, then I left her alone to finish. I started the pants in a soak cycle in the washer and began folding dry clothes as I waited for her to call me in. Finally, she called and I walked to the bathroom. When I opened the door, she was standing stark naked, one hand on the sink, the other on the wall to support herself. She had cleaned herself up, but the bathroom was a mess. She kept apologizing and I finally told her to stop. I kept a light, upbeat attitude about it.

First, I had to dress her wound, which is right next to her crotch. So, I knelt down and began swabbing it with gauze. It is about six inches long and keeps weeping, so we've got to dress it every hour. Then we put her shirt on and then her pants. It was like putting pants on a two-year-old. I had to bunch the whole pant-leg up my arm and then run her foot into it. We then walked to her chair, hugged her down into it, and finished dressing the wound. She was breathing heavily and slurring more than she had in days. Once she caught her breath, she decided she wanted to sleep, so we hugged her back up. I thought it would make her feel better to wear a diaper, so we put one on, careful to avoid the wound and laid her on the blue plastic on the couch. I redressed the wound — the activity made it very angry — and once she was down, I proceeded to clean the bathroom.

I am on the verge of tears, and feel like I have been for four months. My hands smell like Comet from cleaning the bathroom and I feel nauseous.

Chris, how do I keep going? I think that sounds so pathetic, but I really am beginning to wonder. I know I have to stay strong for her, but I feel like I'm going to explode. I believe I had the equivalent of a nervous breakdown the day of her last treatment. When I finally recovered, I thought, "Maybe I just needed to fall apart and now everything will be easier." Afraid not. I constantly feel like I'm on the edge of a cliff, ready to take one more step. This whole experience could be likened to that. It's like being perched precariously on the edge of a cliff by a force over which I have no control. An unknown hand presses firmly between my shoulder blades just to let me know that at any minute, I could be sent screaming over the edge.

She seems to be waking. I'd better get to the laundry so she has clean clothes to wear if this happens again.

Wisdom

CHAPTER 1

I am an optimistic person by nature. Some say naive or gullible, even, but that's not what's at the heart of me. I simply expect the best outcome, or assume others will live up to my positive expectations of them, until they prove differently. This outlook, though, is inherently loaded with underlying pressures. I don't assume good comes easily; I work for it, which allows me to expect it.

When it came to Mom's illness, I needed to expect a positive outcome, which meant I needed to work toward that outcome continuously. I put a lot of pressure on myself and others to remain optimistic and to work for a cure. Everything in my life centered around this focus, like planets around the sun.

I ordered a bumper sticker that said, "Expect a Miracle!" and plastered it on my car. When I exercised, I did it because I needed to stay healthy to take care of Mom. If I woke up late, I grieved over the lost time I could have focused my energy on Mom, whether by cooking, cleaning, or just talking. I awoke every morning, in fact, convinced that I could alter her routine to precisely the right schedule that day and, miraculously, her cancer would retreat — like tipping our planet one degree on its axis might change our weather entirely. Even switching her blanket seemed critical. I was convinced I had the power to make a difference and bring the cure.

When a day ended and we were seemingly no closer to Mom's complete recovery, I collapsed exhausted and distraught. What had I done wrong? What could I do better tomorrow?

Each dawn, each sunrise, represented renewed hope and I'd bound out of bed. Each dusk brought dark reality.

Beginning in late April and running through July, this was our day, every day. We were waiting, though we never described it that way. We waited for the "little events" of the day to give us a sign and we held our breath for those moments. Prior to this, we could look into the next week, the next month and prepare for diagnosis or treatment. Now, looking forward — even beyond tomorrow — meant a devastation to our mood. What did it hold? What would we face next week? Next month? Could we handle it? Could Mom?

Whereas the first four months of Mom's illness fell into two distinct categories: diagnosis and treatment, the next three months were filled with the routine of pills, food, naps, cleaning, and coping. Good days were easy to define. Basically, everything from the weather to only one major clean-up helped determine a positive day. Bad days were determined by our emotions. When these bad days hit, Aunt Margie and I worked together like a fine-tuned machine. Something in our mutually anal-retentive personalities thrived on crisis management.

Before this experience, my knowledge of Aunt Margie consisted only of her annual visits at Christmas when she and Mom stayed up next to the fire until the early morning hours. They had always been playful together (wrestling in the snow when cabin fever struck), and supportive of one another (talking for hours on the phone at least once a week). They were one another's best friends.

But for the most part, Aunt Margie was one of those relatives whom I loved because she was family, but about whom I knew nothing. Jason knew her much better than I because he'd been stationed near her San Diego home. He frequently visited her and he credited her with getting him to take college courses, and helping him through them. He visited her on weekends and they cooked quiches, corn chowder, and salads. In many ways, he got to know Aunt Margie in the same way I'd gotten to know Daddy.

Aunt Margie also served as Jason's West Coast grounding point during Mom's illness because she flew back and forth. When he wanted news, he knew Aunt Margie would give it to him honestly.

Still, to me, she was just that hip aunt who lived in California, got manicures, and jazzercized. I trusted her because Mom and Jason did.

As Mom's condition waxed and waned, Aunt Margie flew back and forth often to be part of the decisions and caretaking. She was a powerhouse, all 5′ 4″ of her. Aunt Margie doesn't walk, she scurries. She doesn't wander, she commits. She doesn't waste movement, she narrows in and completes. She does this all without seeming pushy or hassled.

When Aunt Margie was in Cañon City, we worked into a groove, a routine. We assumed the roles for which we possessed the right amount of energy or desire, and completed our tasks. And, unconsciously, we took turns relieving one another. Not coincidentally, just when one of us let the fear take over, or the fatigue forced us down, the other would jump to the rescue. It was like we took numbers from a butcher's tape at the market. She'd find me leaning over the kitchen sink, staring out the window blankly, my hands soaking in dishwater, and she'd tap me on the butt, saying, "Why don't you get outside for a while?" We both needed this kind of permission to shut down.

As the illness progressed and changed, we adjusted our concept of normal and strange. The routines we developed as a family would probably have made most healthy people sick – especially our jokes.

Table talk included everything from the "orgasmic burps" to the color of Mom's diarrhea. Stella Benson wrote in Pipers and a Dream, "Family jokes, though rightly cursed by strangers, are the bond that keeps most families alive."

"Yellow? Let me see ... yep. That's yellow alright. Hmmmm." We stood over the toilet for a few moments, flushed and wandered back to coffee. "Could be the dairy from last night, though stuff seems to pass quicker than that these days ..."

If treatments highlighted the spring, then preparing for a miracle highlighted the summer.

During this phase of the illness, I found myself in conversations with Mom that I'm certain never would have happened without the threat of death. We never said, "I may not get to talk to you about this later." In fact, I didn't even feel that kind of urgency. Of course, I felt urgency for a cure and urgency — panic — over Mom's declining health, but our relationship seemed to grow without this urgency, without force. It was a natural progression. We explored each other in ways unavailable to us previously. We owed this honor, ironically, to time constraints. Before her illness, we believed we had infinite time to discover one another and yet work, school, and hobbies all pulled us from the moment. Now, with a potential limit on the horizon, we found the time opened up easily. Work, school, and hobbies were effortlessly set aside. But, again, these decisions weren't made out of desperation; they were obvious, natural, no-brainers.

I also realized a voracious curiosity in my own childhood. I wondered, if Mom died, who would remember what I was like as a child? I only saw Daddy once a year and Jason couldn't remember. I wanted to know my first word, the date that I first walked, and letters I couldn't pronounce. What was my reaction to Jason's birth? What games did I like to play? I feared losing myself with Mom.

Gradually, we started having "what if" conversations. Usually, Mom started them and I protested. One afternoon, she asked me to get a pen and paper. I sat next to her on the couch trying to guess her next words, the pad and pencil perched at attention in my hands. Her sudden decision to have me complete a writing task for her — a job she could easily do herself — made it clear that my presence was more important than as a mere note-taker.

"I don't think Jason would want the oak table yet," she began. "He's got no room for it. You should have it for now."

My heart and mind seized up.

"Oh no," I said angrily, immediately placing the pad and pencil on the coffee table. I stood up and walked a few paces away. My heart raced and I wanted to jump up and down, do jumping jacks, run. I wanted to ignore the psychological and physical tremors by diverting my energy.

"I'm not doing this, Mom." I began crying. "No. I can't do this ... dammit."

I breathed hard, trying to stop the tears, leaning on the fireplace mantle with one hand, my other fist on my hip.

Mom paused, let me breathe, and then said, "I want you to be part of this, Janalee. I need your help. I want you to have a say, now. You won't want to do this, later."

"You're not dying and I will not sit here in your living room and talk about your stuff like you're dead. No! You can't ask me to do this." I was shouting, furious. We stared at each other. The moment felt surreal. She looked at the mahogany rocking chair that had been in the family for generations. I followed her gaze. I remembered my childhood when I wasn't even allowed to sit in the chair because I couldn't haul myself up into it without pulling on the fragile arms. The inlaid wood in its back attracted all our guests to comment on its beauty. Mom loved that chair. She wanted her kids to have it and to love it as she did. She wanted to be sure of its care.

I looked back at her. "Mom, I promise that, if we need to, we will care very much for your things."

"Janalee, I trust that you would, but this involves more than the oak table and the rocker. We do need to discuss this." Her voice grew stern. "Come here, honey."

I knew that if I went to her, two things would happen: I would cry and I'd end up participating in this horrifying exercise. But I trusted her and I wanted to ease her mind. My resolve — my fury — collapsed. I crawled next to her on the couch and cried. I wanted to hear that she didn't think she was going to die. I wanted her to tell me this was just precautionary – that she didn't think we'd use the list.

As we began the project, I felt nauseous. We remembered all the times we jokingly said "who gets what" as I grew up. She had once joked, "When I die, neither of you two rotten kids are getting that table! They'll flip it over and bury me between the legs!"

Now, I was creating a two-column list with the headings: "Item" and "Name." We started with the easy stuff — the things she wanted to give to me and Jason.

Oak dining table	*Jana*
Mahogany rocker	*Jana*
Oak bedroom furniture	*Jason*
Necklace Grandpa gave Grandma when Mom was born	*Jason*
Diamond ring Daddy gave Mom	*Jason*

I discovered there were things that were important to Mom, though we did not yet understand their worth. This new knowledge of Mom's values was important to me.

"Teenagers" poem	*Jason*
Picture of Mom and Jason fishing	*Jason*
Hand tools	*split*
Ruby ring	*Jana*
Books	*Jana*
Joy sign	*Jana*
Raccoon cookie jar	*Jana*
"Bookworm" painting	*Jason*
Mug rack Mom made	*Jason*

I also learned that Mom wanted to leave various items to specific people who were important to her. It had less to do with the items themselves and more to do with the gesture.

Mendoza paintings	*AA Club*
Antique ceramic chamber pot	*Jane*
Maple chair	*Pat*
Spring flower painting	*Kathy*
Opal ring	*Annette*
Plaque of the location of the star Chuck named after Mom	*Chuck*
Picture of Mom hugging a tree	*Chuck*
Caricature of Mom and Aunt Margie	*Aunt Margie*

Had this task been left to me later, I may have vainly assumed Jason and I were to receive it all, offending Mom's friends and Mom's intentions.

The effort was tremendous and I balked several times. Mom waited patiently. Finally, I was glad to be involved in the process because I knew Jason would be pleased with the results, not only what we might receive, but the gifts she bestowed upon others. However, I kept it so external that I never believed any of us would possess Mom's possessions. I imagined giving the gifts to people, and their joy at the thought and expression of love. I couldn't associate the distribution with her death.

AT THE END of April, Mom and Aunt Margie decided it would be good for all three of us if Mom went to Aunt Margie's home in California for a few weeks. Aunt Margie needed to work and since she worked from home, she could care for Mom at the same time. Mom wanted to feel less a captive of cancer. She wanted out of her cancer-ridden surroundings. Informed of these plans, Daddy sent me a round-trip plane ticket to visit him in NJ.

Initially, I railed against every aspect of the plan. I thought it would be hard on Mom. I thought I should stay in Denver and work. I realized, though, that I was terrified of being away from Mom. When I was near her, taking care of her, I could focus on the daily routine and details, and ignore the big picture. I also found strength in her peace. I drew on her serenity and balance. Away from her, I knew I'd likely fall victim to big, bad "my mother is dying" thoughts. Before she left, I put together a care package and wrote her a note:

> *Dear Mommy,*
>
> *It's Tuesday afternoon and you leave tomorrow! I'm beginning to realize how much I'm going to miss you. You're leaving the state! For the first time since this all started I won't have the option of jumping in my trusty, overworked car to go see you whenever I want!*
>
> *HORRORS!*
>
> *Then I also realized that you won't be able to see me! Who is going to make you laugh at stupid things? No one in the world has the warped personality your daughter has, eh? I don't think I can depend on Chuck to lie down on the floor, kick his heels, and scream when he doesn't get what he wants. I doubt you will see the humor I could point out in a funny-looking stewardess throwing you an attitude over your very odd diet requests.*
>
> *For heaven's sake!*
>
> *Who will entertain you? Who will let you tuck them in at night? Who will give you the honesty moments? Who will analyze your urine? Who will get clingy with you? Who will ask you "How are you?" 14 times an hour?*
>
> *Well, as of now, consider yourself tantrumed, entertained, a bed-tucker, honesty-ed, urine-analyzed, clung to, and questioned.*
>
> *The enclosed gifts are completely unconnected and silly, which makes them kind of like my current train of thought. The pictures are so that you can see me and your rotten son whenever you want.*
>
> *I will miss you!!!*
>
> *And I love you more than you love me!*

WHEN I RECEIVED the plane ticket from Daddy, I went through several confused days. I wasn't sure I wanted to go. I put so much pressure on myself to find a cure and to make Mom's life comfortable that being apart felt like a cop-out. I thought I was shirking my duties. If I rested, would the cancer grow?

Little did I know that I was going to visit the one person who could understand every fear I faced, as well as help me sort out facts. Daddy also provided much-needed comic relief.

While I was in college, Daddy and I established some rituals and traditions I only dared commit with my whacky father. Many stemmed from movies we'd seen together. We'd rent silly movies, order a large pepperoni pizza, and sit around eating until we both got sick. We loved Steve Martin movies and Daddy does an excellent impression of the "wild and crazy" guy himself. From "The Man With Two Brains," we learned the song, "Duke Duke Duke, Duke of Oil Oil Oil," which we sang together spontaneously in restaurants and over the phone. We rented, "The Little Mermaid," and broke out into a dance to the song, "Under the Sea." However, we sang, "I Have To Pee. Under the Sea." Whenever Phil Collins's song, "You Can't Hurry Love" came on, we jitterbugged in our socks on his hardwood floor.

The ultimate Daddy moment came one night when he drove me to my dorm in his hot little RX-7. When I got out, he pulled the parking brake, blasted Michael Jackson's "Off the Wall," and started dancing in the parking lot. A couple of my friends came outside when they saw the display and we all joined him.

This was precisely the person I needed to see, though I didn't know it until he wrapped his arms around me at Newark airport.

"Hi, babydoll!" he said. "Did you get to sit near any cute men?"

We grabbed my bags and, in the very efficient Daddy style, made a bee-line for the car.

"Open the glove box," he said.

I did, and inside was a single-serving bottle of wine, a wine glass, and a bag of cashews.

"Welcome to Joisee!" he said. "Look at that view!"

We laughed at the typical steel-gray skies. The Anheuser-Busch logo that always greeted me upon arrival beamed through the smog from a nearby building, and reminded me of my distance from Mom. I drank my wine and sat back for the stressful ride down the Jersey Turnpike.

"Exit 9. Rutgers University!" Daddy pulled off, paid the toll, and cruised into New Brunswick.

We had been discussing Mom's health and I realized how much I protected the gravity of it all. I wanted to put a positive spin on everything. Daddy didn't push, but he knew how to ask questions others simply couldn't. He'd lived through it. I found myself able to tell him ugly truths that I'd never reveal to outsiders. When others heard one horrible experience or prognosis, they wrote her off. Daddy knew that reality changed every day. He knew how to hope and he did it from a realistic foundation.

I was also sensitive to the fact that he had just lost his mom, my grandma, in January. In many ways, I was facing exactly what he had faced one year earlier. He was aware that he may only be two steps ahead of me — where I could be in the future. Conversations were loaded, but more honest than those with anyone else.

That first night, we drove through Rutgers so I could see changes on campus, and then we hit Highway 27 south to Princeton, and our favorite restaurant, The Annex. The waitresses at The Annex were all overweight and over 75 years old. They wore white, one-piece, zipper-front polyester dresses over their sizable girths. On their feet, they wore white orthopedic shoes. Their aprons were black and orange, which was supposed to be evidence of their Princeton Tiger spirit. These women had bad attitudes, but called us "honey" and "dear." And we adored them! They provided entertainment all night long; it was simply impossible to believe these waitresses treated their customers so poorly, and yet people returned happily and frequently. Often, these old women hustled through the restaurant and grabbed condiments off of our table to deliver them immediately to our neighbor's table. Those diners used them gingerly and then apologetically handed them back to us when the waitresses weren't looking.

Despite the service, the food was always fantastic. Daddy usually ordered the chicken cacciatore, dramatically saying in staccato rhythm, "CHI-ken-CA-cha-TO-ree" to the nonplussed waitresses, and I'd get rigatoni.

As we left that night, I caught Daddy checking himself out in a mirror and I remembered how he'd done that when he was bald in 1986, my freshman year. The man could catch his reflection in a shiny doorknob when he was bald. As we walked, I reminded him of that and he remembered the moments almost fondly. We passed a man with a bald spot, and Daddy whispered, "At least mine came back!" and we laughed.

During my four-day stay with Daddy, I slept a lot. I fell asleep everywhere I sat down. My body was taking a well-deserved break. Daddy didn't push activity and we watched movies, ate pizza, and talked when the mood struck us. By the time I headed home to Denver, I had a renewed source of energy.

I think the trip was good for both Aunt Margie and Mom, too. They visited another doctor in California, and "played" as much as they could. From what I heard, they furthered their already-strong relationship. I imagine they coveted their time together as much as I coveted my time alone with Mom. We understood each moment was precious, even as we hoped our time together contained no limits.

Once Mom and I returned to Colorado — early May — the routine began again. Her strength improved as the second treatment lapsed into distant memory and her bouts with slurring, impromptu napping, and diarrhea subsided. She was still very weak, though. It was the first year in my memory that Mom didn't "dig in the dirt" or have a garden. I bought her a big plastic bucket in which she could grow a very tiny garden, but even that proved too difficult.

Ironically, my journaling also took a back seat. Ironic, but not coincidental. Until this time, I wrote about my emotions when I didn't feel safe expressing them verbally or physically. I didn't know how to express my feelings to people any more. No one understood no matter how much I tried to explain. Ultimately, I ended up bottling it up or journaling it.

WEDNESDAY, MAY 12

I think I'm hiding my real feelings from others by writing in my journal, but I can't help it! I don't want to express my doubts. I'm certain my fear hinders the cure. Still, I'm forcing optimism on myself and others. I think that all of my optimism contributes to a cure, but the pressure is starting to overwhelm me and anger others. I push very hard. I push myself to ignore fear and to maintain an upbeat pace and attitude. I feel like a balloon filling with helium — the stuff of parties and happy children. But the helium keeps coming, filling my skin beyond its capacity. Even when I can tell I've reached my limit and I try to hold it back, it gushes in with the force of a fire hydrant. I drift higher and higher, beyond rational heights, ignoring the feelings that might bring me back to a livable level. Am I losing all balance? If I don't release some pressure soon, I'll burst.

I mistrust my thoughts and emotions so deeply that I won't allow myself a moment of self-reflection. When I'm in Denver, I work continuously. When I'm in Cañon City, I make sure I am continuously moving. I can't sit. I'm running a lot, sometimes two or three times a day. Mom lives on a hill upon which the homes are situated in a large oval, like a horse track. When I don't want to stray far, I circle the track over and over. If Mom needs me, she puts a signal of some sort in the front window and on my next round, I run inside. Aunt Margie and I use the same signal on the days she's there when Mom requires more than two-handed care.

ALL THAT RUNNING made me feel healthy and people often told me how good I looked "despite the difficulties." (No one ever said, "despite your Mom's cancer.") But running was an escape. Yet another escape. Keep moving. If the feelings get too close — move faster! Run! I didn't realize it at the time, of course. To me, running was a positive way to take care of myself. It fit a category of my definition of care-taking: If I stay healthy, I can better care for Mom.

All the moving, running, and cleaning also helped me to escape one of the worst times of the day.

SATURDAY, MAY 15

When my mind is idle, the demons creep in. I try to get so completely exhausted each day that the second my head hits the pillow, I'm out. Honestly, I'm terrified of nighttime, even before I go to bed. Everything is so quiet ... except the phone. I need constant distraction and activity, but at night everything slows down, gets quiet. I'm alone with scary, scary thoughts. I clean, blast my music, and go running. Anything. Chris keeps telling me I should take hot showers or baths to relax before I go to bed, but that response — relaxation — completely terrifies me. I'm certain that if I were to just lay out in warm water and bubbles, nothing to read or write, I'd start crying. I'd start thinking horrible thoughts. I can't stop them once they start. I feel like I'm at the top of a dirt hill and suddenly the rains come, turning the hill to mud, and I slide, twisting and turning. I can't grasp trees or roots. It's messy and scary and out of my control.

I know how to control my fears. I turn everything off. That's not good, but I can't go around being a basket case all day. No wonder I dream.

Nighttime. It's so lonely. When I'm not with Mom, I'm here at my place, usually alone. The walls that surround me are far more familiar to me than my own fears — and much more stable. God, I fear quiet. Not quiet rooms, but my own quiet mind. That moment, those long moments before sleep rescues me, I lay like a child in bed, afraid the boogie man is in my closet. Only now, I'm 24 years old and the boogie man is in my own head, locked way in the back. I just want to fall asleep before he finds a way out.

THE ONLY PERSON who helped me pay attention to myself was Mom. She was doing what came naturally to her — helping me grow. I suppose this was also a form of nesting to her: preparing a safe place for her children, safe room to grow, safe thoughts of the future, and safe feelings of self-confidence. If she was going to leave us, we needed to understand that we possessed the tools to continue our lives, as her children, as adults. She's the one who suggested I find a support group.

SATURDAY, JUNE 19

Obviously I have been avoiding this little form of therapy and it shows. I haven't done any real crying in months and that shows also. I don't want to backtrack and talk about everything that's happened with Mom because that's not the issue here. The issue is me.

I've joined a Cancer Support Group with an organization called QuaLife. They charge $60 for four sessions. At first I was very skeptical of every aspect of it, especially the charge. The money is used to pay a counselor/facilitator to moderate the meeting. Mom's AA meetings required no fee, just a buck here and there. I was also convinced that no one was suffering as badly as me, no one could understand, and no one would really listen (that's what I'd learned from other friends). I also didn't want to sit and listen to other people's problems. I couldn't imagine how that would help. And I really didn't want some therapist/shrink telling me how to "feel better."

What an awakening I had! Not only has the group helped me express some difficult feelings I cannot express to anyone else, but it's made me realize I'm not alone — at least I don't have to be.

That group is the reason I've decided to write again. I've been four times and the last time was probably the most productive for me personally. I've learned something valuable every time, including gratitude and awe.

But this last time was the best for me because the group forced me to take a long look at the way I'm treating me — not how well Mom's doing. All I do at these group meetings is talk about how glad I am that our relationship is so strong, or how happy I am to have such a wonderful family. I tell them I'm worried about how hard this is for Mom, or I tell them how strong Mom is. They told me that I need to take better care of myself. So, I launched into all the things that I thought I was already doing for me — exercising, eating right, sleeping, taking vitamins, maintaining a balance among work, Mom, and friends. Then the counselor, Pat, asked me how I was doing, and the only way I could answer was by making some statement about Mom or the family. She said, "No, Jana, how are you doing?"

I pride myself on "knowing myself" very well. When all this started, I wrote and wrote and wrote to keep up with all the emotions that were taking over my life and somehow I kept up. But since I stopped writing and asking myself the question, "How do you feel?" I've lost touch of myself. Usually that's followed by weakened "copers," but I've carried on quite well, which has led me to disillusion myself into thinking I'm fine. It becomes apparent when a very stressful situation reaches a climax and then comes to a close — I get terribly sick. I've had two bouts with illness, both of which kept me from work and in bed for three days straight.

Patricia said, "Jana, I want you to uncross your legs and arms and lean forward in your chair. Now, say the first two things that come to mind when you think about your Mom's illness."

I said through tears, "I'm angry. I wish she didn't have to go through this."

Patricia said, "Can you say, 'I wish I didn't have to go through this'."

I started sobbing. I couldn't say it. I was shaking and just stared at a wall ahead of me. Finally, I said it and it felt awful and fantastic at the same time. I was wrecked.

Patricia said that the fact that it was so hard to admit that such a horrible experience was difficult for me should tell me I need to do some soul-searching. I need to figure out how I'm doing and how I feel.

I've been running around like a fool. I have tried to stay so busy with everything else in my life that there's been no time to sit and think. I've been very afraid to sit and think — for the same reason I've been afraid to write. I'm scared that I'll get so upset and I'll be down and bring others down, neither of which I like to do.

The "bring others down" part is interesting. Why should I be so concerned about how others perceive my moods? Everyone has said that they understand I'm going through a difficult time and they all ask how Mom is doing. I've also found that people may ask how Mom's doing, but they don't really want to know. People hate to feel helpless and so they want me to say, "She's fine," so they won't have to think of the right thing to say. I have friends whom I've known for years who haven't contacted me in months. They're afraid to ask about Mom, let alone see her. I feel like saying, "How selfish can you be? If you would show a little guts and try, maybe you could be there for me!" But I know people are afraid of death and dying. They feel like the terminally ill are different people than they were the day before they were diagnosed.

Boy. I'm angry, eh?

Anyway, I don't like to express too much because if some people knew how I felt, they wouldn't know how to deal. Why bring others down, too?

I CONTINUED MEETING with the QuaLife group and discovered many emotions within myself that previously had been unrecognizable or unacceptable to me. Early in the illness, I'd felt some anger and even expressed it in my journal but I had never, in months, expressed anger to another person. To me, anger bordered on self-pity which made me feel guilty. I wasn't the sick one; I was lucky compared to Mom. I thought I had no reason to feel sorry for myself. Also, anger felt like a completely pointless emotion because I wanted to be angry at someone or something. I wanted to lay blame. Like a child who feels wronged, I wanted to point at the wrong-doer and say, "It's your fault!" I wanted to hit the person responsible for putting us in this situation. Never before had I experienced an anger that wasn't generated by a controllable experience gone awry. Throughout my short life, I'd only faced situations that I could look back on and say, "If I had only done that differently." Or I could look at another's actions and say, "Look what you did!"

For the first time, I faced a demon that entered my life through no fault of my own or anybody else's. I wanted to blame someone. Someone had to be responsible! Otherwise, random forces like this could occur at any time, no matter how well I led my life, or if I made right or wrong choices. I wondered, "What's the point in trying to live well and do right if things like this could destroy it all?"

Occasionally, I found myself sitting alone, staring at my surroundings blankly, palms up and open, looking for a reason. When I felt anger coming on, I'd stop because it felt so useless and absurd. Mad at what? What's the point? What a waste.

Then I discovered I wasn't alone.

THURSDAY, JULY 15

I'm feeling very angry and it won't go away. I feel destructive — like I could hurt somebody or something and not feel any remorse whatsoever. Yesterday, I was walking by a pumpkin patch and instantly imagined myself in a huge truck with monster wheels, turning donuts in the patch, tearing leaves and vines apart, laughing hysterically, and turning the wheel like a madwoman.

A woman in my cancer support group said she wants to steal a mobile home and run away. We all thought that was a riot, but the facilitator, Patricia, said that was a very "safe" fantasy for the woman. Susan has been taking care of her husband for over five years and he will not allow anyone else to take care of him, so she hasn't had a break in five years. Whenever she thinks about leaving for even a day, she gets guilty, so she thinks and dreams about all the places she'd love to go and says that someday she will just get a nurse for the weekend and go … but she never does. I wonder if she ever will. By fantasizing about stealing a dream home, she stays grounded, while also doing something reckless. Stealing a mobile home! I imaged Susan backing her truck up to an attractive, two-bedroom trailer, hitching up, and moving out!

The same woman, who is also very angry and deals with her anger better than me, said that one day she sat down at her computer and wrote "fuck" over and over for a full page and said it felt wonderful. Another man told me to take a baseball bat to my bed. Scream, yell, cry, swing, and beat. He said it releases a lot of stress. The same man said that he has good days and bad days, like everyone, but the bad days are really bad. Everyone in the room agreed with him and I think that if there had been a person in that room not going through a cancer-related situation, he/she would have been scared and shaken by the anger expressed that day. The man, Jack, whose mother also has cancer, said on his very bad days he has violent fantasies. When he's being tailgated, he said he wants to slam on his brakes, forcing the "asshole" behind him to ram his car. Then he said he would get out, grab a crowbar from the passenger seat, and walk up to the car to smash the "asshole's" windows. Then he'd grab the guy from the driver's seat, bounce his head against the hood of the car till it was bloody, and break his back with the crowbar. He said he'd back over him as he drove away. For tailgating! Everyone hates a tailgater, but good grief …

THAT NIGHT, I went home and found the closest thing to a baseball bat — a rolling pin — and proceeded to beat my bed. I swung so hard, the muscles in my back ached. I fell down on my knees to get a better angle on the bed for a harder impact. Grunts turned to yells and my vision tunneled to just one square on my bed. I hit harder with every swing and imagined myself inside Mom's liver, beating the cells to a pulp one by one. Then I glanced to my right and saw myself in the full-length mirror on my closet. I looked so ridiculous that I started laughing hysterically, which I thought couldn't be all bad. I rolled back on the floor, proud of myself.

Wisdom

CHAPTER 2

It usually started something like this:

"Kids, turn off that TV and come take a look at this sunset! Now!"

We'd drag our little tails out the back door to find Mom planted square in the middle of her garden facing west, coffee cup in hand. I'd make a bee-line to her side while Jason turned it into a game of war. He would point his finger at any willing target, rapid-firing a round or two, roll behind a tree and finally sprint behind enemy lines (rows of carrots) to land — armed and ready — next to Mom and me. We hardly noticed.

The three of us would stand in the warm summer evening appreciating our own favorite parts of the sunset. I liked the way the Rockies became silhouettes against the sky, like construction paper cut-outs glued against an orange background — all angles and tilts. Jason preferred quietly aiming his fingers like guns at the birds that were even more apparent against the fiery sky. I'm not sure what Mom noticed, but I now realize those types of moments were how I found spirituality.

Then, Mom would say:

"I believe it's time to camp!"

Woooo Hooooo! It took all our reserves not to plow through the burgeoning garden in our dance of excitement.

Quickly, however, the excitement turned to determination as Mom recited her Camping Mantra: "I've got 99 million things to do before we go." She then proceeded to make herself crazy preparing for the trip. Mom didn't camp like most single women with two kids. Mom always said, "I don't want to camp unless I can go long enough to forget what day it is." And, since you could set a watch by my mother, this goal required some serious time. We usually camped for two weeks. The other requirement for our camping trips was that we "completely abandon civilization," meaning we did not want to see another human (bears were fine) the entire time we camped. We usually planned one excursion to the closest town for supplies mid-way through the trip, but given Mom's solitude demands, this was no minor trek. It took a full day, especially given the fact that running water was as novel to Mom on a camping mission as fire to cavemen. Often, we hit every public rest room in town! Once, Mom even took us to a public pool so we could shower and play in the water. Jason and I leaped from pine needles and pitch into gallons and gallons of clean water. Mom was no dummy.

Frequently, we scheduled our camping trips around an annual event held in Leadville, Colorado, the highest town in the U.S. Some people may migrate all over the world for annual events like marathons, car shows, spring thaws, or garden exhibits. My mom was an avid follower of Leadville's "Get Your Ass Up The Pass" race. (That's what Mom called the event. I'm not sure what the town called it.) No small feat, this race involved sometimes more than 40 burros and their trainers. They literally raced through the elevations around Leadville, which required stamina and patience on the part of both teammates. As donkey owners, we knew that the animals are not stubborn, as the stereotype suggests, but cautious. Very cautious. One spring on Ashley Lane, Mom needed to take Alice a few blocks to the vet ("Gotta haul my ass to the vet!") and it took more than 10 minutes to get Alice out of the yard because she wouldn't step over the garden hose, which laid lifeless at her feet. Imagine the training involved in a mountain donkey race where time and speed are of the essence.

On the day we went to town, we'd wake early to watch our own private sunrise as it crawled over the peaks, descended into our own private valley, and shuddered the dew off the grasses. Then we'd gather kindling to make breakfast. Mom's coffee took longer to boil and percolate than the eggs, bacon, and hashbrowns combined.

Finally, as she enjoyed her crunchy coffee, we cleaned up our home and dumped water and dirt on the fire. Jason checked to be sure the refrigerator we'd built in the creek was intact. I put the cooler in the truck. Mom placed other items like spatulas and the cast iron skillet high up in trees. Then, we piled into the truck for the long ride to town. Sometimes, Mom let one of us drive. We would stall the truck out a lot, which meant lots of wood collecting. Every time we stopped she would spy valuable kindling and out we'd bound as though Mom had installed eject buttons on our seats.

Finally, we'd hit Leadville, looking no different from many of the locals. The three of us wandered among the contestants, sizing up their chances and, finally, we'd each pick our winner, putting our initials next to the names on the program. One year I picked AppleJack, an underdog by all accounts, but that was always my style. Our picks gave the three of us something to compete over throughout the day.

"Your donkey's really a goat!"

"Oh, yeah?! Well, yours is cross-eyed!"

The problem with "Get Your Ass Up The Pass" was that the donkeys were gone half a day as spectators wandered around waiting for updates. Leadville-ites turned their little town into a fair much like the arts and crafts fairs of Little House on the Prairie. Ice cream, popcorn, quilts, jellies, and jams lined the vendor counters, which resembled the lemonade stands of my childhood.

Then, suddenly the entire crowd hushed as though a giddy electric current shocked us all at once, letting us know word had come on the race. Strangers quietly smiled at each other, daring not breathe, waiting for the announcement. Even the monetary exchanges paused. Then, like a brushfire or a wind pushing across the tops of a wheat field, we'd hear the buzz racing our way from ear-to-mouth-ear-to-mouth-ear-to-mouth.

"AppleJack's ahead by a hee haw!"

I was the big winner that day because my pick came in first. I felt as though, by picking him, I'd somehow marked him as the winner before the race started. That's how good those trips made me feel. Our little circle of three was so filled with unconditional love and support that I believed my positive energy could influence donkey performance. I thought my energy somehow found AppleJack rumbling through the course and pushed him along due to sheer hope. AppleJack and I were a team. I was so happy and comfy that nothing seemed silly. Anything was possible. AppleJack won!

During the rest of the two-week trip, we hiked, read, floated on lakes, and bathed in creeks. We generally loved one another. I look back on those trips and realize what a gift Mom was giving us and herself with those precious days of solitude and serenity. We learned so much about each other — three people who thought they knew everything about each other.

Sitting under the graspable stars and the protective evergreens, near the healing fire, we asked normally unconsidered questions. We answered with the luxury of thoughtfulness granted only by peace and pause. Little embarrassed us in our tight circle. We feared no judgement and felt free to hug trees when the joyous mood grabbed us. Sometimes we ran scared back to the fire from a lonely trip into the dark woods with a flashlight and roll of toilet paper.

One fireside game I remember clearly, probably because Jason always ruined it. After dinner, we'd sit around toasting marshmallows. One of us would start a story with, "Once upon a time," and begin a yarn. After a few minutes, that person would stop and look to one of the other two, who would continue in his or her own way. These stories usually followed similar patterns. My portions took on fairy tale elements, with talking dogs, gnomes, and magic sticks. Mom's chapters beefed up the plot and sometimes added suspense. And then there was Jason. When he became bored with the game, he introduced the element of destruction. We could always count on

Jason to bring the story to its climax and ending in one short sentence: "And then a big, Mac truck came out of nowhere and ran over everyone. The End." No matter how peaceful, magical, or pristine a setting, Jason could pull a Mac truck out of nowhere and kill all the characters in one final accident.

We were safe. Safe to be curious, to explore, to be silly, to anticipate, to hope. And this safety gave us power, energy to approach all of life as though joy and miracles waited at the end of every adventure should we choose to embrace them.

Wisdom

CHAPTER 3

The more we settled into the routines of cancer, the less we wanted to think about cancer. Mom said she wanted to do things unrelated to cancer but that was impossible. Everything from the meals she ate to the relative distance from the bathroom ruled her living space, her wandering allotment. Even her pills had to be hauled around in a fishing tackle organizer.

THURSDAY, MAY 20

Maybe this is how new moms feel. But I'm feeling this way about my Mom — not about a child. But then, Mom is a child now in so many senses. Specifically, I'm thinking of transporting her around. I can't believe the time and energy involved in travel, and I don't mean long distances.

Today, I drove Mom to Colorado Springs to see a therapist she saw years ago. (That was news to me!) She wanted time with him no matter the physical cost. The easiest part was setting the appointment for a time she thought she'd be awake. We had to be sure she ate things she'd keep down; load the Nissan with pillows and blankets; and flatten the back seat so she could nap before and after. I put together a bag of supplies like wet wipes, high-nutrition drinks, and plastic bags for messes. I divvied up her drugs into hourly doses. I left to get gas before I came back to load her up, and I made sure we had several soothing meditation tapes. For a one-hour drive! I felt responsible and mature at getting it all together and making her appointment happen, but life has become so complex! Since when did I become someone who jumps out of a car, slings a baby bag over my shoulder, and runs to the passenger side so that my precious cargo doesn't toddle into oncoming traffic?

I'm taking care of my mom. The basics. I'm scared. I'm capable, apparently. I'm willing. But this happened without my consent. When do I get to be cared for again? Where is my mommy going?

DESPITE THE DIFFICULTY of travel, Mom didn't want to live like a dying person. Hence the decision to go to my cousin's graduation in Minnesota. Her brother, my Uncle Willis, had carted his family all over the country when Jason and I graduated from high school. Mom felt an obligation and desire to get back to her native state for her nephew Ryan's graduation. Aunt Margie and I were extremely hesitant about the whole thing, but I figured that if Mom wanted to do it, we'd pull it off. Additionally, I was whole-heartedly into Mom's theory of living over dying.

The graduation was the first weekend in June. Mom and I planned to fly out June 3. Aunt Margie would fly from California and meet us there the next day. The Navy wouldn't let Jason attend.

Mom and I spent a couple of playful evenings trying to figure out what to pack and what she would wear to the graduation. All she wore those days were humongous men's boxer shorts and colorful jogging suits. They didn't cramp her stomach and were soft against her fragile skin. With all of the water retention and bloating around her tummy, and the significant weight loss everywhere else, her skin looked stretched and old against her diminishing frame. She bruised easily. After trying on many of the sharp suits she used to wear daily, we found only one that still looked even reasonably appropriate. The long, loose black skirt had an elastic waist, covered by a bright red jacket with black ribbing. The looseness of it hid her tiny limbs as well as her extended stomach, while the shoulder pads held it all up straight. She looked as strong and vibrant as I'd seen her in weeks. I think she was excited to dress up.

I was a wreck over the logistics of the trip itself. We experienced disasters going to the grocery store. What would happen when we were trapped on a plane? Mom sensed my fears and the two of us called Aunt Margie to get some advice. "Auntie Em," as Jason had begun calling her while stationed near her home in San Diego, had already thought it all out. She was concerned and didn't think the trip was wise, but, like me, she knew that if Mom wanted to do it, we'd make it happen. Aunt Margie told me what to take on the plane, what to tell flight attendants, what to do during layovers, and how to handle any resistance. She bolstered me and helped me pull out the old "pit bull" persona I'd not used in weeks — thanks to less contact with doctors.

When the day finally arrived for the trip, my emotions were loaded. I was very concerned as to how our family would react upon seeing her. I was convinced that she looked like a walking corpse most of the time. I also wondered if I was up to the task of caretaking en-route.

THURSDAY, JUNE 3

It's 10 p.m. Minnesota time and we are ..."cruising at an altitude of 23,000 feet. We're just above the cloud cover, which tends to make the ride slightly bumpy, so the pilot has turned on the fasten seat belt sign ..."

We're between Sioux Falls and Fargo after an hour lay-over in Sioux Falls. Mom is lying down in the three seats across the aisle from me. It really emptied out in Sioux Falls. (Why would anybody get off in Sioux Falls?) We deplaned at SF so Mom could stretch a little. She laid down on the ground in the terminal because she was in pain. No one was around, so it didn't inconvenience anyone. When it was time to board, I waved at the man who was calling for passengers and said, "Just a few more minutes, OK?" He said, "No problem, I'm in no hurry." He could see me talking to someone on the floor but could not see Mom. A couple of minutes later, he said, "I take it you've got a baby over there?" Mom and I both laughed and I said, "It's my mother." He thought that was really funny until Mom yelled, "She's the kid!" He said, "It really is your mother!" I think Mom gets off on the shock value sometimes.

There was one thing that happened earlier that really pissed me off. We got on the plane and there was a young guy in Mom's seat. We said, "We specifically asked for an aisle." He said, "I have a bad stomach. I like to be in the aisle." And he made no offer to give it up! It was assigned to Mom who was obviously weak! I almost went into my "pit bull" routine, when a lady said, "You can sit here," and pointed at two seats next to her. We did, but Mom made a huge production out of how weak and feeble she is. When she sat down, she said, "I wanted to overdo that. He should have gotten out of my seat." Anyway, when we landed in SF, that jerk (who had slept the entire time) stood up and he was wearing an Air Force jacket! Not only was he lying about having a bad stomach during flights (he slept!) but he's in the Air Force! I saw him walking through the airport and felt like walking up to him and saying, "You are an ass!" but why waste energy?

later …

I'm in my aunt and uncle's living room right now and Mom is lying on a couch across from me. I really have a great family. Everyone was nervous to see her, but after a few minutes, everything was normal. We're picking on each other, joking, laughing, and talking like normal. This is a nutty, goofy, resilient bunch of people. I'm so grateful for the love we've all developed and nurtured. I know I can count on these people for anything. And we're all such fun when we get together. It reminds me of Mom's surprise 50th birthday party just last December. It took us over eight months to plan and lasted several days. Doing things like that has become somewhat of a source of pride for us — who can get the last laugh.

Life here seems to be even more laid back than Colorado. My Uncle Willis says things like "by golly" and "son of a biscuit."

Everyone also seems to be pleasantly surprised at Mom's condition. We painted a pretty grim picture before we came, so they were expecting worse. My cousin Ryan said she looks like she's been on a diet! Geez! If only! Part of me is glad they are seeing her when she's doing so well. Another part of me wishes they had seen her when she was so weak that I was changing her diapers. I guess that's selfish, but I can't help wishing they had gone through some of that.

I SLEPT HARDER and longer that night than I had in months. Uncle Willis set up a mattress for me in the basement away from graduation festivities and I must have cocooned into complete hibernation. The next day, I awoke late with a screaming sore throat and aches and pains throughout my entire body. I had gone from feeling healthy and happy the night before, to feeling like I deserved more medical attention than Mom the next morning. Even walking hurt. I was dizzy from the effort. Luckily for me — maybe — I had every family member there to assess my condition. Also, Aunt Margie was there to run interference and to keep me away from Mom, who definitely didn't need more bugs in her system. Uncle Willis took me to the emergency room the following day and I was diagnosed with a roaring case of strep, given antibiotics, and told to rest. Mom was convinced that I had gotten sick because I'd worn my body out and the first moment I'd relaxed, my body gave up the fight. She said it proved to her that I needed to "take better care of me." We remembered the time that I had the lead in the school play and I'd rehearsed, built sets, and run around with the rest of the cast so much that two nights before the opening, I got sick. Luckily, the play was English with lots of tea-drinking and I pulled it off by toting a teacup — pinky high in the air — throughout the performance. Such crescendo and collapse is my nature.

I didn't recover until I was back in Denver in my own bed, where I stayed for three days. Mom was very glad to have taken the trip, but she, too, was a little worse for wear. We all needed recovery time and, though the routines continued, the rest of June turned into a journey of a different sort — we journeyed deeper into each other than we'd ever done before. It set the tone for July, when Jason would be home from the Navy for good.

I was concerned about Jason's return. I regretted that he had not been able to share the time with Mom that I had. At the same time, I resented that he didn't have to face her daily depletion. He was still telling me that I was overreacting to the situation and his optimism for her certain cure alternately bolstered me and unnerved me. I'd talk to him on the phone and frequently decided he was in denial, which made me more bitter. I wanted him to clean poop, change diapers, see the spaces where Mom's teeth used to be, and wake to dry heaves randomly throughout the night. I was feeling a lot of self-pity.

At the same time, I wanted to protect Jason from everything. I didn't want my baby brother to hurt; I didn't want him to lose his characteristic "this-aint-the-end-of-the-world" attitude: I didn't want my little brother to lose his mother. Jason deserved to be happy. I wanted him safe, free of fear, free of mental anguish. If that meant he stayed in denial in the Navy, so be it. We'd deal with it when he left the Navy for good and came home. I realized I was spending June waiting for his return as though it portended some change in our activities.

FRIDAY, JUNE 25

Dear Glen,

Things are tough, but I'm doing my best to cope. Mom is "in the sixth month of an illness in which she was predicted to live six to twelve months." I'm quoting her. She is such an incredibly courageous woman. She has good days and bad days. She's lost a lot of weight and has to take lots of naps, but if you let her do what she needs to do for herself, she is generally in good spirits. When she doesn't get her nap or eats something out of the ordinary, she gets weak and sick. They won't do the treatment on her like they did the last two times because they don't think she'd live through it. We almost lost her the last time.

Anyway, she was supposed to start systemic chemotherapy today, but decided against it because she's not absolutely certain she wants to do it. The doctors say that it provides zero chance for a cure, but that it may extend her life. They don't even guarantee that, though, and she would go through some pain and a lot of discomfort, so she has to weigh the risks and the benefits. A lot of people are approaching it with the attitude of "What have you got to lose?" But I think if you look at the situation from an insider's perspective, she may have a lot to lose. Quality of life is of supreme importance right now and why give up an unknown number of days of fair comfort and real happiness for extra days of discomfort and frustration? It's tough, because I don't want to lose her. I still can't imagine life without her and my life is RULED by cancer, but I cannot bear to see her in pain. After the last treatment, I experienced what it would be like to have to care for her 24 hours a day and I don't want to have to go through that again. I would do it without question and without regret, but the frustration, pain, and fear was more than I want her to endure ever again. I now completely understand euthanasia. This woman deserves dignity in life as much as she deserves peace in death.

AS JUNE PROGRESSED, my expectations changed; I began to expect Mom's death. However, there is a huge chasm between expecting and accepting.

I remember the conversation with Brooke when the internal conflict revealed itself to me. We were getting new carpet in our apartment and as the installers hauled all our furniture onto the front lawn. We ate lunch outside and moaned about our brown, leather couch. We had heaped scorn upon it for years. It must have weighed the same as a vintage VW van and was built similarly. And brown! Like the brown of old, smoky bar stools, or the bench seats on tractors.

We ate our sandwiches and chips, staring at the couch as the leather collected the sun's heat.

"Maybe I should just break down and buy a new couch," I finally said, squinting.

Silence.

As soon as I said it, I realized that deep in my subconscious, another idea lurked. It struggled for expression and made its way to my throat where it formed a lump, forcing me to stop eating. I set down my food and exhaled. I hoped my hesitation hadn't shown — that the little thought wasn't apparent. It felt like weakness.

But Brooke was way ahead of me, not only in minutes of the conversation, but probably in weeks or even months. The thought hung between us like a boulder over a glass table. It had to come out, but I was incapable of forming the words, and she feared seeming insensitive. Finally, it fell.

"You should wait, Jana."

I looked at her, tears forming, and I nodded.

"I know."

My mind flickered to Mom's couch, placed it quickly in my living room, and then, like a drop-kick field goal, booted it back into my subconscious. It was gone and the carpet installation continued.

I was living with my heart in one arena and my head in another. Soon, they would have to battle it out and the only livable solution would be a truce.

Acceptance

CHAPTER 1

THURSDAY, JULY 1

Jennifer!

I'm at work and I'm taking a break. I've started coming in around 7-7:30 a.m. because nobody else is here and I can get a shitload done before they arrive. So, now it's 10:30 and I need a break. I'm kinda low and want to update you on what's going on.

Jason is home from the Navy and the timing couldn't be better. Mom is not doing well. In just one week her health went from fairly stable to very unpredictable. I was down there the weekend of the 18th and 19th of June and she was weak and slurring a little, but nothing dramatic. After her last treatment in the hospital, she was slurring very badly because her liver was not removing the serum ammonium from her body. (I can't remember what I told you at the time, so I'll go over it all again.) When your serum ammonium level gets too high, you can go into a coma and die. It affects your muscle coordination and after her last treatment, she couldn't hold glasses without dropping them; she was impossible to understand when she spoke … it was awful. So, when I heard her slurring that weekend, I obviously got scared. I told her to go to the doctor and get a liver analysis done. She promised she would. On Thursday she went to the doctor. She had been scheduled to start systemic chemotherapy, meaning it would go all over her body, not just to her liver. The previous treatments were directed strictly at her liver through her aortic artery (that's why she almost lost her leg during the last treatment). That form of chemo is way too risky now because she is too weak and it would definitely kill her. So, she was supposed to start the systemic chemo on Thursday, but for some reason she didn't want to. I told her to go with her gut feeling, even if she couldn't explain it. She told the doctor that she didn't want to start the treatment, but she wanted a liver analysis done. He did and said she would get the results Monday. He also said that she had gained five pounds, which would be great except that the weight is all water retention — a very bad sign that her kidneys are not functioning properly. She told me all of this and I started to get scared — the slurring, water retention, nausea, dry heaves (which have become routine in her life), increased weakness. The doctors had told us that the treatments would slow the cancer growth for a while but that it would kick in again and the deterioration would be rapid. Naturally, I feared the worst. Then I saw her the next Saturday — June 26 — and could no longer control my fear. She was completely jaundiced. Her skin was yellow and the whites of her eyes were brown. Panic struck. My mother turned into some kind of horror film monster. She looked disgusting. It's the only way I can describe it. She smiled, and I wanted to tell her to stop — she's skeletal to begin with, and yellow-skinned and sickly-eyed on top of it. She looked disgusting and terrifying.

She told Chuck and he saw her that day and called Aunt Margie. Aunt Margie took a midnight flight on Monday and arrived at 1 a.m. Tuesday morning. Since then, Mom's had blood work done to check her kidneys and she has had an appetite, but she still has trouble keeping stuff down.

Jennifer, this is a nightmare I've been living for six months now. And the hardest part is yet to come. I've talked to Mom about her fears and she says she doesn't fear death. She fears the discomfort and pain of dying. She doesn't want to be dependent on others for her survival.

This woman, who is so full of strength and courage, is losing everything that made her identity. She hasn't worked since the day they found the tumor. She relies on others for simple things. She is in pain constantly, finds eating to be a monumental chore, has lost 40 pounds ...

It's the physical changes that are the hardest part for me because they bring the whole thing home. It's easy to ignore the ultimate "end" to this when she looks OK, but when she is not doing so well, all I can do is look at her and think, "I'll never get to hug her enough. We'll never have enough time. I have so much more living to do with her. I want her to see her grandchildren. I want her to know the man I marry. I want to share the rest of her life — a life that's been so FULL and so difficult."

It's more than I can understand.

I'm sorry if this is a downer. I just needed to get this down on paper and wanted you to know where things stand.

I BELIEVE PEOPLE facing a terminal illness can choose when to die. Jason's homecoming was a turning point in Mom's illness. She still had work to do with him. His denial was distancing him from her and from the rest of us. Initially, though, it was more than he could handle to be involved in the rituals that had become simple routines for the rest of us. Whereas we had been given six months to ease into Mom's current appearance, illness, weakness, surprises, Jason was thrown into it like a child dropped into a house of horrors. Everywhere he turned, gruesome truths leaped out at him, slobbery, pestilent, and impossible to ignore. He watched me walk Mom to the bathroom, arm-in-arm and when I came out, he wouldn't look at me. When Mom called out for help getting back to the living room, he glanced my way and his look expressed both fear and anger. I could tell he wanted to help, but he felt like an outsider. He could not accept that she was so helpless. The last time he saw her, we went gambling in Cripple Creek. Such a trip would literally kill her now. That was history — forever. Jason wanted everything to be the way it had been before he entered the Navy. He went through multiple, speedy cycles of denial, fear and anger.

One night when I was in Cañon City and Jason was in his newly found home in Colorado Springs, I called him to talk. He had moved in with a high school buddy and was in the midst of getting into the University of Colorado at Colorado Springs. He thought he wanted to be a nurse.

We chatted about school, his plans, and how it felt to be out of the Navy. Then we cut to the only topic either one of us really thought about these days.

"Jason, do you think about her dying?" I asked. We had not discussed this possibility. We'd only discussed how to fight.

"No. Never." He said it abruptly, as though the conversation was closed as soon as it was open. He acted convinced that Mom would live. But I was growing more convinced that he was too afraid to consider the alternative.

There was silence on the line during which I struggled to decide whether to let him continue ignoring the possibilities, or to help him confront it. Then he spoke quietly.

"Jana, I really don't think she will die. But I don't know what will happen."

I knew exactly what he meant. Her death would mean permanent absence from our lives. That simply was too extraordinary to be real. So, what else could happen? It had to be something else.

"Jason," I said, "I need to tell you something difficult, but I really need to tell you."

"OK." Again, he was abrupt, steeling himself.

"Jason, you may not want to face this now, but if what the doctors are saying comes true, I'll need you to face it because you're the only one who knows how I feel. I'm going to need you."

Without pausing a moment, he said, "Jana, I'll be there for you. I may not be of any help to anyone else, but I'll do anything for you. I probably won't even be able to take care of myself, but I'll take care of you."

We were both crying.

I said, "I won't be able to take care of myself, either, so I'll take care of you."

It felt like a pact between two children in a treehouse; it felt that honest and that reliable.

At the same time, the lull of pills, meals, heaves, and naps changed again and, much like the confusion of the first three months, we faced new diagnosis surprises. Mom was getting sicker.

THURSDAY, JULY 1

Mom is not doing well. She went to the doctor today. He told her she'd waited long enough and she needed to start systemic chemotherapy. He also said the analysis indicates that her liver is failing. I had expected that, but it's so different when a doctor says it.

Jason came up to Denver for lunch today and we bought the nutrient enriched drinks that she can eat. She's having such a bad time keeping food down that those drinks are all she eats. So, Jason drove from Colorado Springs to Denver, to Cañon City to Colorado Springs again in one day. He called me when he finally returned to Colorado Springs and told me about the chemo and warned me that she looks worse than she did last weekend. He said it was real hard for him. When he left her house, he drove as fast as he could with the music as high as it would go.

Then I talked to Mom tonight and she said they'd had a bad day. She said they'd "hit a wall" similar to the ones we hit in the beginning when doctors were trying to diagnose her cancer and come up with a treatment. Those days, the bad news was so bad that we went through phases of re-grouping: we cried, accepted that we were scared, and then looked forward to a new day. If today's news was that bad, I'm very scared. I hated that process.

Tonight, she told me the doctor had some "discouraging" news, but said she wouldn't tell me over the phone. I immediately thought of Jason. He had seen her today, so I assumed he wasn't telling me everything. I talked to him later, compared notes, and learned that she hadn't told him, either. So, now we're both petrified because she's obviously waiting until we're together. I told her that guessing was worse, but she still refused to tell me.

So, tomorrow, Friday, I head down to Cañon City and pray it's not as bad as my creative imagination. I fear it's even worse.

I feel like I did in January. It's like I've regressed. I'm shocked. I, once again, can't believe this is happening. Not MY mother! She's my best friend. I need her to survive. It seems that after the treatments were done, we all were lulled into a "routine" of sorts. Cancer was ALWAYS there — never a moment without thoughts of the "C" word — but we could ignore it. Now, it's hitting us with a sledgehammer again. It's screaming, "I'm still here! In fact, I'm worse! Deal with me NOW!" It laughs at us and mocks our prayers with each new transformation of her appearance and each new pain.

I'm scared to see her. That makes me feel so awful. Why should I be scared to see my own mother? But she no longer looks like Mom.

* * *

God,

I want my mom back and I'm very angry with you for taking her and hurting us all so much in the process. How can you be so cruel? Not only are you killing a necessary person in my life, but you're twisting, wrenching and cracking her body and spirit in the process. How could you? How could you! How dare you!

JASON AND I returned to Cañon City the next morning and learned that the doctors now were "giving her" less than six weeks, unless she chose to start systemic chemotherapy. Again, I listened to estimated timelines in fury. How do doctors determine the length of life left in a spirit? They just look at a body and assume the spirit has nothing to do with life. That aside, we faced new options for treatments, which returned us to the basic questions regarding quality of life. What were we willing to do? More important, what was Mom unwilling to do?

"After the last treatment, I almost lost my leg," Mom said. Aunt Margie, Jason, and I all listened to her. The living room windows and the front door were wide open, letting in the warm, summer breeze.

"Since then," Mom continued, "I've tried to imagine what it would be like to battle cancer as I also learned to function without a leg."

She looked around the room at each of us individually, making us soak in that image. She was not musing about random thoughts. Mom was making a point.

"I am not willing to go through something like that. I am not willing to sacrifice the quality of my life for some unknown, uncomfortable quantity. I've told you that I do not fear death; I fear dying. If I'm going to be here, I want to be as comfortable as I can be."

Mom decided to begin systemic chemotherapy, but of a lesser dosage than the doctors recommended. Also, he suggested that marijuana would help ease the pain, but Mom was dead-set against the use of illegal substances. She'd lived the last 17 years of her life fighting alcohol and drug abuse. It was a sacrifice she would not make.

By mid-July, Mom required 24-hour care. Aunt Margie was flying back and forth with more frequency.

THURSDAY, JULY 15 — 3:00 PM

I'm down in Cañon City with Mom and I'm actually having a good time. I've been cooking and cleaning, waking her, and putting her to bed (she takes a lot of naps) and keeping her comfy. I think that my main goal is to help her maintain her dignity. I look at her yellow eyes and scrawny legs and wish I could take it all away — I want to reach into her belly with both hands and carve out her liver. But since I can't, I plan to do EVERYTHING I can to make her happy and comfortable.

Looking at her is the hardest part. It's so frustrating. I can see where the liver is, can almost see it growing, can touch her stomach and feel it harden as the day progresses, can watch her eyes become browner as she weakens, and can pinpoint the exact cause of all of it — cancer. But I can't do anything about it. I feel like I should have more power than this. I feel like I should do more. It's right there! In her body! And it's eating her alive, but all we can do is watch. So many times I've wanted to poke her stomach, grab it and pull it off of her skeletal frame, punch it into submission, shake her until her liver slides out her vagina … just get it out. But no, it sits there and rapidly gnaws out her insides, burrowing a bigger home for itself. I'm very frustrated.

AT THE END of each day, I tried to remember what I had done. I was busy all day, but accomplished little of lasting value, and it all flew so quickly.

FRIDAY, JULY 16 — 6:30 P.M.

Mom woke up about 7:30. I waited to get up until 8 so that she could do as much as she could by herself. I ate and made myself some coffee. At 9 a.m., I fixed her a bowl of cereal (very small) and half of a nectarine. At 10 a.m., she took a shower — sitting on the chair in the tub — and I stayed in the living room in case she needed me. After her shower, we put on her bathrobe and she rested in her recliner. She gets wiped out after showers. Today, she fell asleep in the chair. At 11:15, we got her out of her recliner, put her pajamas on and put her to bed. She slept until 12:15. In the meantime, I washed the front windows, weeded the front flower garden, made new flower bouquets out of the daisies from across the street, began watering the back yard, and figured out what we'd have for lunch.

When I woke her at 12:15, she took her usual time to fully wake up (about 20 minutes sitting quietly in the living room) Then we ate. I made sure she took her vitamins, too. Then, we figured out what we needed from the store. I prepared a bank deposit. By 1:30, she was back in bed and I headed to the store. I woke her up at 3:30 and we tried to get some health insurance stuff straightened out with the state. We got nowhere. She had a severe bout with diarrhea, which required me to change her, clean her, and put new clothes on her. I am getting better emotionally with all of that, though. It only upsets me when she's in pain. After that, she had to sit and be still for a while because it wore her out. I prepared dinner — waffles with bananas — as she lounged. At 5, the news came on and we watched until 5:30, when I griddled the waffles and we ate. She ate half a waffle and I ate three. But she did get her medication down and now, as she lies resting on the couch, it looks like it all might stay down. I'm watching her as I remember this day. She looks like an infant with her blankets all tucked in around her shoulders.

At 8 p.m., we'll get her into her PJs, which takes about half an hour. Then we'll sit together in the living room as she gets her breathing back to normal. By 9 she's in bed. I washed her sheets today, so she's got fresh linen to crawl under. She napped in my bed so she could get into a "new" bed tonight. After 9, I'll be alone with my thoughts.

EVERY DAY BROUGHT new physical signs of her body's deterioration. I was fixated on them and recorded them diligently.

SATURDAY, JULY 17

Her color was not so good today. The skin around her eyes seems really yellow and her eyes were worse. As soon as she wakes up from her naps, she looks great, but as time wears on, she gets worse and worse — it's like watching a time lapse video of newspaper getting old.

I BEGAN TO see the world entirely differently, knowing that soon, I may not get to share it with Mom. One day in mid-July, I went for one of my runs. I left as the sun began its descent behind the Rockies. It rapidly turned into one of the most gorgeous sunsets I'd ever seen. The sun filtered through clouds that reached almost to the peaks and rays of golden silk fell from the clouds like a waterfall from the sky. Deep purple shadowed the backs of the clouds and with each moment, a new dimple was revealed as the sun sank lower. Every time I looked up, I found new colors cascading into view. I decided Mom needed to see this sunset and, though I was certain it would disappear by the time I arrived back home, I had to try.

When I ran inside, Mom was dozing on the couch where I left her. I hesitated momentarily, wary of disturbing her rarely found peace. However, I knew that Mom would prefer a tough walk outside and a view of Mother Nature to the safety and comfort of the couch. I woke her and quietly explained that she needed to see something outside. Without a word, she pushed off her blanket and we slowly stood her up. She held my arm as we walked out on the front porch, down the steps, and onto the lawn.

"It's over to your left, Mom," I said.

Mom concentrated on her feet, turning her body in tiny steps toward the horizon. She didn't have enough strength in her neck to turn her head and hold her chin up. I watched her feet, too. This was a monumental effort.

As soon as we turned to the west and she slowly looked up, we both gasped. It was even more breathtaking than during my run. Pink, gold, purple, white, and blue. It was like a rainbow couldn't contain itself in an arch and exploded excitedly all over the Rockies in a ticker-tape parade of color.

"Incredible," Mom whispered. I had the feeling she was complimenting God.

Moments later, she said, "How can I fear death when there's such beauty to look forward to?"

At that moment, I felt safe to talk to her about her death. I took a deep breath and spoke.

"Mom, I will see you in every sunset and know that you made it for me."

We weren't looking at each other. We watched the changing scene before us.

She squeezed my arm and quietly said, "That's the way I would want it. I'll do that for you, babe."

I cried silently and when the show was over, we walked back inside.

Later that night, I was massaging her feet and she suddenly asked what I was thinking. I thought she had gone to sleep.

"Honestly?" I asked.

"Honestly."

"I don't want you to die, Mom," I said, and started crying.

She became visibly concerned and said, "I don't want to die."

It was surreal, talking to her about her own death, and what my life would be like if she were gone.

"I feel sorry for everyone who loves me," she said. "I'm very frustrated. None of this feels real. I can't believe I might have to leave so many people who mean so much to me. It just doesn't feel right."

We both had tears in our eyes.

She said, "A miracle is still possible, but I think we also have to begin accepting that I may die."

"Have you begun accepting it?" I asked.

"Yes, I believe I have. But that doesn't mean it feels right, or even real," she said. "That's all part of the acceptance process, though. I guess I've learned that."

Very suddenly she had to go to the bathroom …

THURSDAY, JULY 15 — 9:30 P.M.

She's thrown up twice and I'm very upset. I don't want to write long because I don't want to relive it all, but I just have to write about how I'm feeling. I'm scared and angry. I want to make her peaceful and comfortable and her guts keep coming up and her bowels keep sliding down. She throws up and poops at the same time and she's miserable because she can't control anything anymore. Not even her own body.

The episode began at the couch and ended with her in new clothes and in bed. Afterward, she felt bad that our conversation ended because she didn't want me to sit alone in the living room upset. I promised her that if I got upset, I'd call Aunt Margie. That seemed to make her feel better.

Imagine. This woman still wants to take care of me — still knows how to take care of me.

TAKING CARE OF Mom, however, was becoming more difficult every day. Aunt Margie and I simply didn't have the resources or experience to take care of her every need. She had become increasingly bed-ridden.

"Your mom and I have been discussing Hospice care," Aunt Margie told Jason and me one afternoon out on the back porch. We both looked at her quietly. As Jason and I became more traumatized by Mom's decline, Aunt Margie had stepped up her role as all-around caretaker. Her energy seemed infinite, and we increasingly saw in her the wisdom we used to seek only from Mom.

"Hospice can help us to anticipate and prepare for changes in Sylvia's health," she continued. "They can give her sponge baths, and they offer a spiritual person who can come and talk to her. She said she really wants that."

Aunt Margie looked at both of us. I wondered what conversations she'd shared with Mom about death.

"I've researched the organization a lot," she continued. She seemed to be leading up to something. "They have a very kind, benevolent mission. But before we let them into our lives, we have a lot of soul-searching to do."

She had several pamphlets in her hands and I thought she wanted us to read them, but she decided not to take the easy way out. She told us in her own words what Hospice does.

"Hospice believes that terminally ill patients deserve dignity." She paused, letting the full implications of her words sink in. "They would help us maintain that dignity for Sylvia."

She was crying quietly, clutching the pamphlets.

"Kids, you only call Hospice when you are done with invasive treatments and you simply need help controlling pain, feeding, bathing, and other daily routines."

She stopped. Jason and I processed the information.

"So basically, you bring them in when you admit defeat," I said angrily.

"Jana," Jason said in a voice filled with warning. He was protecting Aunt Margie from my anger.

Aunt Margie cried harder. She nodded.

"I think we need help, Jana. She is going to be in a lot of pain very soon. She's going to need a catheter when we can't get her to the bathroom. We need to admit that we can't do it all."

I felt like she was convincing herself as much as she was convincing me. Jason was quiet. I could see his jaw moving as he ground his teeth together.

"How much do they have to be here? How often will there be a stranger in our home?" I asked.

"Their nurses will work with Sylvia's doctors to help administer treatments and pain killers. They'll bring in a hospital bed and a wheelchair. Their counselors will work with all of us. That is, if we want them to," she said. "Sylvia really wants us to do this."

Aunt Margie looked at the mountains for a while.

"Sylvia knows we can't administer medication, but she also wants to be at home. She does not want to be in a hospital. I think we can all respect that."

Jason and I nodded. I considered what this step meant. It was over. We were done diagnosing. We were near the end. Was I ready to believe that?

I resented that strangers would come into our home at such an important time. I didn't believe they could be sensitive. My only experience with medical personnel had resulted in quite the opposite. How could Hospice maintain peace in a vicious environment of hospital beds, and wheelchairs. How could outsiders understand, let alone participate?

But we made the decision to let them in and within a day, I was soothed by their presence. These were people who had lived through exactly what we were facing. Most were volunteers who were giving back their time to Hospice after receiving Hospice's gifts when their own loved ones faced death. Their gratitude and respect showed in everything they did.

Mom's home was immediately transformed by Hospice. They moved a hospital bed into the living room, angled so that Mom could look out the window at the neighbor's daisies. Soon, they told us, she'd need a catheter and she'd be in bed continuously. For the time being, though, she could use a wheelchair to get around and it sat next to the hospital bed. We all sat in that wheelchair to chat with her. It quickly became part of our living room furniture.

I anticipated that I would want to avoid the Hospice people, but I found that I looked forward to their visits. A woman named Anne came three times a week to give Mom a sponge bath and a counselor named Cheryl came once a day to talk to Mom and to the rest of us. They did their work with immediate love, not only for Mom, but for the rest of us, as well. Aunt Margie and I had no idea how hard we had been working until we got the breaks made possible by Anne and the nurses. At first, we felt guilty and we also were convinced no one could care for Mom as well as we did. Finally, though, we learned to let go.

As soon as that happened, Cheryl, the counselor, had a bigger and more difficult task for us.

When I first met Cheryl, I had all sorts of walls built up to her presence. It did not help that she drove an old, convertible Cadillac, wore a lot of jewelry, and she seemed to be perpetually smiling. Then I discovered she was from New York, and I nearly shut her out entirely.

However, she had a patient spirit and as I learned how helpful she'd been to Aunt Margie and Mom, I opened up. I was most curious about what to expect. I didn't want to talk about the here-and-now. I wanted to talk about what was coming. Of course, I had meant Mom's health. Very cleverly, Cheryl explained the process Mom would go through, but at the same time, she taught me what I would need in order to make it through the next few weeks, and the next several years.

"Janalee, your mom only has a couple of weeks to live," she told me one afternoon on the back porch. I looked at her in shock and my immediate reaction was to run inside to tell everyone, but Cheryl must have read my mind.

"I've told your Aunt Margie. Jason's not ready to hear it yet."

I felt stuck. I wanted to get away from her, from the house, from everything. I wanted to go for a run. But I sat there with her.

"I understand from your mom that your family is very big on acceptance and serenity," she said.

The words sunk in and I knew she had spoken with Mom. She was not lying to me or playing games with me.

"The next few weeks are all about acceptance, Janalee," Cheryl continued. "If I understand your family's spirituality, I think the only way for you to begin the process is by saying goodbye. You need to say goodbye to your mom."

I bordered on laughter and sobbing. She had no idea what she was saying.

"How can I accept something I don't even understand!" I shouted, staring at the mountains. "I don't think I even believe it. How can I accept it? Say goodbye? Are you kidding? It is most certainly not OK with me if she dies."

"You can say goodbye any way you want," Cheryl said. "It doesn't even have to be with her. This is your way of releasing her spirit and letting her go peacefully. It doesn't mean that it's OK with you, or that you've accepted it. But it is the first step toward serenity. Your Mom is learning how to say goodbye to you right now."

I shook my head. "Cheryl, I don't understand. If I say goodbye, it's like saying it's OK with me that she goes, and it's not. I can't just waltz in there and say, 'Well, I've done some thinking and I know you're leaving me, so go ahead. Good bye, Mom.'"

I stood up angrily. "I don't want to say goodbye."

"Goodbye can mean anything you want it to, Janalee. You will discover what that is when you least expect it."

I looked at her. I just didn't understand.

Acceptance

CHAPTER 2

Mom's neighbor, Earlene Wolfers, came over to chat. Throughout Mom's illness, Earlene had arrived at random moments with munchies, flowers, video tapes, and gossip about the neighborhood. Usually, her arrival felt like opening all the windows on a great aunt's stuffy home — we breathed deeply, noticed new things about our surroundings, and sat still for longer than we ever imagined possible.

When she arrived that day, Earlene plopped herself down easily in the wheelchair. She was completely at ease in such a bizarre environment. Normally, her visits brought the laughter and respite we all needed.

This day, however, her conversation pressed on me like a wet blanket thrown over my head. Aunt Margie and Mom seemed just as cheered by her company as usual.

"Oh, and Mrs. Alper's dog needs shots," Earlene said, smiling. "Mrs. Alpers is just a mess over it. You know, since her husband passed away, that dog is all she's got."

"Well, of course," Aunt Margie said. "It's understandable."

"Your garden is looking wonderful this year," Mom said. "Thanks for all of the veggies you keep bringing over."

"Oh, it's been a good year for carrots," Earlene said. "It sure has."

"So, I see that Mr. Tilley is walking around the loop again," Mom said.

The chatting started to make me angry. Incessant stories about people I didn't know, recipes I'd never make, weather that came and went. All of it pushed closer and closer to me, like the walls of the hospital when I accompanied Mom into the operating room. It made no sense to me; none of this chatter mattered at all in the grand scheme. How could they make small talk when every time I looked at my mom I saw death?

Every time they laughed, it felt like tiny shards of glass cutting into my skin. My eyes felt like they were expanding in my head. I struggled to breathe, and I raised my chin to open my throat. I thought I was going to fall out of my chair. I kept petting Chelsea, Mom's dog, who sat at my side. Their conversation probably meant just as much to her as it did to me.

Yet they kept prattling. I became extremely angry. I felt like putting my arms out around me to push the words away, forming a protective circle for myself within this room of chit chat.

Suddenly, I stood and walked into the kitchen. Mom's sickly image flashed in front of my eyes. The image smiled and I physically jerked away. I imagined her teeth falling out one by one. She stopped smiling, but her skin began to droop, to drip. Yellow and thick, it looked like a snow slide. Her entire cheek was sliding right off her face, pulling her lower eyelid down, exposing the brown spots on her eyeballs. Then I heard her laugh in the other room and that sound mingled with the image I held. Her yellow cheeks were made of liquid, sliding down her face. Her snaggle-toothed grin pulled at colorless lips, and her loose eyeballs rolled helplessly. I felt shaky, trapped, and hot, like the first day Mom told me about her tumor. I collapsed on the kitchen floor and I cried silently.

No one seemed to hear except Chelsea, who came eagerly to my side. I sat on the floor and tried to catch my breath. At the same time, I wanted to scream, "Shut up! Goddammit! Shut up! Just shut the fuck up!" Instead, I breathed. I shut my eyes and tried to put my head back on my shoulders. When I opened my eyes, I saw feet, ankles, calves, and knees bending to show me a face: Aunt Margie.

"Janalee, what happened?"

"I can't take it," I said. Then, I suddenly stopped crying. "What the hell are they talking about? How do they come up with those stupid topics when she looks like that? She looks like she's dead now and they're talking about good tomato plants? She'll never grow another fucking tomato again. And who the hell cares about what the Smiths barbecued last night or if Mrs. Alper's dog needs shots? What are they doing? I can't take it! I feel like I'm going to explode. Or implode."

I had ahold of her arm and pulled her down with me. I jerked at her like a life preserver. With her other arm she stroked my hair. She looked at me thoughtfully for a moment and finally said, "You haven't said goodbye. You need to say goodbye."

I shook my head back and forth. She was telling me the same things she was trying to tell herself.

"Janalee, you need to let her go. Soon you will need to tell her that it's OK with you if she goes. Before you can do that, you must figure out how to say goodbye to her."

Suddenly, Cheryl's words came back to me and I finally understood why I needed to say goodbye. I was holding Mom so tightly, denying that I could go on without her, that the pressure was pulling me away from her and the final stages of her life — a time that Cheryl said could be the most rewarding and important in Mom's journey. In order to fully participate in and to appreciate the end of Mom's life, I needed to first say goodbye in my own way.

And, as though the answer was there all along, like Dorothy's red slippers, I knew exactly what I needed to say and I knew where I had to go.

Almost exactly one year earlier, Mom and I had celebrated my 24th birthday together at Red Canyon. We packed a picnic, threw Chelsea in the van and headed out. We sang in horrendous harmony to "Rocky Mountain High" on the way. We slowed down when we hit the red dirt road and hit the brakes for several wild turkeys. Once we found a good parking spot, we headed out on foot.

Red Canyon is about 15 miles north of Cañon City and consists mostly of large, red rock formations and cedar trees. As we hiked, we shared observations of the dirt, the sky, plant life, and animal life. We played.

We came across a glen of piñon trees, though I didn't know what they were at the time. Mom proceeded to wiggle her way between the needles of a tree and hoisted herself up a couple of feet within the tightly packed branches. Next thing Chelsea and I knew, we were being bombarded by small pine cones.

"Open 'em up! There's nuts in there!" she yelled.

She descended the tree and emerged with a sap-stained chin. We grabbed the pine cones, popped out the nuts, cracked them between our teeth and munched on the soft pulp inside. Chelsea didn't get it and tried to gnaw on whole pine cones before realizing the sap was too sticky.

We kept hiking up the red rocks and found a flat spot for our picnic. After eating fruit, cheese, bread, and cookies, we laid back and absorbed some sun quietly. That day was her birthday gift to me.

With Aunt Margie's help, I escaped out the back door, dove into my car, and drove toward Red Canyon.

As I drove out this time, my little Subaru jostled around with every pothole and washboard. I left a trail of red dust in my path. I tried to think of last year, the smiles, the happiness. Everything had seemed so easy then and I'd thought it would never end.

I parked and began the hike in earnest. I attacked the rocks rather than ascended them. My heart pounded and my breath was short. I needed this badly. I felt like I was racing, just one step ahead of a reality I was getting ready to confront. I tried rehearsing what I needed to say, but the words couldn't come. I needed tranquility to say — feel — the right thing and for the moment, I was attacking a mountain. Spontaneously, I stopped before reaching my destination, turned around to be sure I was alone, and let go of a scream that had been building since the first moment of this ordeal. My eyes squeezed shut, my hands balled into fists, my ears popped. In that moment, I saw myself in every role I'd played since January 5. One, long, desperate, heart-wrenching scream against the unfairness. I suddenly realized it was OK to feel bad for me and not just for Mom. I screamed at the unfairness cast upon me — not at Mom's cancer, or her pain, or her frustrations, or her shortened life — but for me. And I felt my head reattach to my shoulders.

When I reached the site where Mom and I sat together just one year earlier, I turned a slow circle and took in my surroundings. I was perched atop a round boulder sitting high in a low valley, surrounded on all sides by mountains. The air smelled of fresh cedar and the blue sky stretched its fabric out from peak to peak. I sat down and hung my legs over the edge. I stared at the mountain ahead of me, almost pleading with it to say the words for me. I believed strongly that if I said the words out there, their meaning would one day be shared with Mom. I fully intended to look her in the eye and tell her that I was ready to let her go, but those words could not be simply words. I had to say goodbye this way and know that in releasing her from this world, I'd feel her presence always in nature. When I released her, I gave her to God and to the Rocky Mountains. Much of me believed her spirit already resided there and her body was simply winding down in the living room.

"Mom," I spoke aloud. My voice was so shallow compared to the scream of moments before. I didn't feel self-conscious speaking to her as I faced the mountains. I did feel scared. Was I really accepting her death? I was. Her absence would require much more time and courage to accept. I understood that now.

I took a breath and said it again.

"Mom, I've come to say goodbye. I can't believe this is happening even after facing it every day for the last seven months. But I know I've got to let you go."

I looked down and grabbed a small red rock, holding it tightly in my palm.

"I think, though, instead of goodbye, I want to say thank you. That is the only way I can let you go. When I thank you, I realize all the things you've given me and I know you've prepared me well for a full life. I'll miss you ..."

I began crying as I squeezed the rock.

"I'll miss you so much. But I do believe that you taught me how to live a good life and you gave me the tools to make wise decisions. You also taught me what's important, like gardens, wild flowers and brothers, and you gave me the best of all three."

"I miss you already, Mom. Goodbye. Thank you."

That's all I could say, but I felt so much more and I sat there thinking of my childhood, my adolescence, and my new adulthood. I couldn't think into the future, but the past was crystal clear and, thanks to Mom, it was very, very good. I felt the mountains hug me.

I stood up, dropped the rock into my pocket and headed home.

Acceptance

CHAPTER 3

Jason had made himself scarce after returning from the Navy. He said he was spending time with friends he hadn't seen in four years. He was partying hard every night, sleeping until noon every day, and avoiding Mom's house at all costs. Beginning in early July, I was staying in Cañon City quite a lot and had hoped Jason's return to Colorado would mean a little companionship. Months earlier, my friends had stopped visiting; Mom's appearance was too much for them to handle, so they preferred to call. However, since I had stopped answering the phone during the first few months of Mom's illness, I rarely spoke to people on the phone. Without Jason's presence, life in Cañon City was solitary, particularly as Mom began sleeping more. I grew resentful of his insistent denial, realizing that not only was he ignoring Mom, but me as well. I needed him there for emotional support and also to pitch in with the work. Instead, he'd call from Pueblo to "check in," explaining why he couldn't make it to Cañon City. In his mind, they were legitimate reasons.

"Jana, I've been away for four years. There are things I want to do. I need to see my friends," he said during yet another frustrating phone call.

"Don't you think I'd like to see my friends? Shit. Don't you think I'd like to see you? I went away to school seven years ago. We haven't hung out since then."

"Jana …" he warned with his voice.

"Jason, you know why you're not coming here and you're going to regret it."

"Dave's here. I have to go. I already made plans. I'll call you tomorrow. I promise."

I began to felt like a nag. I also felt panicky. He needed to be with Mom.

Finally, he called one afternoon in mid-July while I sat in the living room with Mom. When I heard his voice on the machine, I snatched up the receiver. We chatted about his wild night and then I handed the phone to Mom. They spoke briefly and then I was back on for my daily appeal for a visit. He, again, tried to back off and I flew into immediate fury. I wanted to control what I said in front of Mom, but couldn't.

"Jason, you may not want to be here but I need you here. I'm lonely. No one comes to see me and I can't leave." I paused and looked at Mom who nodded understandingly. I didn't want to make her feel like a burden, but I had to give it to him straight.

"Jana, I'm busy. I'll come tomorrow."

"That's not good enough. You're being selfish. Don't avoid us …"

"That has nothing to do with it …"

"Bullshit!" I interrupted and then, before I knew what I was doing, I hung up on him. I had no idea where he had called from so I couldn't make amends.

Mom smiled at me.

"Good for you," she said.

"I'm sorry if I made you feel like some sort of inconvenience, Mom. You're not. I just need to see him."

"So do I," she said. "You didn't do anything wrong."

A few minutes later, she fell asleep. I tucked in her blankets, grabbed a beach towel, and headed into the backyard to read. I had long ago abandoned the Bernie Siegel books and the Rabbi Kushner books. When I had any free time, I wanted to escape. I read what I called "McNovels:" Grisham, Stephen King, and Clive Cussler. I never read romance. I stripped down to my bikini, laid down, and began my escape.

Within half an hour, Jason walked out the back door. I heard the door and watched him walk up to me, but neither of us said anything. He must have driven mach three from Pueblo.

He walked straight over to me, sat down on the grass, and said, "I'm sorry." He fiddled with his car keys.

"Me, too," I said.

We let that sink in for a bit. It was clear we had a big conversation ahead of us. He didn't just come to apologize.

"Jason, you need to be here. You need to talk to her."

He shook his head more out of frustration than in a negative response.

"I don't know what to say, Jana. What do you talk to her about?"

"Everything, Jason. You can talk to her about anything, just like always. You can talk about the weather or you can talk about the last time she threw up. Just talk to her!"

"I can't. I don't know ..."

He looked at me and I realized he was crying. I put my hand on his knee. He kept shaking his head and played with his keys.

"Jana, what do you believe? Where do you think she's going?"

He looked away, still thinking and I remained quiet.

Finally, he said, "Where does she think she's going?"

When Jason was seven, he'd gone through a long bout of fearing death. I can't remember what inspired it — only mom would remember that — but I remember he had nightmares and wanted to talk about heaven and hell. He often asked Mom where people go. I realized that he was again battling with the same fears, a fundamental spirituality usually decided for people by their religion. We'd never attended church but had been raised in a very spiritual environment. Our faith revolved more around a partnership with a higher power and was grounded in the serenity of nature. I knew Mom's life was organically linked with nature and so, too, would be her death. But I'd never asked her "where" she thought she was going. On those rare occasions when I thought about visiting Mom after she died, I thought less of a place and more of a feeling — the feeling I experienced in the mountains. Among the new aspens, the fallen pine cones, the tender grasses, and the timeless rocks, there was no beginning or end. Only renewal. A continuity, a dependability, an enveloping that felt safe, and unconditional. My spirituality grew its roots there. Mom's grew wings. I could imagine no resting place with her name carved in stone. Only good grass for romping and tall trees for climbing would harbor this woman's spirit. But had I assumed too much? I looked at Jason.

"Where do you think she'll go?" I asked.

Without hesitation, he said, "Oh, the Sangre de Cristos." The mountain range where we once had a cabin.

I cocked my head. "That's pretty specific. I thought you didn't know."

"I want to know what she thinks," he said as he began crying again. "I don't want her to be scared."

I remembered all the "honesty moments" I'd had with Mom over the last six months and realized what a gift I'd been given. I had no idea what Jason was going through. He needed to talk to Mom. Like so many others who hadn't faced the daily realities, discussing the ultimate reality felt more than awkward, it felt rude. How do you broach the topic of death with someone who is dying?

I told Jason that he needed to talk to Mom and that she should be woken from her nap anyway. He balked, thinking he couldn't even wake her properly. I laughed, explaining that she was still our mom and she'd tell him what to do.

"I'm scared," he said.

"I'll bet she's waiting for this, Jason."

"I love you, shithead," he said to me.

He stood up and walked inside. I watched his back and understood from experience just how scared he was. Not only was he asking Mom questions that he didn't think she should have to answer — questions about her own death — but he was going to have to face death himself.

I couldn't read. I stayed away from the house because I didn't want them to think I was listening. I sat up and looked at the mountains. I couldn't help but get excited at the prospect of talking to Jason about everything. I hoped he would finally open up.

SUNDAY, JULY 18

Our society hides its dying like its prisoners. We look away in shame as though they just murdered. They apologize for their slow pace, and they receive scowls for special menu requests. Throughout Mom's illness, when I've wanted to talk to friends, I've heard, "keep your chin up," "don't talk like that," "don't cry," "be strong," "she'll be fine." The moment I let myself reach out, I am strong-armed back into control. I've had to control myself. I'm learning that I can only rely on myself.

People seem to think that they help by bolstering me or trying to cheer me up, when all I want is to lose control, lose my cheer, be weak, and cry. I want to turn my back on the illness. I want to walk aside with my arms open and find one, good hug containing no prescriptions to feel better. Just one person who will say, "It's OK to cry and I'll hold you until you stop. And I'll hold you the next time, too."

Jason will understand. Maybe not today, but someday. I wonder if I will ever find anyone else who will.

ABOUT HALF AN hour later, the back door opened and Jason stood there with red eyes and a puffy face.

"She wants you in here, too," he said, raising his shoulder to wipe his eyes on his shirt.

I sat still, staring at him. I sensed the conversation ahead. He looked back at me steadily and nodded, as though he was jeering in his brotherly way, "Come take some of your own medicine."

I put my clothes on over my swimsuit, walked up to him, and grabbed his hand as we walked into the living room.

Mom was perched on the couch, a blue blanket I hadn't seen in months wrapped around her legs. It looked like Jason wrapped and wrapped and wrapped that blue blanket around her legs, turning her into a human cocoon. It was clear from this humorous state that they'd been playing. I imagined that she probably told him how to tuck her in and Jason did so with gusto.

Jason sat next to her on the couch and I sat in the recliner. We were silent and we studied each other calmly.

"I have a very special favor to ask you two," she said.

"Name it," Jason shot back immediately. I nodded.

"I want you to scout out a place for my ashes."

I saw Jason's eyes fill with tears, and my own streamed down my cheeks. I think I was still nodding. Mom took a breath and continued.

"Jason and I have been talking about where I think I'm going to go when I leave," she said. "I'm not leaving you. I will be here. Remember Grandma?"

Grandma's death six months ago seemed so distant. Despite myself, I smiled at a memory of her tap dancing. I saw Jason smile, too. Mom nodded.

"That woman has not left. That incredible woman only became more part of life when she left her tired body."

Mom smiled now, too. Then laughed.

"How in the world do you contain a spirit like that in one body, anyway?"

We all giggled.

"I'll bet as soon as she died, she caused a racket with those tap shoes of hers in whatever environment she calls heaven. And she's singing! Could that woman ever sing!"

"And I'll bet Daddy still feels a little shiver up his spine when she takes those long, noisy yawns," I said.

We sat quietly with our thoughts of Grandma.

"I want to be taken to the Sangre de Cristos, up above Westcliff," she said. I looked at Jason and he looked surprised, but pleased. "I'm not sure where, but I'd like you two to go find the place and tell me about it. Take Aunt Margie. Go love each other up there and find a place for me in God's country."

Again, the tears, the fears.

"Mom, have you accepted that you're going to die?" I asked. I gripped the arms of the chair.

"Come here, babe," she said, tears forming in her pale eyes.

I sat on the other side of her and the three of us snuggled into a small ball on the couch. Her arms were around our shoulders and she played with our hair. She was thinking.

"Yes, I have. I have accepted death," she said. "But I have not accepted what that means for you two, and Chuck, and Marge. Accepting death is very different from accepting loss. Yours is a more difficult journey. You two must find peace, serenity. That will take years."

I tried to breathe deep. I tried to record her words, to etch them onto my memory. They felt like my last access to her wisdom.

"I am very proud of you two, my kids, my friends. You have given me so much to be grateful for. I leave you believing I've given you all the tools to live good, joyous lives. I am proud of who you've become. I am proud of us. We have always shared a special joy and I trust you both to spread that joy for the rest of your lives," she paused. "And I will be with you, in that joy, in the Rockies, in your triumphs, sharing your sorrows, for the rest of your lives. We have shared a lifetime of love."

After a moment, Jason said, "I'd rather have 23 years with you than a lifetime with anyone else."

I hugged her gently in agreement and we sat for a long time holding one another.

That night, my mind yanked at me and wouldn't let me sleep. I kept considering Mom's memorial service even though it still felt so impossible to me. I'd think of words I'd want expressed for her at that moment and then block it out of my mind. Finally, in order to exorcise them, I had to write the words down on paper.

MONDAY, JULY 19 — 1:45 AM

WRITTEN FOR THE MEMORIAL SERVICE BUT NEVER READ

Jason and I have often tried, through tears, to figure out why God would need this woman so early in her life — so early in our lives. And, if he needed her, why he took her like he did.

We will probably never know, and acceptance comes so very slowly.

But there are a few things Mom said and did throughout her life that provide examples of the peacefulness she experienced in life.

Mom told Jason and me what she believed happened to a person after they die. She talked about her father's death and the recent death of my father's mother. She smiled as she discussed the power of their spirits. Mom said she believed that the more integrity a person possessed in life, the more powerful their spirit after death. She smiled as she thought of her father's spirit — memories that kept him alive to her, glimpses of his presence in her children's faces, wisdom he shared that she sought even after his death. He was still very much alive to her. After Grandma died, Mom said she could instantly feel her spirit bouncing off every living thing on earth. Mom said that since Grandma had touched so many people and shared so much joy in life, her spirit had energy and power immeasurable after her life. And we shared a smile thinking of those two spirits and their influence in our lives.

Now, Mom's spirit has been released, and though I can't help but feel cheated and angry, I also know that a great energy has entered my life — every life. She has not departed.

Mom always said that God lived in the Rocky Mountains. When we camped, she'd point at tree tops, curl up next to flowers, inhale the stars, and soak up the serenity. At the times she most needed Him, she found God, her higher power, in the mountains. Now, when I need my mother most, I know I will find her in sunsets behind the Sangre De Cristos, cloud bursts in the afternoon, and aspen trees in the forests.

Mom always said her father was the first feminist she knew. Sylvia Chmel was the first nature lover I knew. Her love, courage, and wisdom will forever live in everyone she touched and everyone who enjoys a sunset.

Good bye, Mom, and thank you for the love.

MONDAY, JULY 19 — 2:15 AM

Dear Daddy,

I'm at Mom's and I can't sleep. Like father like daughter. I must share what I just did. I'm upset that I wanted to do it so badly. Now that it's done, I don't ever want to use it.

I wrote a eulogy for Mom's funeral. I don't even know how funerals work — I've never been to one before — and here I am in the middle of the night writing about this woman as though she's already dead. I feel awful, but I've been writing it in my head for weeks and I decided that I just had to get it out. I know that I won't want to read it. In fact, no one may ever see it. But I thought that there may be a good chance I'd want something special said at her funeral and I'd be in no shape to provide anything then. (I hate how that sounds like I'm planning her funeral, but lately the thoughts keep coming.)

Daddy, why would God do this and if He needed her, why did He do it like this? I'm sure you asked the same questions only a few short months ago. Jason and I can't figure it out and we feel so cheated. Jason said he's so angry he hasn't spoken to God in months. I find myself badmouthing Him incessantly.

I like being here for her because my feelings of helplessness are alleviated when I can make her dinner, tuck her in, and share a moment. She is so incredible, Daddy. She's skeletal with the stomach of a woman who's eight months pregnant. The other night, we were sitting at the table and her stomach started making a funny noise, like a toy that you wind up and then let it go. All of a sudden she looked up at me and said, "BOOM!" It was so hysterical we almost fell off our chairs.

Her courage is boggling.

She's so frail. When she breathes, her cheeks flutter in and out. She walks like a toddler because she's so uncertain of her legs. Her eyes are yellow and getting worse as weeks progress. She sleeps most of the day and eats baby portions. I run around like a madwoman while she sleeps, making sure everything is clean, cooked, and picked up so that when she's awake, there's little activity around her and her life is calm. I'm happy to do it for her, but why do I have to do it for her? Damn it.

Daddy, will it ever stop hurting?

Acceptance

Chapter 4

We borrowed an old CJ-5 Jeep from a friend of Jason's and headed for the hills. We had scoped out a four-wheel-drive road on a map that appeared to lead to a small, glacier-fed lake called Hermit Lake. It was due west and about 3,000 feet above Westcliff in the Sangre de Cristos. Since the top was off the Jeep, Aunt Margie wanted to climb from the back tire into the back seat instead of using the door, but her little legs limited her reach. Most people put one foot on the top of the tire, and threw the other leg into the Jeep in two easy steps. Finally, Jason grabbed Aunt Margie around the waist and tossed her onto the back seat. He yelled "buckle up" as she howled laughter and turned around to face the front of the Jeep. Jason pushed on the broken screwdriver that served as a key and suddenly the ripped vinyl seats were alive with a quivering anticipation. It seemed to rumble, "Get me to dirt!" Aunt Margie howled some more in the back seat, hanging onto the roll bar with her head thrown back. Jason and I glanced at each other and shook our heads, giggling.

"Let's go!" he said.

"Tally ho!" Aunt Margie yelled. "Up up and away! Yeeee-haaaaaw!"

At the time, I thought Aunt Margie was overwhelmed by the novelty of the Jeep, hidden roads, glacier-fed lakes. I thought it had gone straight to her head. I still had a lot to learn about this little woman who always seemed to express her pleasure with gusto. It *is* a gift.

The drive from Mom's house to Westcliff took a little over an hour. The winding dirt road between the two was filled with potholes. I tasted dirt on my teeth, and felt it on my skin. It was so good to be outside and moving. In Westcliff, we spied the dirt road that headed to Hermit Lake and began the journey into Mom's mountains. Our mood became slightly more somber as the trees became taller around us, but still we laughed and smiled. Just as a sad thought approached, that old, primer-colored Jeep pitched itself into a hole and leaped up on the other side, sending the old springs in our seats into a hip-hop frenzy. Then Aunt Margie screamed delight again and the sadness departed.

"What the ... ?" Jason said, hitting the brakes.

The Jeep had suddenly gone from a light purr to a staccato baritone. Aunt Margie unhitched herself and hoisted herself onto her knees on the back seat, facing the back of the Jeep.

"We lost a part!" she said gleefully. "It appears to be the muffler."

"Oh," Jason said casually. He hopped out, grabbed the old, rusted part and tossed it into the back next to Aunt Margie's feet. He jumped back into the driver's seat, pushed the screwdriver, and drove on. I looked at Aunt Margie and shrugged.

"I guess that's OK?" she yelled.

"Just means everyone will know we're coming," Jason said.

Farther up, the hood started rattling. I peeked at Jason who was studying it casually as he maneuvered the rocks, holes, and mud. Then, suddenly, the entire hood slid off the side of the Jeep. He hit the brakes and we all just stared at the exposed engine, prattling away cheerfully. Jason began laughing ... hard ... which was the cue Aunt Margie and I needed. We joined in. We were at least five miles into the mountain and hadn't seen another person or vehicle since Westcliff. The muffler. The hood. Luckily, they were superficial parts.

Jason turned off the engine and studied the situation.

"Looks like you have a job, Jana," he said. I smiled. He

unhooked a couple of joints on the front window and lowered it forward so that we no longer had a windshield. Then he grabbed the hood and put it back over the engine. He sized me up.

"Think you can hold this on?"

I smirked, and jumped into the passenger seat. I hooked my fingers through a joint hole in the hood and yanked on it a couple of times.

"I think so," I said. I leaned on the dash where the windshield was supposed to stand. "Drive!"

They jumped in and we continued. Every so often, the hood would rise completely free of the Jeep and then slam back into place.

"I think I want a Jeep," I said seriously.

"Isn't this great!" Jason yelled back. "Can't do this in your little Subaru."

"Or your silly Mustang," I retorted.

When we reached timberline, we stopped. Suddenly, the only vegetation was knee-high and the air was cooler. All around us, towering over us, were bald peaks, rocky crevices, snow patches, and long tundra meadows. We neared the summit.

"Look at this flower!" Aunt Margie squealed.

In unison, Jason and I yelled, "Don't pick it!"

Jason explained the little patch of purple and white flowers were Columbines, the state flower, illegal to pick. He kneeled down with Aunt Margie and pointed out the small, golden bulbs at the back of the white petals, clinging like honey drops. He pinched off one of the orbs and tasted its sweetness. Aunt Margie did the same, respectfully. Then she took a picture of the flowers huddling among the rocks.

"Thanks," she said to Jason. I realized he had just given Aunt Margie a little of Mom. She taught us about flowers.

"Only a little farther," Jason said.

I looked up at the peaks around us. We were very high.

We assumed our positions in the Jeep again. Aunt Margie maneuvered the back seat with ease, now. We rattled on up the road.

"Look!" Aunt Margie yelled.

Jason and I followed her gaze across a long valley to our left and saw a narrow waterfall about 300 yards away. It gushed from a tall plateau feeding the dense valley below. We followed its course with our eyes, taking in all of the valley life.

"That's where we're going," she said instinctively. We silently agreed and our jolly mood ascended to reflection.

Jason took us farther up the road and we realized the waterfall's origin — the plateau — contained Hermit Lake. We were still below the plateau, so we hadn't seen the lake, but the plateau was surrounded by a huge mountain bowl of snow, which we could tell melted to create the lake. Our road led us to a foot path below the lip of the plateau. We got out of the Jeep silently.

Mom would love this place, this space.

We left the Jeep and hiked up only about ten feet to look down on the small, crystal green lake. From that vista, it looked more like a large pond. Our perspective, our sense of depth, was distorted. The towering bowl of snow opposite us, the plunging valley behind us, and the lack of sound played games with our senses. We struggled for breath; the oxygen felt as negligible as our very presence. We were a moment, a whisper, a sigh in this sanctuary of peace. We participated only in spirit; our bodies got us there while our spirits released themselves, seemingly old friends to the energy swirling in the space. I tingled.

As one, we descended toward the lake silently and then followed its edge to the creek that fed the waterfall. The ground reacted to our footfalls like a sponge, seeping water two feet in diameter from where we stepped. The earth was as soaked as I felt when I couldn't stop crying. We walked carefully.

When we came to the edge of the plateau, we climbed down a few rocks to locate a spot near the waterfall. We could hear its rumble and feel its mist, but shrubs and grasses crowded around its life-giving force. It was so dense that we couldn't get close. Finally, we found an outcropping of rock that jutted above the waterfall's most vigorous plunges. The three of us sat silently amid the roar. I slowly followed its entire path with my eyes, imagining Mom's ashes touching, enhancing all the life in the valley. By bringing her body here, we would set her spirit free to roam the Rockies. This place was so right. When Jason put his arm around me, I knew he agreed. Aunt

Margie placed her head on my shoulder as though she read our thoughts. Even our spirits seemed to say, "You done good, folks."

We couldn't talk near the loud waterfall, so we were left to our own thoughts. I tried to imagine the moment when we would release Mom's ashes, but I couldn't even imagine the container in which we'd receive them. I couldn't imagine their color or texture. I looked at the trees in the valley and knew Mom's spirit would live happily here and everywhere there was natural beauty. But I could not conjure the moment we would let her go physically into this space. I accepted the fact that we had found the right space. I knew her joy would go on.

We headed home to share the moment, the space, and the energy with Mom.

Acceptance

Chapter 5

Wednesday, July 28

Well, it's been a long week. Last Friday, I found out that Mom had been told by her doctor that he believed she has less than a month to live. I was shocked. I had been thinking that she probably wouldn't be around for Christmas, but less than a month?! Suddenly, everything hit. That hand that has been touching my back for the last seven months, threatening to push me over the cliff, shoved with all its might. I'm careening at a screaming pace to the invisible bottom.

I was alone Friday night and tried to call everybody on earth to get someone to help, but no one was around. I found myself lying on the floor sobbing. Then suddenly, I'd stop and stare at the ceiling thinking about everything from baseball to egg whites. Then I'd start crying again uncontrollably. When I finally went to bed, that's how the whole night went. I'd cry until I fell asleep. But then I'd wake up crying.

Jason and I talked to Aunt Margie about how angry we are that someone would have to go like this. We asked why God would make somebody go through this suffering if He planned on taking her from day one. She said there was another way of looking at it. She said that Mom's experience has actually been very gentle. She has been surrounded by people who love her from the very instant. Everyone has had a chance to say what they need to say. The will and memorial service are set and planned. She said other people might rather go in an instant, feeling no need to accomplish the things Mom has accomplished over the past seven months. But Mom is the kind of person who would want to comfort others. She'd want to find a peace and serenity in herself before she died, and to make sure Jason and I are taken care of. God knew this and gave us all time. And now, only days after the last "loose end" was tied (Jason), Mom is dying.

She really is. Her memory over the last few days has deteriorated rapidly.

I'm tired and must continue this later.

"AUNT MARGIE?" I said tentatively. We had a basket of clean laundry between us and we were folding clothes on the back porch.

"Yes?" she said.

"Mom's so skinny." I kept folding, not looking up.

"I know, Jana," she said with tenderness.

"She's so skinny it looks like her teeth have grown, Auntie Em?" I said it in a question, almost pleading.

Aunt Margie stopped folding a towel and hugged it instead.

"I know." She looked out at the mountains and tears streamed down her cheeks.

"Have you looked at her urine? It's getting really dark," I said. Mom was on a catheter, as Hospice said she would be.

"It's going to get darker, Jana. Her kidneys are shutting down," she said.

We both sat quietly. She looked at me and then she tried to look deep inside me. I could tell she wanted to relieve my fears, but she had so many of her own to face. We gulped back our tears and continued folding.

After the doctor's dooming news, the atmosphere in Mom's home changed. It became foggy. Moments whispered to me, images drifted in and out like waves, emotions welled up and then dried up.

I spent hours sitting in the wheelchair next to Mom's hospital bed, looking through the window sheers at the daisies across the road. They were so thick that I couldn't see the ditch on the other side. I read the titles of books on the huge, wall-to-wall bookshelf that Mom had specially made. I wanted to ask her which books were her favorites, why, and when she had read them. I sat on the floor next to Mom's bed with Chelsea and considered her future. That dog stuck near Mom's bed just like the rest of the family and occasionally thumped her tail when the tension and anticipation became too thick.

Jason, Aunt Margie and I were constants while others dropped in and out.

"Look at that wool on your head!" Sharon said to Mom as soon as she arrived. Sharon had been Mom's hair stylist for 15 years. She had come to the home after Mom requested we give her a call. Anne's sponge baths had done wonders for her comfort and she thought a good haircut would, too.

Sharon teased, "It's all flat in back! Have you been laying down a lot?" and she gingerly thumped Mom on the shoulder with her plastic comb.

Mom smiled her snaggle-toothed grin. By now, her smile repulsed me. Her face was gaunt and yellow, and her teeth looked like horse's teeth. When she smiled, you could literally see the fine lines of her bone structure, down to the pointed bones of her nose.

Sharon made a huge production of Mom's "do." It seemed she brought every hair dresser's tool at her disposal. She even brought a portable adjustable chair. With our help, Mom pulled her skinny butt out of bed, carrying the catheter with her, and sat in the chair in the middle of the living room. Then we all left them alone so that Mom could be with a new person all by herself.

When Sharon called us back into the house, Mom was tucked in bed. She looked thrilled with the results. Mom felt pretty for the first time in months. She smiled and winked at me. I wished she could be that happy all day.

The next time she took a nap, Aunt Margie and I checked out her catheter bag. The Hospice nurses changed it, but we knew it contained all kinds of clues. That little plastic bag became a barometer of her health; the color, consistency, and quantity all told a story about her insides. We usually covered it up to allow her a little privacy and dignity. When the end is inevitable, why make a spectacle of the process? We simply tried to accept and become part of Mom's journey.

WEDNESDAY, JULY 28

The hours pass. I'm slowly realizing ... how can I write this? I want her to die. I want her to have peace. I want peace. How can death come so slowly and viciously?

ONE AFTERNOON, I sat in the wheelchair and studied her as she slept. I began to believe that her marathon naps were helping her to prepare for the death of her body and the release of her spirit. Her eyes and neck moved and twitched as she slept and she said completely incomprehensible things.

"Turn the crank!" she yelled during one of her naps. "Did you turn the crank?"

"I got up last night," she said in her sleep very matter-of-factly. "There was the potato masher and it was like Spaceship Potato!" Her voice crescendoed and then trailed off like a kid saying "Superman!" I cracked up as I watched her fade into deeper sleep. She must have heard me laugh, because she smiled.

She also spoke aloud to people both dead and living.

"Daddy?" she said more than once. Grandpa had died many years ago, but she had always been close to him. When she spoke his name, it was as though she was asking his permission.

As she slept, I began to feel peace, and to accept her death. I could not even force my mind to consider the moments, days, and years after her death, but I did grow to accept that she would die. That acceptance hit me in waves of guilt and peace. I was so used to fighting death that accepting it felt like defeat. I grew to understand that acceptance is the real battle, and apparently, I was winning.

THURSDAY, JULY 29 — 9:30 PM

Today was OK. Pretty much the same, so I want to write about something else.

How has this changed me? Has it been good or bad? For the better or worse?

I spoke to David Bird at DU's employee assistance program on Wednesday morning before I came down here. Our talk became one of change. He said that he admires how I'm dealing with everything and he thinks that because I'm being so honest with my feelings, I will survive very well. But instead of talking much about that, he asked about my stomach. I haven't thought much about my stomach lately because it hasn't been too bad. There was a time when a hang nail made my stomach act up so badly I'd buckle over in pain. Now, as I go through the worst experience of my life, the pain has been minimal. David asked why and at first I couldn't answer. I said that maybe I was eating better and exercising more. He recalled that I had been doing that several months earlier and that I still had lots of pain. He was right.

So, then he suggested what he thought it might be. He said that his previous impression of me was that I was a very control-oriented person. I need to have control of not only my situation, but my emotions, as well. I was convinced that if my emotions were "let loose" I would appear weak to others and I've always wanted to appear strong. I want to be considered independent and self-reliant, and that has not changed. What has changed, perhaps, is my concept of strength. I still do my damndest not to let others see me cry or break down, but when I really need to let it all hang out, I find a way to do it rather than keep it in.

He described emotions as fluid. Each person has a reservoir for their emotions. When the reservoir fills up, I need to open the spillway and let some out so that I can deal with the next emotions that flow in. If I try to build up the walls surrounding my reservoir, I'll only weaken the whole reservoir.

The emotions build and push upon the walls. If I allow myself a spillway, I can be more flexible and prepared for the next wave to enter.

He said he believes I have begun to learn how to open my spillway. I believe that I am learning to be more comfortable with my emotions. Hopefully I can learn that experiencing these emotions does not make me weak.

THE WEEK OF July 25, Hospice suggested that we let a volunteer come in a couple of nights a week to stay up with Mom while we slept. Though I was hesitant, the real decision fell to Aunt Margie because she was the one running around at all hours of the night. She needed sleep.

At 8 p.m., Linda rang the doorbell and Aunt Margie let her in.

"Hi!" Aunt Margie said. How did she sound so chipper all the time?

Mom was asleep on the hospital bed and the lights were dim. Chelsea sidled up to Linda's leg fondly and looked up at her with those big, brown eyes.

"Hi. Marge, right?" Linda opened her arms and Aunt Margie gave her a hug.

"Thank you for coming," Aunt Margie said.

"My pleasure," Linda said. "May I see her?"

Aunt Margie led Linda to Mom. Jason and I had been watching television in Mom's bedroom, which we had commandeered for our own. We stood nearby after introducing ourselves quietly.

Linda instinctively sat down in the wheelchair and reached for Mom's hand. She was reverent.

"She's beautiful," Linda said, and turned around to look at us.

We must have looked dumbfounded, or puzzled at the very least. She smiled and explained.

"I watched my son go through something just like this several years ago," she said. I thought that her son must have been very young. Linda looked no older than late 30s. "I've been volunteering for Hospice for many years now, and this is the most beautiful part of the dying process. She is experiencing so little pain when she sleeps. Look at her peace."

For the moment, I couldn't look. If I saw something like what Linda described, I wanted to be alone with Mom. I tucked away Linda's thoughts for later reflection. However, I found solace in the fact that Linda had gone through the same experience and still she saw such beauty in a process with which I had grown so impatient. Linda possessed serenity.

On August 2, Mom's condition became markedly worse. She was sleeping most of the time. During fits of activity in her sleep, Mom yelled things out and spoke more often to invisible presences. The words carried significant meaning.

"I'm ready to go now," she said. "Yes, I'm ready."

Her tone reminded me of the same tone she used when she had errands to run. She was matter-of-fact, not sad or frightened. A couple of times, however, she became adamant.

"Let's go folks!" she yelled. I smiled, thinking that if there were a presence in the room helping to decide her departure date, it was surely having to deal with an impatient, self-directed spirit.

As I heard her demands and pleas, I knew my time had come. I knew that the hike in Red Canyon had brought me to this moment. I sat by her bedside and studied her, and I knew I was ready to let her go. I had to. I couldn't bear that she be in this condition much longer.

That afternoon, when she awoke in her hospital bed, I was sitting next to her. I had asked Aunt Margie and Jason to let me have some time alone with her.

"Mom?" I said. She looked at me carefully. I struggled, but I knew I had to go on. "I want you to know that it's OK with me if you die."

She didn't say anything, but I knew she understood. She opened her hand for me to put mine into. Tears trickled down my face and she gripped my hand as tightly as her limited strength allowed.

"Does this make you sad?" I asked.

"Yes, this is very, very sad," she said. "I don't want to go."

"Are you frightened?" I asked.

"No, I'm not frightened."

We sat quietly for a moment. I thought about how hard it was for me to say goodbye to Mom when I boarded the plane for college seven years earlier. This permanent goodbye was impossible to fully comprehend.

"I'm going to miss you," I said, bowing my head. "I'm afraid to live my life without you."

She reached her other arm up to hug me and I leaned over her so that she could rest her skinny arm on my back. A tear slid from her eye onto the pillow.

"I know I'll be OK, Mom, because of everything I've learned from you."

I pulled away to look at her. I wanted to hug her so hard, but it would have crushed her. I had to be gentle. She smiled a big smile and winked at me. I winked back and I kissed her.

"You are so beautiful, Mom."

"Thank you, babe. Thank you."

The next day, August 3, Mom slipped into unconsciousness. Hospice had told us to expect that. The Hospice nurse came once more to give Mom a sponge bath and to smooth her bedridden skin with baby lotion. Aunt Margie, Jason, and I wandered. It was hard to stay still in one place but we couldn't go far. It was like all the waiting we'd done over the last seven months — for diagnosis, treatment, results, miracles — had suddenly all piled up into each breath Mom took. We were waiting for death.

TUESDAY, AUGUST 3

Watching Mom die forces me to consider questions that wouldn't have occurred to me earlier. I sat next to her today. Only seven months ago, this woman was motorcycle riding with Chuck, belly-laughing, climbing trees, and hiking mountains.

Her body is giving in, but I can feel her spirit strengthening. I stared out at the daisies and thought about the balance we all must keep between our physical and spiritual selves.

Once the physical grows weak, how do we continue cultivating, nurturing the spiritual? One question most intrigues me, perhaps I am obsessed with it: what determines that precious moment when physical life ends? What click in the universal clock? What hiccup in the physical being? What burst of the spiritual energy?

This experience has led me to believe that there is a moment of exchange when spiritual life leaves a physical body. That moment cannot be random. Living requires such a balance of physical and spiritual matter that I believe death does not happen merely due to physical weakness. As the physical dissolves, the spiritual develops. Then, at some perfect moment, the physical releases itself to spirituality, the balance tips only when our spirit has strength enough to carry on alone.

Because of this realization, I can understand why Aunt Margie thinks Mom's illness has been gentle for her. I cannot imagine the trauma people face when they get that phone call in the middle of the night saying a son, daughter, wife, husband is dead. A car crash. A plane crash. A fire. An accident. Accident. How to you reconcile death when it presents itself so immediately? We are fortunate.

THE HOURS WORE on through August 3 and 4. Mom never fully awoke. We grew weary, tired of the constant "any time now" thoughts. August 5 found us doing the same thing. Jason and I rented two movies: "Sneakers" and "Raising Arizona." I watched the video clerk scan the videos and I wondered what she would think if we told her we were taking these movies home to watch as we waited for our mother to die. It struck me as particularly morbid to rent "Raising Arizona," one of the funniest movies ever made. But Jason had never seen it and I wasn't convinced there was a correct movie selection for such a moment. We chose what sounded good.

We set the movies aside during the day. Chuck came to visit Mom and we let him sit by her bed while the three of us sat on the back porch. All day, Jason, Aunt Margie, and I would do our own thing, but when we gathered on the back porch, we came together tightly in a little ring. Sometimes we spoke, but usually we just shared space.

That afternoon, Jason and I wandered out into the middle of the backyard with Chelsea, originally to find her ball. When we found it, we looked at it like it had dropped from outer space. We couldn't even gather the steam to play catch with the dog. So we sat down right where we were.

"Jason, I think that I want Mom to die," I said, picking at the green grass.

"Me, too, Jana," he said. "I've been praying that she'll die. She needs peace."

"God, I'm so glad you said that," I confided. "I've felt so guilty praying that she'll die, Jason. I keep asking God to take her. Just take her already."

"Me, too," he said, and he sighed deeply. "You know what, though?"

"What?" I said, squinting at him in the sun.

"I think she'd be proud of us," he said.

I looked at him for a couple of seconds and nodded.

Finally, on the night of August 5, Mom's breathing changed. That moment I'd feared for seven months had come. In all the times I'd considered her death, I'd only considered the absence that would result from her death. I had not been able to imagine that pinpoint of time when she died. I'd considered what death meant, the transition from physical to spiritual, but what would that moment be like? Would I watch? Could I watch? Hold her? Touch her? Talk to her?

I never imagined I could be part of the moment, the miracle. I never thought death could be beautiful nor did I think death could be shared.

The Hospice volunteer, Linda, arrived at 10. Jason and I were trying to watch "Raising Arizona." Aunt Margie was going to try and get some sleep. However, Linda stood for a moment next to Mom and said, "You all need to be here. It's happening."

Jason and I turned off the television and stood next to Linda, looking down on Mom. How did she know? I wanted her to be wrong and I wanted her to be right.

"I'll be in the backyard," Linda said, and she quietly left us.

Mom's breathing had become very shallow. The three of us sat around her bed in silence. She was on her back with her right hand up near her ear and her left arm across her stomach. I kneeled on the floor near her right side and held her right hand. Jason sat in the wheelchair on her left side next to Aunt Margie, who was on the foot stool. They stroked her left arm. Occasionally, we told her we loved her and let her know we were there, but for the most part it was quiet except for her unsteady breathing. We watched as life left her body.

Mom quietly and without struggle gulped little drinks of air. Her teeth clicked with each swallow and a couple of times her right arm twitched. She even smiled a childish smile once or twice. Her eyes, though mostly shut and unfocused, were very expressive. At about 10:40, her eyes opened partially and her breathing became even more shallow. She took fewer breaths with each minute.

We sat and cried and told her we loved her. With each gulp, I thought she was gone, that I had witnessed her last breath. I fought battles inside of wanting her to stop breathing and have it all be over, and wanting to shake her and say, "Stay with us! Please, Mommy, don't go!" For almost 15 minutes, I breathed only when she breathed. Each time she surprised me by taking another breath, I gasped for my own.

Finally, one breath did not lead to another. She stopped. We cried, resting our heads on the white sheets, holding her hands. And then, in a single moment, I realized I was no longer holding my mother. This was just her body. I studied her face and instantly knew, without a doubt, that something had left her and it was the most important part of her: her essence. That essence would live on while her body could not.

That moment was the most important gift Mom gave me throughout her illness. I knew she lived.

FRIDAY, AUGUST 6 — 11:15 A.M.

Mom died last night at 11 p.m. and it was the most beautiful experience I've ever had in my life. We were with her, holding her hands and talking to her. She was surrounded by our love and we were surrounded by her peace.

It was beautiful and, as Jason said later, "I loved it." I was with her when God took her, when she crawled into His arms and giggled her way to the heavens.

I know my life changed last night. My life has been unalterably changed by the last seven months.

Last night was Mom's final gift to me. She shared her most precious moment with me. She shared her death. And as her energy, her spirit, left her body, I understood that Mom had always shared the best of her life.

Acceptance

CHAPTER 6

The days immediately following Mom's death were wrong. That's the best way to describe them.

I felt like a child on one of those kid leashes so popular today. I followed instructions, thinking others must know better than I how to handle these moments. The problem was, they handled them as though the best solution was a big cover-up. "Oh! Big, bad Death knocked on this door. We must get rid of it and get on with it."

About 30 minutes after Mom died, Linda suggested we go sit on the back porch while she called the city's morgue. They had to come get "the body." We sat in the backyard on the phone, each of us calling a select few friends who were important to us and who were important to Mom. I called my ex-boyfriend Chris, to whom I had written my most traumatized thoughts during the past seven months.

"Chris?"

"Jana." His voice said he knew why I called.

"She just died." I sobbed and held my forehead. I was sitting in the staircase leading into the basement. I wanted to be away from Aunt Margie, Jason, and the morgue people.

Chris was silent. Finally, he said, "Were you with her?"

"Yes."

"I'm sure that meant a lot to her," he said, trying to say anything.

"It meant a lot to me."

Suddenly, I heard a zipper. It was a body bag. I almost threw up.

I quickly told Chris I had to go and I ran into the backyard and handed the phone to Aunt Margie. She called Uncle Willis and he said that he, Aunt Pat, and Grandma would begin the drive from Minnesota within hours.

After that call, we sat on the back porch and stared at one another. We had only one day to be alone. The wind chime caught a breeze and tinkled slightly. Aunt Margie looked at it and said, "Sylvia is with us."

The next day was peppered with more phone calls and funeral arrangements. I couldn't believe how quickly people expected us to make decisions. Luckily, Mom had made some for us, but there were still so many details to decide. We made an appointment with a funeral director in Pueblo for the next day. While on the phone, we picked a day for the service. Then we had to call everyone we hadn't called the night before. We also called the newspaper to make sure an announcement was printed.

That night, the house felt more like death than the night before. The empty hospital bed lay in the living room. A commode stood in the bedroom. The steel bars were still affixed to the shower walls. Yet, Mom was gone. The reason we had changed our lives over the last seven months had disappeared in one moment.

We sat in the living room like zombies. We had nothing to say. Among the three of us, we needed to say nothing. We understood.

That night, Jason and I slept in Mom's room as we had for several nights prior. He took the floor and I had Mom's big sleigh bed. We talked in the dark.

"How are you, bro?" I asked.

"I think I'm OK," he said. "It hasn't hit me yet, though."

"Me neither," I said. After a few moments, I continued. "I don't think I understand what forever is. Whenever anyone used that word before, like as in 'I'll love you forever,' I guess I never knew how long that was. I think I'm beginning to feel it now, though. She's gone forever, Jason."

I cried quietly.

"I hate to say this," he paused. "I'm feeling relief. Is that horrible? I thought it would hurt more than this. I feel like I'm not showing how much I loved her if I'm not falling apart."

"I know what you mean," I said. "But I think this is what Hospice told us we'd feel. Just kind of numb."

"Yeah, I'm numb," he said.

We laid quietly in the dark.

"Can I make a confession, Jason?"

"Of course," he said.

"I don't want anyone else here. I don't want anyone else in this home. I don't care if they're family. They can't understand."

"Oh, I know," Jason said. "Aunt Margie said the same thing today. I'm glad they're coming because we need help. Otherwise, I might just lay here forever. But it's kind of like being invaded."

"Yeah! Invaded! That's how I feel," I said. "Why can't we just take a week? Huh? Why can't we just be here, alone with Aunt Margie, thinking about Mom for a week. Robin told me that's what Jews do. They don't do anything for a week after a loved one dies. They don't even cook. Friends bring food. They just sit and think about the person who died." I paused. "God, that sounds so good."

"Things are going to get crazy tomorrow," he said.

"Yeah," I said. "And they need to be here. I know that. I am looking forward to Unc's hug. I don't know. I guess I just don't know how to be."

"Don't worry about it, Jana. Screw what other people think. If you want to be alone, or cry, or laugh, just do it. We don't have to be any certain way. Our mom just died. Fuck 'em all."

I laughed. "I sure do love you, Jason. You keep it all in perspective, no matter how crude."

"Do you think you can sleep?" he asked.

"I guess we'd better try."

"Catch you on the flip side," he said. Then he said, "Jana?"

"Yeah?" I said.

"I love you."

"I love you, too."

Grandma, Uncle Willis, and Aunt Pat arrived at 6:30 the next morning. Jason and I heard them pull up and we sat up to look at one another.

"Here we go," he said.

I started crying immediately. "Jason, I can't do it. I can't face people. I don't want to talk to anyone."

He looked at me, then looked at the window.

"Then, let's escape!"

"Are you serious?" I asked.

"Heck yeah! You know I used to sneak out all the time in high school."

"Yeah, but ..."

I heard poor Aunt Margie scrambling out of bed, trying to act excited. She said something about putting on a pot of coffee.

"OK, let's do it!" I said.

We both wore shorts and T-shirts to bed, so all we had to do was lift the window and go. Jason went first, and then he helped me through. Since our bedroom door was closed, everyone thought we were still sleeping. We sat on the back porch watching the sunrise.

About 7 a.m., we heard Aunt Margie through the kitchen window.

"Oh! You two!" she hissed.

She came creeping out the back door with two cups of coffee. We explained our escape.

"Go ahead and stay out here," she said. "I won't say a word."

"Why don't you stay out here, too," Jason said. "They'll have to find us sometime."

She took no convincing.

"OK."

We had about 10 minutes before Uncle Willis came out the back door. Just looking at his big blue eyes and his understanding smile made me cry. I gave him a tight hug, but all I wanted to do was run away. I didn't want to face people.

Aunt Pat and Grams followed him and we all sat at the picnic table drinking coffee. Aunt Margie told them about the appointment at the funeral home in Pueblo. It was scheduled for that afternoon. In the interim, I just wanted to sit in the backyard.

Unfortunately, the reality was that Aunt Margie, Uncle Willis,

Aunt Pat, and Grandma would all be gone in a little over a week and Jason and I would be alone in Colorado. Because I couldn't even see beyond noon, I had little concept of our need for help. I didn't want to deal with people and, therefore, I wanted all activity ceased. All people gone. I wanted to be alone. Perhaps forever.

Uncle Willis and Aunt Pat, on the other hand, knew that they only had a week and they had jobs to do. Before Mom died, she'd asked Uncle Willis to take care of all her financial affairs. While Mom wasn't wealthy, she had the financial concerns that any responsible, single mom would have: life insurance, the house, health insurance. It was amazing to me that Uncle Willis found so many documents in Mom's files. Left to me, they would have rotted there forever.

Aunt Pat decided to organize the house since Jason and I needed to put it on the market. I lived in Denver and Jason lived in Colorado Springs. We needed a realtor in Cañon City whom we could trust, especially since neither of us had ever bought a home, and here we were selling one. We also needed to pack. We needed to pack an entire house full of our mom's stuff. Our mom, who had only died two nights earlier. We were packing up her things as though she never lived there. It felt so disrespectful. I wanted to ask her ridiculous things like, "Are you sure you won't need this waffle iron any more?" The finality of her death had not sunk in.

That first day, the idea of packing was too much for Jason and me. We let Aunt Pat go to work in the kitchen where neither one of us cared much about who got what. Whenever she had a question, she asked.

"Either of you need a good mixing bowl?"

"Who gets the Kitchen Aid?"

"OK if I just pitch this?"

We were like ghosts in the home, wandering from Uncle Willis in the office to Aunt Pat in the kitchen to Chelsea in the backyard.

The activity made real thoughts and deep emotions impossible. We were surrounded by physical activity and all we wanted to do was feel. Aunt Margie, Jason, and I sought solitary moments to dig into, discuss, and express our gratitude for one another, and for the experiences we had shared. With the activity, those important moments were stolen from us. I felt as though my emotions were inappropriate.

Aunt Margie, Uncle Willis, Jason, and I drove to Pueblo to meet with the funeral director. We adamantly insisted that the service be a memorial not a funeral. Two of Mom's friends had volunteered to play the piano and sing "Amazing Grace," Mom's favorite gospel. I remembered her playing a Mehalia Jackson album in my childhood.

"Do you want flowers?" the funeral director asked.

We looked at one another. I increasingly deferred to Aunt Margie because her instincts seemed so sound at a time when mine failed me. But she looked at Jason and me with the same glazed look we offered her.

"I just can't see roses strewn all over the place," Aunt Margie said. "It's so morbid."

"Me neither," I said.

The funeral director bristled a bit. "We can do quite tasteful work."

"You didn't know Mom, though," I said. "She wasn't a roses kind of person."

"Daisies!" Aunt Margie said.

"For an arrangement?" Jason said. "I think we'll need aspen trees. Maybe pine cones."

We were quiet. Uncle Willis sat with his hands folded in his lap. His patience reminded me of Chuck.

"Hey, what if we have a big basket of daisies and we hand them out to people as they leave the service," I said. "Kind of like giving everyone a little gift from Mom."

"I like it," Jason said.

Uncle Willis closed his eyes, smiled, and nodded.

"And I think we can get a neat arrangement with a lot of evergreens, and aspens, and pine cones," Aunt Margie said. She looked at the funeral director and said, "We'll take care of the flowers."

When the other plans were finalized, we headed next door to the florist where we divided to conquer. This was one well-stocked florist because of its convenient proximity to the funeral home. We started grabbing things that reminded us of Mom, and then returned to the counter.

"We need an arrangement — a HUGE arrangement — on Thursday made out of this kind of stuff," Aunt Margie said.

The clerk looked at our hodge podge with a smile on his face. We had collected spruce, pine cones, aspen twigs, vines, daisies, willow branches, and cat tails.

"This will be fun," he said.

Aunt Margie's face lit up. "Good! That's how it should be."

We headed back to Cañon City. It occurred to me how long it had been since we had been able to stray so far from Mom's home. I thought about the fact that Mom wouldn't be waiting there for us and a severe pain gripped my heart.

SUNDAY, AUGUST 8

I now know why there are so many songs and stories about breaking hearts. Hearts really can break. I've never felt this pain in my chest before. It's like there are two iron fists clamped around my heart and wringing it out like a kitchen towel.

Love must be centered in the heart, because mine hurts so very deeply now that I clutch my chest from the pain.

I say that I miss her and it seems so empty. So vacant. Those words don't begin to express my sorrow. I'm in pain.

WHEN WE RETURNED to the house, Aunt Pat was ready for us. She had jobs for us to do. She handed me a big sheet of little, green, circular stickers. Jason received the same, only his circles were blue. She also gave us a sheet of red, and a sheet of yellow.

"Anything Jana wants, she puts a green sticker on it. Anything Jason wants, he puts a blue sticker on it. If you want to sell it in a garage sale, yellow, and red is for storage. If you put a red circle on something, write your name on it so that I can put all of Jana's stuff together in boxes, and the same for Jason."

I stood with the sheets in my hand, dumbfounded. I don't know how I expected the house to get packed, but I was not ready for such a systematized divvying up of Mom's property. I did as I was told though.

Jason and I began wandering through the house. Nothing had

been packed, except in the kitchen, so we had to claim every picture frame, every memento, every piece of Mom's favorite collectibles. I faced the floor-to-ceiling bookshelves and shuddered. Sea shells from the Pacific coast, photos of me as a child, candles, Grandpa's pocket watch, handmade wooden boxes that contained everything from an old butter press to antique knitting needles. Jason and I simply walked toward it and started at one end.

"Do you want this?"

"Not if you do. You can have it."

"Yeah, but do you want it?"

"I really don't care."

"Me neither."

"I don't want any of it."

"Me neither."

Long pause, looking at the ground, rubbing the sheets of stickers between our fingers.

"OK, let's do this."

"Yeah. OK."

"Do you want this?"

"Sure. Whatever."

Of course, most of the items did matter us, but we hated wandering around Mom's home, sticking little circles on her property so that it could eventually end up in our homes. I kept thinking, "I don't want any of it. I want Mom."

A couple of items made us uncomfortable. Mom had specified who should get the most meaningful property, such as the oak table and the sleigh bed. However, other items of real material value held us up. The washer and dryer, for instance. We both needed a washer and dryer.

"What do you think?" I said.

"I could sure use a washer and dryer," Jason said.

"Yeah, me too," I replied.

Our words were more frustrated than competitive. I just couldn't face my brother and declare, "I get our dead mother's washer and dryer!" He couldn't either. But it made no sense for us to sell the set with the house if we both needed it. He ultimately got them. I wound up with a lot of the linens. Most of the time, we ended up deciding by saying, "Who really cares?" and placing a sticker on it.

Many hours later we finished. I felt like I had just ransacked my mother's privacy. I collapsed on the couch.

"Jana, I need you to come into your mother's room," Aunt Pat said.

Like a zombie, I followed her. I didn't even have the energy or will to ask questions. My heart and mind were numb.

"Do you think you were the same size as her? Before she got sick?" Aunt Pat said, holding up one of Mom's Pendleton suits.

I just looked at her and held out my arm for the suit. I walked into the bathroom to try it on. As soon as I opened the jacket to put the sleeve on my arm, I caught a strong whiff of Mom's perfume, Chanel No. 5. I clearly smelled her own body on the clothes, too. That smell only Mom had. I remembered when she used to come home from teaching when I was young, and I smelled the school on her. She smelled different than when she had left for work. Or the smell she had after playing in the garden — the salty sweat flavored her smell.

With one arm in the suit sleeve, I sat down on the toilet and started sobbing. Simultaneously, the smell repulsed me and drew me in. I realized that once the smell left those clothes, I would never smell my mother again. At the same time, I couldn't believe that a smell lingered after a person had died. Why couldn't she take everything with her that accosted my senses. She took her touch and her voice. Why didn't she take her smell, too? It was like sensing her presence when she came home from teaching at school; I'd hug her around her knees and she'd lift me up into her arms. But this time, it was only her smell. No voice. No hug.

"Jana?" Aunt Pat said through the door. "I have some more out here."

I wiped my nose. "OK," I said. I felt powerless to stop the momentum. I reached through the crack in the door and pulled in more of mom's clothes. I forced my mind to shut down and I went through the motions.

From that moment, throughout the next week, I simply went through the motions.

The day of the service arrived. I had begun to think we only needed to go through this motion for everyone else. I certainly didn't think a memorial service was necessary, and I thought Mom would feel the same. I imagined that she would have preferred that any memories be of the personal type; not the kind conjured by a group of sad mourners gathered in one room for the sake of a formal service. Admittedly, though, I also dreaded seeing all the people. I wanted to be alone. The thought of a huge group of people focusing their attention on me and my family scared me to death. I wanted to stay home in the backyard.

Before leaving Cañon City for Pueblo, we all gathered in the backyard to take pictures. Even though our family had been together just eight months earlier for Mom's 50th birthday, we wanted pictures of all of us together again. Grandma hugged me tight and whispered how proud she was of me. Uncle Willis put his arm around me and told me to hang in there. Jason lifted me in his arms attempting humor, but I felt such relief at my weightlessness that I hoped he would just carry me inside, lay me on the couch, and let me sleep. Our poses were so difficult to hold. We merely stood, staring out of our hollow bodies at cameras poised quietly before us. Normally, people shout, "Smile!" when they point a camera. These cameras clicked with no warning. No one even imagined we could push out a smile.

The late summer breeze shuffled across the grass, lifting my long navy skirt slightly. We looked like zombies in drag.

We arrived at the little chapel before anyone else and set up the arrangement, which was spectacular. It was filled with evergreen branches, aspen leaves, vines, willow branches, pine cones, driftwood, and daisies. It stood more than five feet tall on a table at the front of the chapel. We placed items of importance to Mom on the table, including a conch shell, the AA Big Book, a picture of her taken in the mountains, more pine cones, and aspen leaves.

Once all the pews in the chapel were full, we walked out from a side door. We filled one row: Aunt Margie, Jason, me, Chuck, Uncle Willis, Aunt Pat, and Grandma. From the moment we sat down, I ignored the service. I couldn't concentrate on what people were saying. I held Jason's hand and I thought about him throughout the service. What was next for him? Once all our family left Colorado, how often would he and I see one another? Was he crying? If he was crying, I couldn't, but if he wasn't crying, I could. We'd take turns.

Some of Mom's friends spoke and others sang, but most of it was lost on me. Finally, it was our turn. The chaplain explained that the family wanted to give everyone a final gift from Mom as they left the chapel. Everyone would receive a daisy. The florist next door had filled three big wicker baskets with single daisies. As people filed out, they hugged us and we handed them daisies. I was very proud of this gift, knowing Mom would be tickled with the results. I imagined people pressing the flowers to keep forever, and I even imagined little kids plucking the petals out of the yellow centers. Still, these were living symbols of Mom's joy and grace. Everyone seemed touched.

The line of mourners, however, never seemed to end. I wanted everyone to be gone so that it would finally be all over. Once the last person left, I could go back to Cañon City. I never wanted to leave her backyard. I never wanted to be a functioning member of society again. I wanted to be alone forever.

Finally, we piled into our cars and headed back to Cañon. The drive was quiet, and suddenly I thought, "What's next?" For so long, I had asked that question of doctors. Now, I had to ask myself. I couldn't bear the thought of going back to work. In my heart, I knew I could curl up in bed and stay there forever. I never wanted to work again. I didn't want to be around people ever again.

Jason reacted just the opposite. He wanted to find his friends and blow off steam. He wanted to get rip-roaring drunk, start a fight or two, and hit somebody or something really hard.

But before we attempted to start our lives over, we had one final task to complete for Mom.

The Saturday after the service, Aunt Margie, Jason, Chuck, and I headed for Hermit Lake. Jason and I took the old Jeep again, while Aunt Margie and Chuck took Mom's wimpy, powder blue, Nissan Stanza wagon. We didn't want to rely entirely on the Jeep, but we weren't sure the Nissan could make it up the last stretch of the road to the lake. So, we headed out in two vehicles.

The ashes were with Jason and me in the Jeep. The funeral home gave them to us in an institutional-looking, black, plastic box because we planned on scattering them in the mountains. None of us wanted to keep any of her ashes, so we didn't need an urn. That black box mesmerized me. It was nothing like what I expected. The edges were rounded and it stood about ten inches square. The box was a lot larger than I'd expected and, disturbingly, a lot heavier. It weighed about eight pounds, which seemed like a lot of ashes. Worse yet, it rattled. Apparently there are just some things in the human body that cannot be cremated. I was repulsed at the sound of hard objects hitting the inside of the plastic walls. Were there possibly recognizable elements of my own mother within? Her teeth, perhaps? It was too gruesome to imagine, and yet too compelling to ignore. We put it on the back seat for the trip.

"That's not really her, you know?" Jason said. "We saw her die. We saw what happens when someone dies. That was just a body. Not Mom anymore." He paused. "So, that's not really her in there."

"I know, Jason," I replied. "It's just that I didn't expect it to be so heavy and to rattle. In the movies, they always show these tiny little vases with about two ounces of ashes inside. I guess this makes more sense, but it's gross."

We hit a big rock and the box jumped a few inches. Jason laughed.

"Well, she is getting one last, good ride in," he said.

Chuck hadn't been to the spot before. When he saw the lake for the first time, I watched him nod his head and smile to himself. He approved. I walked over to him and hugged him around his belly.

"Think Mom would like it?" I asked.

"She's gonna love it," he said, wrapping one of his arms around my shoulder as we looked at the clear lake.

The four of us descended toward the lake and then walked around to the waterfall that poured from the lake into the valley below us. Jason carried the ashes, and we each walked at our own pace. We wanted to be alone in our group. I remembered how remote and impossible this moment had felt only a week and a half earlier. Now, here we were fulfilling our dreaded promise. I thought to myself, "I guess this means Mom really died." I walked around the lake and struggled to understand what that meant; I still didn't grasp the concept. Something about the moment up there — maybe the altitude and a lack of oxygen — made everything seem like it was moving in slow motion. I remembered dozens of little details from the last seven months. I remembered doctors telling us they couldn't do anything. I remembered standing over her bloodless leg, wondering how I could make such a decision. I heard one of her orgasmic burps. I felt the warmth of her hug as she held me in her lap. Could those moments really be gone? Would I really, truly never feel her hug again?

I looked behind me to see Chuck and Aunt Margie trailing. Jason was ahead of me. About five minutes later, I came upon him standing very close to the falls. We couldn't speak because it was so loud, but he was struggling with a screwdriver to pry open the box lid. Aunt Margie and Chuck arrived right as we cracked it open. We didn't lift it off immediately, though.

The deafening water relieved us of any attempt for profound words. We simply stood in a circle with the box on the ground at our feet. I looked at all three of them slowly, studying their eyes to find readiness. We were all ready. This was the private moment for which the four of us had longed since Mom died. We had been with her throughout the toughest moments, and we each had shared many years of her incredible life. Not only was this natural ceremony a fulfillment of Mom's wishes, it was our final thank you to her.

Jason picked up the box and we watched as he leaned over the falls to release some of the ashes. The pounding water overcame any rattling noise I had feared, and the white ashes blended immediately with the water. She literally became part of nature. We each took turns silently pouring her ashes into the waterfall, and then we stood looking out over the valley. I smiled, thinking of the blessing we had just bestowed upon the Rockies.

We stopped to eat a picnic lunch on the way back and we allowed ourselves to talk about Mom; not her house, her clothes, her books, or her dog. We talked about her death, her life, and her love. The moment we released her ashes, we released her. It would take the rest of us years to achieve such release.

A Note ...

October 8, 1998

Dear Reader,

God, how I have struggled with this last section. When I began it, I foresaw this wonderful journey called "healing" in which I would impart, through my experiences, the wisdom and peace I'd gained after Mom's death. Here it is five years and two months after that day and I'm afraid this is the best way I can describe it: Healing is messy.

Healing is not chronological like the rest of the story I've told you. I don't even think it's definable in "phases," as I was told by so many professionals. I know that there are moments when I felt at peace with Mom's absence and there are still times that I curl up in a ball on my bed, heaving tears from my heart.

A friend recently told me that healing is like a drain. Imagine water in your tub swirling in large circles around the drain, and as it draws closer to the mouth, the circles become smaller, the cycles move faster. Picking up speed, the water swirls 'round and 'round, smaller and smaller circles, down to the bottom of the drain. That analogy feels the most accurate to me. I feel like I go through the same emotions over and over, but the cycles used to be much longer. When I was sad right after she died, I was sad for weeks. Slowly, I've learned how to pull myself out of those cycles more quickly. However, I don't think that my low points are any less intense than they used to be. They just don't last as long, and I trust that they will end so that I can get on with my day or my week.

So much of this process requires trust.

I was surprised to look back on my journal and discover many entries about how happy I was! I wrote about intense happiness only months after Mom died. At the time, I interpreted that as healing. In fact, at those moments I thought I was well on my way to this great goal I'd set for myself: serenity. I look back now and realize that, because I had wondered how I would even survive Mom's death, any smile I experienced felt like winning an Olympic gold. I was so excited by any form of happiness in my life that they all seemed transforming. I wrote about them, shared them, shouted them. I felt so alive simply by giggling. It was like saying, "Look at me! I'm living and laughing!"

But still, healing is messy, and thus, it is terribly hard to capture on paper. I tried! Believe me! That's why I'm writing to you directly now. I'm offering the next section as my personal journey, told through stories, conversations with friends, and journal entries. But it's been messy! I wanted to lay out this wonderful little section about the Process of Healing, and my Road to Serenity. I've written it three times and have come to realize that I cannot capture it as a process, as I did Mom's illness and death. How can I write about something I may not fully understand? How can I end this book if I now know that healing never ends?

But I can tell you about moments and people who have helped me to answer questions that plagued me, who shared in my joy, who hugged me when I cried. Like life, these moments didn't necessarily come at the "right" times (as I perceived them then), but they all led to a critical mass of knowing, of trust. That trust is what I hope you feel at the end of the book.

And, with all humility, I can tell you that I have achieved serenity. However, I have learned that serenity is nothing like what I expected it to be. I had imagined that serenity meant I would never feel such sadness again. I thought life would be easier. Basically, like a child, I expected to feel safe from the world's potential harm — the way Mom's lap made me feel.

Today, I understand that my serenity requires that I experience pain as well as happiness. Serenity demands courage, wisdom, and acceptance of life's challenges. Serenity means mourning. It means gratitude. It means anger and pain. I have learned that I must experience trauma to revel in triumph. I must find solitude to understand myself, but I must also allow others into my life if I am to grow. Serenity means joy as well as sorrow.

Therefore, I share with you stories from the past five years of my life. I hope that if you, too, face the challenges that I have, that we can share this journey together. As you read this, I hope that at least once, you exclaim, "I'm not alone!"

Serenity

Chapter 1

Two days after the memorial service, Uncle Willis, Aunt Pat, and Grandma drove back to Minnesota. Aunt Margie stayed in Mom's home for a week before heading back to California. She said she needed to be alone in the house. While she was there, she put it on the market.

About a week after the memorial, Daddy came to Colorado. He, Jason, and I went to a town home in the mountains. Daddy's friends from Pueblo loaned it to him. All I wanted to do was sleep. I felt like I was in limbo between the horrors of Cañon City and the terrifying life that awaited me without Mom. I still harbored deep fears of work. I didn't want to be around people. I just wanted to sleep forever and forget that life had ever been good. When we got to the town home in Dillon, Jason and I found bunk beds in one of the rooms and slept for hours.

I slept so deeply that it hurt to open my eyes when Daddy finally woke us for dinner.

"Hey you two urchins," he whispered into the room. "Pops is making his famous 28 pounds of ribs. If you don't hurry, I'll eat them all."

We awoke slowly, alone in the room, listening to Daddy singing in the kitchen.

"Hey," Jason said, leaning down from the top bunk. "You sleep?"

"I think it would be more like going unconscious," I said, rubbing my forehead. "You?"

"Same. Let's eat."

Daddy made a wonderful meal and we sat on the balcony overlooking Lake Dillon. Fall was around the corner and the evening was crisp. The three of us had not been together in over 10 years. Daddy had visited Jason in San Diego while he was in the Navy, and I had seen Jason occasionally during his short breaks, but we had not been together as a threesome. Still, we were all content to sit quietly on the balcony and watch the sunset.

Daddy's presence was no mistake. After Mom died, he immediately turned up the volume on his already impressive Daddy-from-a-distance performance. Because his mom had died only six months earlier, he knew exactly what we faced. His was precisely the unconditional love we needed. I didn't want to entertain a visitor; I wanted to sit quietly with what remained of my family. I didn't want to talk about the weather, or any other form of small talk; breath was too valuable. Every moment felt precious and I didn't want to garbage it up with life's typical concerns. That's the same reason that work and the rest of my life in Denver felt completely pointless. None of it mattered to me any more. I expressed that to Daddy and Jason.

"I'm really scared to go back to work," I said.

Jason looked at me. "Why?"

"Because it doesn't matter to me any more," I said.

"So, are you worried you won't do well any more?" Daddy asked.

"No," I said. "Not really. I just don't want to do it. I don't want to live that life. All that work. For what?"

They thought about it a bit.

"I don't feel like that," Jason said. "But I can see why you would. I'm really angry. I just want to get in a fight. I want to hurt someone. I want to take this out on someone."

"Try a rolling pin on your bed," I said, laughing.

"Leave it to Jana, the domestic Cyclops, to come up with such a unique purpose for a kitchen utensil," Daddy joked.

The beauty of the time with Daddy and Jason was that none of us felt like we had to solve our sadness. Daddy let us nap, went on hikes with us, and fed us. We were free to be cranky, or sad, or mean. He took it all in stride.

His departure meant re-entry into life and I feared it terribly. Jason and I headed back to our respective worlds. He was starting his first year of college in a week and I had to get back to work. Jason's presence in Colorado was still foreign to me. We hadn't lived in the same state since 1986 when I moved to New Jersey. We hadn't hung out on a casual basis in over seven years, and our re-introduction to one another had been during Mom's illness. We had gotten to know each other again during a crisis and it shaped the way we responded to one another for many months after her death. We sought each other for consolation only. We simply didn't know how to hang out like we had in the old days.

The night before I returned to work at the university, I sobbed myself to sleep. I considered calling in sick, and even quitting. Aunt Margie had said she wanted to take a full year off and I wondered if I might be able to do the same thing. I thought I could use the money Mom had left me and I could just exist in a black hole for a year. But the next morning, my alarm clock went off and I laid in bed listening to the radio jocks talk about the weather.

As I'd done since the day after she died, I lay on my back and said aloud, "My mom died." I stared at the ceiling and tried to comprehend what that meant. It still made no sense, so I rolled out of bed and walked to the bathroom. I passed the phone in the hallway and my hand instinctively reached out to call her. I wanted to tell her how scared I was to go back to work. Yet her death was the reason for my fear. These synapses of logic fogged my days.

I got in the shower and the drops shuffled down the curtain. I stared at them thinking, "What is forever, really? If I already miss her hugs, will I ever stop missing her?"

I dried my hair and thought, "I wonder if she ever wrote down that recipe for black cake. I bet it's gone, too."

Brooke was spending all of her days and nights with her boyfriend, Bill. The apartment was all mine, which was a blessing for both of us. I would have been a horrible roommate.

I returned to work to find that the world had, yet again, defiantly rolled on. Projects waited and people, while kind, went about their own jobs. Life insisted on continuing despite the fact that I was kicking and screaming to get out of it. At first I did my best to avoid the real world. I arrived at work precisely when expected and left precisely when allowed. The in-between hours were spent alone in my apartment, avoiding people and their seemingly ridiculous concerns.

Not too much later, however, I made the exciting discovery that the busier I was, the less I thought about Mom's absence. Like a drug that makes everything feel better, a frenetic work pace dulled my sorrow. I soon became addicted. I arrived at work early, left late, and assigned myself all kinds of extracurricular tasks. Slowly, I became convinced that I was replicating my previous life and that Mom's death hadn't changed my life.

I wrote about what I was feeling, but it was only superficial senses, like getting a sudden chill and not knowing its source. I told everyone I was fine and I wrote about grand feelings like courage and wisdom. After all, on the outside, I was an efficiently functioning member of society. Therefore, I reasoned, how bad-off could I be? Less than one month after Mom's death, I expected myself to be well into the journey of healing, if not bordering on its final descent into happiness. I didn't understand that my heart and mind were in hibernation. I was functioning on pure adrenaline.

SUNDAY, AUGUST 29

Dear friends,

I've been receiving so many cards, letters, and phone calls that it has become not only a daunting task to respond to everyone, but probably impossible. Everything helps, though, so I wanted to write and let everyone know what's going on and how I'm doing.

The past eight months have been the worst of my life, but I now think I see the light at the end of the tunnel. Mom's death was a tragedy and a blessing in one final breath and my love for her continues to grow with each day. She was an extraordinary woman and the impact of her absence is still hard to comprehend. I believe I have much healing ahead of me and I have not even begun to understand that she is gone from my life forever. I still pick up the phone to ask her about her day.

Now begins the process of trying to make life normal again. My life has been completely changed by the experiences of the past few months and it's hard to figure out what's important, what's insignificant, and what requires change. My priorities rearrange themselves daily. But, as a wise woman once advised me, I'm taking things one day at a time.

I hope this letter finds everyone healthy and happy. Please bear with me over the next few months if I seem unlike myself. Also, know that I am not walking around like a lost, sad puppy. I'm doing very well. If I've inherited one one-hundredth of my mother's strength, I will not only survive, I will soar.

I love you all and thank you for your thoughts, prayers, and love.

TUESDAY, SEPTEMBER 21 — A LETTER TO A COLLEGE FRIEND

Dear Robbie,

I miss Mom quite a bit but haven't had time to think about it much. I don't know if that's good or bad. It's strange how life really has gone on despite the fact that I don't feel like I'm living it. I feel like I'm being tugged along, tripping and stumbling through the days only to crash hard at night so that I don't dream too much. That's probably very unhealthy but I can't seem to break the pattern ...

EVERY OTHER WEEKEND, I drove 120 miles to Cañon City to check on the house. Jason went on the weekends I didn't.

The first time I was there alone, I couldn't sleep inside. Except for a few pieces of furniture and a bed, the house was empty and it literally echoed. Coupled with the haunting conversations and tremors I heard and felt from the past seven months, the house was impossibly scary and upsetting to me. Instead of turning right around and heading for Denver, I went next door to the Wolfers and borrowed Chelsea, Mom's dog. They had asked if they could take care of Chelsea after Mom died and we felt that was best for Chelsea. I returned to Mom's backyard with the wiggling, excited dog, hauled out a sleeping bag from a box in the garage, and snuggled in under the stars.

Moments like those — comfortably tucked into a beautiful environment with a dog that felt familiar — helped build the illusion that I was healing. Then, without warning, a month had passed since her death. And then two months. I began to recognize the daily, hourly impact of her absence on my life.

SUNDAY, SEPTEMBER 26

Mom's been dead almost two months and there are days when I feel perfectly fine and days like today when I feel abandoned, scared, and angry. The monthly anniversary of her death is particularly difficult and I didn't expect anniversaries to be hard. I always thought that when people said anniversaries were hard that they were talking about the date. I never considered the passage of time. Suddenly it had been a month. Now it's almost two. In some ways, it feels like a week and in others a year. Something in me will still not accept forever. So far, it feels like Mom's on an extended vacation. I know she's happy and having a good time, so I only miss her in a way that makes me feel she'll be back soon.

The constant activity has concerned me. I've noticed that when I'm alone, I do my best to DO something in order to avoid thinking. I'm sure that's why I haven't written in so long. Work is going very well and I'm surprised at my own ability to separate my professional and personal lives. I question if I am facing my emotions or running from them. I rarely cry even when I'm alone. I guess that over the last seven months, tears have come less readily than they used to. Have I become stronger as everyone predicted (as though that were a consolation) or have I become hardened? Closed? Distant?

I want to cry. But I wonder if I'd ever stop. Besides, it wouldn't help. I could cry at any moment, but I always force the tears back. There are people who want to help me, share my pain, hold me, talk to me. But I haven't allowed them.

I've been to the mountains a lot and it's bittersweet. It's fall now and the beauty intensifies my loss. Mom was such a nature-freak and I want to take a walk with her, picking up leaves and pinecones. I can feel her spirit touching every aspect of my life but I long to touch her. To talk to her. To ask her advice.

That only brings me back to "why" and I've learned that question wastes as much energy as regret.

So where does that leave me? The more I allow myself to feel, the more frustrated I become. My choices for "facing it" seem so limited and so undesirable.

I constantly want to call her. I want to tell her how well I did on my job evaluation. I want to make her laugh again like she did before she was sick.

God, I miss her.

IN OCTOBER, I gave myself a big present — a 1991 Jeep Wrangler. The trip up to Hermit Lake had convinced me that I needed to get rid of my tired Subaru hatchback and cruise through the hills in a four-wheel-drive. As soon as I laid my eyes on the bright red, two-year-old Jeep, I had to have it. However, it was a trade-in at a Chevy lot and the salespeople didn't have one clue about Jeeps. This was the first moment I realized that my demeanor might have changed due to my experience since January.

When I went to the lot, I took a friend from work with me — a guy friend. I had dealt with car salesmen before and I knew that they simply took men more seriously. However, I made it very clear that I was the one with the cash.

We drove up and one of the raven-haired salesmen unhitched himself from a display model and sauntered up to my car. He looked like he dyed his hair, mustache, and eyebrows the same shade of oily black.

"What can I get you into today?" the guy said to my friend, Michael.

Michael began to speak and then he simply pointed at me. I said, "I'm here to look at the Jeep trade-in I saw in the paper. I want a Jeep. Not a Chevy."

"Nice Jeep," he said. "Let's take this Chevy truck out to the back lot."

We got in and he proceeded to tell us all the features of the Chevy. I didn't say a word and looked straight ahead. As soon as I saw the Jeep, I elbowed Michael and smiled. He smiled back. It was perfect, except that it needed bigger tires.

"It looks a little low," I said as we drove up. "I'd want bigger tires."

"Little girl like you?" the salesman said. "They're harder to drive that way. With big tires."

I didn't respond. I could hardly believe he was falling so squarely into the car salesman stereotype.

"Would you like to drive it?" he asked.

"Yes. Can we take it out on our own?" I asked.

He looked at us suspiciously only to prove what a good guy he was when he handed over the key.

Michael and I drove it about five miles and turned around. I wanted it. And I wanted big tires. I asked Michael the best way to handle myself. I must have looked like raw meat to the salesman, my eyes all sparkling with hope.

"Do not drive off with it tonight," Michael said. "He'll tell you anything to get you to drive it home tonight. Just tell him you want four new, 32-inch tires. He'll say he can't do it and then you say you have to think about it. It will drive him crazy and you'll get your tires tomorrow."

We got back in the Chevy and the salesman immediately drove to the office to "work up some numbers." I stayed silent.

"That Jeep has both the hard and soft tops, and it is fully loaded with light grills, wiper covers, steel front bumper, back trunk ..." he went on and on. "I'm afraid that price is rock bottom."

He continued to look at Michael, who remained completely silent.

"Sir, I'm the one buying the car. Not him. OK?" I said. I tried to picture him as a doctor who wasn't giving me all the answers I needed.

"Of course," he said, and smiled sweetly.

"I don't want that Jeep unless I can get four new tires. That's not too much to ask."

As Michael predicted, the guy wanted me to drive away that night in the Jeep. Instead, Michael and I made a beeline for my Subaru.

As we were getting into my car, the salesman said, "Maybe your boyfriend can share with you the dangers of driving in a Jeep with tires that are too big."

I shut my door and walked back around to the passenger side where the salesman stood next to Michael. Michael was smiling and shaking his head.

"First of all, just because Michael is a man does not make him my boyfriend. Second, why would I need a boyfriend to tell me how to drive a Jeep. Third, 32-inch tires are not that big and they don't even require a lift. I can handle a Jeep just fine and I will get a Jeep with 32-inch tires."

Michael looked at the salesman, smiled, and got into the car. I returned to the driver's side and the salesman followed me, tapping on my window.

"I'll call you with numbers tomorrow," he said. "You could still change your mind and take it home tonight, though. If we can get you those tires, we could put them on there any time."

"No thanks," I said. "I'll keep looking."

As soon as we drove away, I said to Michael, "I can't lose that Jeep!"

The next day, the salesman called and I had gotten everything I wanted. I could pick it up that day! After some annoying conversations about hardware that I might need to "borrow from my boyfriend" to remove the soft top — what an idiot! — the salesman handed me the keys to my new Jeep. I immediately named it "Jake," Jason's nickname.

That weekend, I drove it down to Colorado Springs, picked Jason up, and we headed for the hills. I discovered roads I never knew existed, and Jason taught me the finer points of four-wheeling.

"So, how are you doing?" I finally asked. We were eating a picnic lunch in a meadow I had never seen before. I felt like I was on top of the world, and closer to Mom.

"I don't know," he said. His voice warned me that I was skating on thin ice. In the three months since Mom died, he'd covered himself with a tough veneer.

"Do you think about her?" I pushed.

"Of course I do," he said, annoyed.

I didn't respond. Finally, he started picking at the grass and tossing pebbles. He sighed and began talking.

"I feel like I don't have time to think about her, though," he said. "I may be doing that on purpose, but with school, I'm completely buried. I've never been a serious student. College is kicking my butt."

"You're going to do great, Jason. I'll drive down to Springs any time you want me to and help you."

"I know. Thanks."

"I'm the same, though," I said. "I try not to think about her. I'm so busy. I feel like I should think about her more, and I should miss her more. But even when I think about her, it's like a dream. It's like it never happened. I was there the whole time and I still don't feel like she's really gone."

Jason nodded and tossed rocks.

"It wasn't supposed to happen," I said.

"What do you mean?"

"You know how some things, even bad things, just feel like they're supposed to happen?" I said. "Even when you wish something hadn't happened, you can feel that it was supposed to be that way. You know?"

"Yeah," he said. "Like when I get a C. Or even when that person broke into my car and stole all my disks. It sucks, but it doesn't feel wrong."

"Yeah," I said, "this feels wrong like the earth-shifted-off-its-axis wrong. It just wasn't supposed to be this way. Usually when something bad happens, you can say that maybe it was fate because you learned something from it. I can't even imagine a positive outcome from this."

"Yeah, it's wrong versus bad," Jason said. "Bad stuff can teach you something. Wrong stuff just never should have happened."

We played all day in the mountains and then, two weeks later, Jason called to tell me he had gotten a Jeep of the exact same make and model. It was only October, but we started making camping plans for the next summer.

Serenity

CHAPTER 2

Janalee, I've decided that I want to buy Sylvia's house and move to Colorado."

Aunt Margie's phone call couldn't have been timed better. It was mid-October, and Jason and I were still taking turns driving down to Cañon to check on the house. Its vacancy only highlighted my aloft feeling. I had begun to feel like a satellite to the rest of my family, beaming back messages every now and then when the sun struck me correctly. I also felt like a very young child. I'd always had a parental presence nearby, both in Colorado and New Jersey. Lately, I was feeling weightless and misguided.

I still reached for the phone at the end of every day to talk to Mom. I felt alone and instinctively thought of her whenever I needed comfort. I couldn't believe that my subconscious was in such denial. I even tried telling myself, "Don't pick up the phone to call Mom," repeating it like an annoying song. But it became gibberish and merely ran through my head out of habit. I picked up the phone even as I said the phrase aloud. Then, suddenly, I was sitting on the floor, crying again. How could I alter the habits I'd formed over 25 years within a matter of days, or even weeks?

"You really want to move to Colorado?" I responded. "I thought you hated snow."

She laughed at my practical response.

"You'll teach me how to get around, right?"

"Of course!" I said. "Have you told Jason?"

"Not yet," she said, "and what I'm really doing is asking you. How would you feel about me living in that home? Would it bother you to visit me?"

"Not at all," I responded immediately and truthfully. "At first, I hated being down there, but now I can't even imagine selling it to a stranger."

I paused and thought about the house.

"I still have a tough time in the living room," I admitted. "But that backyard ... I love that backyard. I want to be free to go there all the time."

"Me, too," Aunt Margie said.

"And Aunt Margie?" I said.

"Yes,?"

"It sure would be great to have you back here. We miss you."

"I miss you, too."

She arranged a trip to Colorado to buy the house from Jason and me, which amounted to little more than a transfer of title. She paid us a little more than what was owed, and she also took that Nissan wagon off of our hands, since she figured she'd need a four-wheel-drive. She made arrangements for new carpet to be installed before she moved her furniture from California, and for the walls to be painted.

I met her in Cañon during her visit and I stayed the weekend. I agreed to fly to San Diego in November to help her pack and to drive back with her. We also had a long, soul-searching talk.

I was relieved to discover that I was not alone in my quest for meaning, for a new purpose. Aunt Margie had sold insurance for almost 15 years. Prior to that she taught piano at the University of Southern California. She loved selling insurance because she truly believed she was helping people and she had seen her policies assist people at crucial times. However, it ruled her life. She had no time to live her own life. Before Mom's illness and death, that lifestyle had been fine with her. A successful career seemed a valiant, completely life-fulfilling goal. Now, she wanted more life, less career. She planned to quit her job, move to Colorado, and kick around until she discovered a way to make a living and live at the same time. She'd survive on her savings and the money Mom left to her.

I, on the other hand, still wanted things to be the way they used to be, but I couldn't figure out why nothing seemed important to me. I assumed that I'd be "healed" once everything became normal again. Aunt Margie's journey helped me to realize that not only was my quest for the past in vain, but that it held few rewards.

SUNDAY, OCTOBER 10

It's been a long time since I wrote and I think it's because I've tried very hard to make myself numb. But the past week has brought much emotion, pain, and clarity.

Aunt Margie is buying Mom's home and moving to Colorado. She is here this weekend to get through some arrangements. I spent Friday night with her. We talked until past midnight and I realized that the past few months I have been sleepwalking. But the talk with her cleared up and strengthened some things for me. I suddenly feel the best I have since Mom died.

It's been a strange process ... After Mom died, her memorial, though beautiful, was stressful. Spreading her ashes was unforgettable, but part of a rushed process. Packing her house was painful and sterile in its handling.

Then I returned to work, hoping to find the normalcy I was craving. In a desire to master my own life, I turned away from my own thoughts, fears, and questions. Instead, I've worked hard to make myself busy and indestructible. I've worn a smile for everyone and joked, laughed, kidded. I was seemingly OK and that's how I honestly felt. I kept thinking, "I'm not thinking about her enough. I should hurt more." I even began to question how much I loved her because any loving person would feel much more pain than I was experiencing.

But a couple of weeks ago, the pain dawned. Suddenly my life is gaining what I had craved — normalcy. And I hate it. No, hate is too strong a word. Indifference is probably more accurate, and indifference toward life is a detestable feeling. I want — need — meaning. Nothing seems to matter to me at all right now. I do my job and I do it well, but it offers no rewards. I suppose I'm proud of doing a good job, but who cares? What am I living for? I don't mean that in a suicidal sense. I simply mean, what am I living for? Surely there must be more fulfilling activities than those in which I currently participate.

"I THINK MY goals are changing," I told Aunt Margie that night. "I keep asking myself, 'Is this really important?' It's like I'm going through the motions because I'm supposed to. Like wanting to move up in my job, make more money. Succeed succeed succeed! I feel like it's plastered all over the foreheads of people my age. But I don't find any meaning in it. None. Not even fun."

She nodded knowingly. We shared a bottle of wine in the living room next to the fire.

"Maybe, underlying this search for meaning is a change in your needs," she said.

"What do you mean?"

"Well, you're at an age, like you said, when society is pushing you to achieve success, but the benchmarks by which society judges success don't matter to you any more."

I nodded.

"You've just faced something that most people your age haven't. And they won't for a long time, generally. You've smacked right into the value of life at a time when your peers are still fulfilling more superficial goals. Not that those aren't important," she explained. "But you've been forced to take a detour into something much more fundamental."

We stared at the crackling fire.

"It's hard to appreciate the importance of the day-to-day grind when you're asking questions like, 'If I die tomorrow, would I have led a full life?'"

"But how do I resolve this?" I said impatiently. "I'm reading all these books about how I'm supposed to feel, but they don't help. I want peace from this constant questioning. I want serenity. But I can't seem to move on."

"Maybe you're actually ignoring how you feel, instead of opening yourself up to it."

"What do you mean?" I asked again. I was frustrated by this kind of talk because I wanted structure; I wanted a plan with precise bullet points of steps I should take to serenity.

"There won't be one magic moment when suddenly you feel resolved and then you'll be able to go on living exactly how you did before she died," Aunt Margie said. "I suspect your search will take you down a different path — like mine is — but it won't happen until you're ready to ask yourself some tough questions."

"Like?"

"Like, 'What's important to me?'" she said.

I found her balanced reasoning as annoying as I did helpful. Then, as if she sensed this, she suddenly said, "I haven't been able to do it yet."

She threw another log on the fire and started crying.

"Sylvia used to talk to me like this," she said, and I immediately nodded in agreement. I began crying, too. "I'm not trying to be your mom, Jana. I used to talk to her about these kinds of questions because she always seemed so centered. Or at least she knew how to ask herself questions. That woman didn't know how to do things contrary to her nature, so the answers always revealed themselves to her, even if it took time. I say all of this because I know it's how she lived. But I can't achieve it yet."

She held my hand and we both stared at the fire.

"I do know what's not important to me, though," she said after a few minutes. "And that's a good start. That's why I'm moving here."

TUESDAY, OCTOBER 12

I'm learning that healing is like one of those wooden, Russian dolls that has more dolls layered inside. I get through one layer and then move deeper into the next layer. Sometimes, though, it feels like I jump right back out to the biggest, most exterior doll, and all my work is meaningless. I feel like I did the day she died.

I don't think I realized how much Mom's death would affect my life. Who am I kidding? I still don't.

The most frustrating part is that I'm slowly understanding that I'll never be who I was before. At least my life won't ever be the same, which means all my expectations of life have to change, too.

That's funny. I was just trying to remember what expectations I had. I don't think I had any. The only thing that comes to mind is a job. I was getting a master's so that I could enter the environmental field, but that was mostly because it looked like a good field. Now I can't even believe it appealed to me — nor that it's the only mission I had.

What's going on? What do I want? What do I need!

I have much higher expectations of myself now than I did a year ago! But I don't have a clue how to verbalize them beyond this feeling that keeps haunting me. I need meaning! Purpose! A higher ... no, a deeper satisfaction.

How do I discover it? How do I achieve it?

"YOU'RE JANALEE CHMEL, aren't you?"

I had seen the petite blonde woman around the office and I knew she was relatively new. I heard that she'd started working at the University during the last two weeks of Mom's illness, when I wasn't around.

"Yes," I said, and smiled. Her face was bright and alert. She wore no makeup, which allowed her naturally translucent skin and bright blue eyes to shine. She wore her almost-white hair straight, no attempts to iron it into the latest bouncy style. She looked like a new daisy.

"I'm Ann," she said, then concern washed over her face and she said, "I heard about your mom. I'm very sorry. You must have amazing strength to be here."

My mouth opened slightly, but nothing came out. This was the most direct, honest statement I'd heard from anyone since Mom died. Most people said, "I'm sorry," but usually they moved uncomfortably right into the next item on their agenda.

"Wow," I said quietly, my hands still loosely holding papers on my desk.

"I'm sorry!" Ann retreated a bit. "You probably don't want to think about it."

I almost stood to grab her. "No! I do!" I gasped. "I do. It just seems like no one else does."

We both became embarrassed. I felt my weight settle back in my chair and I smiled. This was not exactly your standard introduction.

"Would you like to have lunch sometime?" I asked.

She smiled back. "That'd be great!"

That night in my apartment, I thought about Ann. She had a different energy. I was drawn to her instinctively, but couldn't understand why. I looked forward to lunch and, perhaps, a new friend.

"My husband and I just moved down from Vail so he could go to law school," she said, as we walked to a Chinese food restaurant near our office.

I felt slightly awkward and very energized, like a horse in a chute. After waiting so long to find someone who might understand me, or at least let me speak honestly of Mom, I wanted to find out right away if she might be the one, or if she would turn out to be just like everyone else. I had especially learned that no one my age had any concept of death, nor did they seem to grasp this "meaning" search I was on. Ann's energy resonated differently in me. I felt I had something to gain from her. For the moment, though, I had to trust that mysterious process of friendship.

Ann studied fine art, painting specifically, at Xavier College. While she and her husband lived in Vail, she worked at a gallery and did her own work on the side. Todd, her husband, worked for the city in planning and now wanted to couple that knowledge with law. As an employee of DU, she earned tuition reimbursement for him. We also discovered that she lived less than a mile from me.

"Are you painting now?" I asked. I was intrigued by this talent. I had always wondered how an artist took a blank canvas and transformed it into a vision or a message.

"Not as much as I'd like," she said. The move had disrupted her routines. "I've got a room in the basement, but the light is so bad."

Unconsciously, she fiddled with her knife to catch light on its blade. Ann considered her words as carefully as she considered light. That intention helped me to trust her more; she did nothing unintentionally.

"Light inspires me," she continued. "I heard there's a valley in Colorado where the light is different than anywhere else in the country. I'd like to go there sometime."

Ann moved her hands as she talked, but not in emphasis of her words like most people. She seemed to capture invisible objects and even to study them with her fingers. When she described her work, her hands moved toward an invisible canvas and I imagined her playfully finger-painting, though she drew with charcoal, brushed with acrylics, and stroked with oils.

"I love color!" she said with a delighted, silly grin, as though an outrageous periwinkle had just mooned her. "Right now, I'm really into oranges."

Ann's creativity washed through me like hot tea on a winter day. I felt my body relax as it had when I sat on Mom's healthy lap so long ago. Instinctively, I felt safe.

"Liver cancer," I said, when she asked. I studied her bright face to see if that would be enough information for her. I hoped not. I didn't know what I wanted her to ask, or what I wanted to share. I only knew that I needed it.

"What do you miss most?" she immediately asked. With every moment, she set herself apart and I began to wonder if our meeting was coincidence.

"Hugs," I said, poking at my food. My throat got hot and I could feel tears gathering in my eyes. Still, she didn't retreat.

"Is your family touchy? Warm?" she asked, truly curious. I noticed that she used a present tense verb.

"Yes," I said, and, instead of crying, a smile crawled up through my hot throat. "We hug each other and say, 'I love you' all the time. I think it's really important to express all that. Especially now."

This time, when I paused, she just watched me without interrupting. I didn't know how to hold a conversation without stopping at the end of every sentence to allow the person an easy way out.

"If I hadn't had time to express all my feelings to Mom before she died, I'd have so many regrets. But that came easily to us, usually, while she was sick because we had always shared our feelings. We were in good practice."

I thought some more, and she let me.

"The love was unconditional and it was always apparent. We had a lot of joy. Joy was a biggie for Mom."

Ann studied me.

"I haven't met anyone like you before," I ventured carefully, not wanting to overwhelm her. "It feels almost like we were supposed to meet."

My heart pounded. Would I scare away a new friend with my need, my intensity? I wanted so badly to confide in a kindred spirit, but experience had led me to believe no one wanted the burden. Ann did.

"Yeah," she responded with an easy smile. "Something here feels right."

We shared lunch at least once a week and gradually we began calling one another at home. I was still in the habit of screening my calls and she never told me it was annoying, as everyone else did.

We began to explore our creativity and, thanks to her, I soon recognized not only the intrinsic value of the journaling I did, but also that writing held deeper purpose for me than mere self-expression.

"If I could paint your mom, I'd use reds, golds, bright greens," Ann said, splashing her hands against an invisible canvas.

We were sitting on my living room floor drinking wine.

"Why?" I asked.

"Her passion!" Ann said. "And her guts! She was a very courageous woman. I can tell by what you say and by who you are."

"By who I am?" I said slowly. She had just introduced an issue with which I had struggled recently: could I be as strong a woman as Mom? And, even more important, how would my friends ever know her? I had always taken such pride in introducing my friends to her. I was proud of her. Now, how would my friends ever know her? If they couldn't know her, I believed, they could not know all of me.

"Oh, sure," Ann continued in her peaceful way. "You obviously got your strength from somebody. I can tell she loved you very much."

From the day we met, Ann and I never had a trite conversation. We joked that within 10 minutes of meeting one another for coffee or a meal, one of us would be crying. We cut right through the small talk to the issues plaguing our hearts and minds. We began to truly believe that we were meant to discover one another at the precise moments we did.

"I hope this doesn't anger you," she said, and paused to look at me. I only gazed back to let her know that everything was safe between us. "Well, I've been talking to your mom."

"What?!" I said, a smile jumping across my face.

She just looked at me peacefully, waiting for my next response.

"I don't ... I can't even talk to her."

Still, she waited. It was as if she felt no compulsion to explain; it was natural.

"I've drawn from her based on the stories you've told me." Ann laughed. "That woman didn't take any bullshit!"

We both laughed aloud, and then I started crying. But, because that was naturally a part of our friendship, Ann didn't stop the moment.

"I was raised to be the good little girl. The good wife," she said. "I remember at the dinner table, the girls always made dinner, set the table, and cleaned up. My brother and dad showed up to eat and then left. I got so pissed off one day when I had just had soccer practice and I was famished. I finished everything on my plate and there was one pork chop left. Without even asking, Mom picked it up and put it on Tom's plate and he wasn't even done with his first helping."

I watched Ann and realized that it took a lot of self-esteem to even recognize that as an injustice.

"I think I've spent half of my life doing the supposed right thing and the other half pissed off at myself for doing it," she said. "It's not like your mom talks to me, but I can feel her. I know for a fact that she put you in my life."

I thought of Mom arranging this friendship and could believe it in the same faithful way I believed in guardian angels. Why not believe it? It's rather comforting and it certainly can't hurt. Still, why would Mom think I'd be any good for someone else in my confused state? Ann wondered the same thing about my need for her friendship.

"Well, I'm glad Mom provides you some comfort," I suddenly said, almost angry. "The only time she visits me is to die repeatedly, in grotesque ways, in my dreams."

Since Mom's death, I'd had recurring, violent nightmares about her. In some, she died — by drowning, cancer, car crashes, everything — and I usually stood by helpless. Those were very bad, but in the worst of my nightmares, I was dying in violent ways and she usually stood nearby without attempting my rescue. Those terrified me.

SUNDAY, DECEMBER 12

It's 5 a.m. and Mom just died again. I woke up sobbing. My pillow is soaked, so I must have been crying a while. This time, she was drowning and yelling my name. It was like I was under water watching her because I could see her frail body thrashing and her head kept popping to the surface but something pulled her. I hate that. I just watched! I watched the whole thing from beginning to end. I watched her struggle, fight, and die.

She looked like she did at the end of her life. All ravaged. Her skin was loose and floating like a sail around her bones.

Why do I keep focusing on her physical being? I can't even picture what she looked like healthy. Maybe that's just the most tangible part of this whole disaster right now. I can't even begin to understand what her absence means — absence forever — so maybe the physical part is the most real.

Yesterday, I decided to buy some skirts and pants to go with some of Mom's jackets. But when I smelled them, they smelled like her and suddenly it was even less believable that she was gone. Time literally stuttered back upon itself, like a child sliding across a linoleum floor on a sheet, fold upon fold of time gathering up with lightening speed, retracing the last 12 months, back to when she wasn't even sick — it's hard to believe such a time existed. Her smell still lingers, four months later, and yet the woman is gone.

I miss her so much.

But why does she have to keep dying every night? It's like a bad movie. Those Freddie Kreuger movies. "Don't go to sleep! Freddie will get you!" Only now, it's, "Don't go to sleep! Mommie will die again!"

I've also heard that women closely associate their own physical health and image with their mother's. Maybe deep inside I feel her death killed part of me? No. That's not right. I do know that I don't think I'll live past 50, which means I'm halfway done with my life.

Wow. If I'm halfway done, I have a lot to do! Like what? That's the million-dollar question.

Geez, what a way to wake up.

Serenity

Chapter 3

In February 1994, a college buddy came to visit me. Her name was Nancy, and she had been to Colorado three years earlier, right after we graduated. Nancy, born Anunziata Scala in Italy, was a passionate and introspective friend. I looked forward to her visit because I knew we'd share important conversations, not to mention a lot of homemade pasta.

She got in on a Wednesday, I worked Thursday, and then on Friday, she and I drove up to a friend's cabin in Breckenridge. We had the place to ourselves and we stocked up on red wine and all the pasta fixings Nancy needed for the long, cold weekend.

After a considerable amount of wine the first night there, Nancy asked, "Have you accepted it?"

"What?" I asked, "That Mom's gone? Forever?"

She nodded.

"No way," I said. "I keep trying, though."

Nancy giggled.

"What?" I said.

"You said that like you're cramming for an exam."

"Really?" I asked.

"Yeah," she said, taking her legs off the table to bring her chair flat on the floor. "'I keep trying.'" she mimicked me. "It's like you think there's a cheat sheet, or an answer key."

I thought about it a bit. She continued.

"What do you think acceptance means?" she asked. It was a rhetorical question. I could tell she didn't have the answer, though I'd have preferred that she did.

"I feel like I'm holding my breath all the time," I said. "It's like I'm this little kid and I'm going to hold my breath until I get what I want. And I want acceptance. Maybe if I hold out enough, I'll be given acceptance and I can move on. Does that make sense?"

"Yeah, I guess," she said, and she smiled. "Jana, you've always been able to just move on every time you break up with a guy, or he breaks up with you. It's always amazed me. When we were in college, that stuff was black and white to you. It would either work or it wouldn't, and it's like you just told yourself, 'It wasn't meant to be,' and you just moved on. Are you trying to do that with your mom?"

"Maybe," I said. "But usually that stuff with guys was my decision. I had control over what happened. Or, maybe it's that I always believed there was someone perfect out there so what was the big deal if Mr. Wrong got away? But with this ... well, there's no one else out there, you know? So, I guess my main goal is to accept her death and I'm sure I'd love it to be as easy as when I realize I'm dating Mr. Wrong. Just move on."

"It doesn't seem that easy," Nancy said.

"I know. It's not. Believe me," I said.

"I think you said it yourself. You're not in control. You can't suddenly decide that you're healed, though you want to," she thought a bit. "Maybe the acceptance is in the details."

"Like what?" I said.

She smiled. "Well, maybe these kinds of conversations."

"OK. Sure, I can accept that," I said. "How much longer, though?"

"You mean, how much longer should you expect to heal? Like on a timeline?"

I realized the question was ridiculous. Point A: begin healing process. Point B: healing process reaches climax. Point C: invite everyone over to celebrate completion of healing process.

"It's like you're sprinting and someone just pulled the trigger," Nancy said. "I can tell that you want to hit the finish line, but it's like you're missing all the hurdles."

She paused, and the air became tangibly energized. Something was clicking inside me.

"Maybe the hurdles are the lessons you're supposed to learn and you can't get to the finish line until you clear all the hurdles."

It was so profound that I stared at her to determine if she'd scripted this entire conversation. She was absolutely right. My main goal was to accept Mom's death and I thought I could accomplish this as I had accomplished other goals in my life: set my mind to it, organize it, put it in a time line, achieve it. I chased that goal with the zeal of a sprinter, starting block and all. But I was so busy racing toward acceptance — demanding acceptance as a sprinter demands adrenaline — that I was missing the tiny, daily opportunities for growth.

Before we left the mountains on Sunday, we went for a long walk in the snow. It was crisp and bright. We could see our breath as we talked, but the cold air felt good in our lungs. We'd been cooped up inside for too long.

"So, what do you think you've learned from her death?" Nancy asked.

I laughed instantly.

"The truth?" I asked. "The first thing that came to mind? I can't believe it. It's the first thing that came to my mind!"

"What?" she said, smiling.

"My first thought was, 'I'm a pretty incredible person.'" I shook my head and laughed quietly.

"Well, you are," she said. "You went through something horrible, and you did it with grace. And your mom died with dignity. That's amazing by any standards."

"OK, so what else?" I asked myself out loud, uncomfortable with the self-congratulations. "Well, in the end, all you've got is love, and that's all that matters in life."

We walked on.

"So, I guess if love is what matters in the end, people are the most important priority in your life," I continued.

She nodded. I thought some more.

"This last thing I'm thinking about is less tangible, but I'm beginning to realize the deep value of it. Even this trip has helped the idea gel. It has to do with peace. It's the way I feel in the mountains. It has to do with inner peace and tranquility. Mom called it serenity. We need it, I think, to understand ourselves and to truly open ourselves to love, and to the people who love us."

Nancy smiled, as though remembering a distant memory. She shook her head.

"What?" I asked, smiling myself.

"I was just thinking about that guy you dated. Rob, I think. He was from Spain. Or his parents were."

"Yeah, Rob!" I said. "Why in the world ... ?"

"Well, I don't know. You just said something like 'open ourselves to the people who love us' and I thought of him."

"Oh, God," I said, instantly knowing why. "Was I evil, or what?"

"Not evil," Nancy said. "Very, extremely honest."

We both laughed and walked a while. Then, Nancy recreated the conversation with a Rob voice and a Janalee voice.

Rob voice: "Janalee, I think I love you."

Janalee voice: "No you don't, Rob. Finish your laundry."

We stopped hiking and she laughed, holding her tummy. I stood staring at the peaks, feeling like a schmuck, but laughing anyway.

"Honesty is a good thing!" I reasoned out loud at her, smiling.

* * *

WINTER THAWED TO spring and I received news that four of my friends were getting married. Good God! That thought was so far from my reality that they seemed to be pursuing life on Mars. All four of them asked me to be in their weddings, and one even said, "I figured you could use some good news and happiness to look forward to."

That sounded reasonable enough, except the more I thought about it, the more nervous and angry I got. I was thrilled for my friends, but images of the four respective events floated through my mind and two things kept jabbing my emotions: the grooms and the mothers of the brides. I had neither, and both felt equally distant.

Since Mom's illness and death, I had dated little. I found the routines of first dates tedious and I found most men the same. I had lost the art of small talk somewhere between, "It's cancer," and "good-bye, Mom." I hated pointless, superficial chatter. To a lesser extent, small talk still cornered me as quickly and completely as it had that day in Mom's home when Earlene came over and I sank down crying on the kitchen floor. Not exactly conducive to getting to know people — men and women alike. Ann was the only person with whom I could start a conversation saying, "My idea of happiness is shifting," and have her meet me right there on that level. Others talked about their jobs, the weather, whatever popped into their line of vision at that moment. I needed more depth, and I needed to get there without all of the build-up to it. I was impatient and I began to accept that dating — though a nice diversion sometimes — would not be fulfilling for me for a long while.

Then there was the idea of "mother of the bride." I pictured all four weddings and I knew the moms of three of the brides. I could envision their smiles and tears of happiness. I could hear them welcoming the grooms into their families, and I knew I would never see that pride and love on my mom's face.

And I was angry. At first, this feeling so alarmed me that I set it aside like stinky garbage. I had felt angry before, but this anger was very different. Its focus frightened me even more than when I had been angry at God. I realized I was furious with Mom.

For months, I fought it. In fact, I beat myself up. How could I allow myself to be angry at the woman who raised me, gave me unconditional love, and then died too soon? I was confused and scared of the thought. Why was I angry at her? And how could she ever make up for it? The feeling was so deep that I imagined it may never subside if I gave it life, so I continued to ignore it. I thought that if I wrote about it, the words would be permanent and, somehow, I would do damage to her memory. I wanted her to be perfect, even in her absence.

By August 1994, I had spent over $2,000 on three bridesmaids' dresses, gifts, travel, and other wedding necessities. I also had a marvelous, joyous time at each wedding. I understood that my dearest friends had found happiness and I was honored to be among the significant witnesses at those events. Still, I watched the grooms and wondered how in the hell I'd ever find the companionship I sought, and I watched the moms wondering if I even wanted a husband since he would never know my mom.

On August 5, 1994 I reflected on the past year. I'd lived an entire year without Mom. Still, the overriding emotion was anger, so I decided to put pen to paper and discover its essence.

FRIDAY, AUGUST 5, 1994

Dear Mom,

(oh, how it's hard to write those words and know that you will never read them.)

I'll try this again.

Dear Mom,

I'm down in Cañon City at what was once your home and is now Aunt Margie's home. I have been struggling quite a bit lately with your absence, your death, and all the little spaces and holes I've encountered in my life since your departure. It's pretty hard to be here. Aunt Margie played Amazing Grace on the piano last night and it reminded me of your memorial service.

Geez, Mom, it is all so hard to believe, still! I say "memorial service" like I've accepted that you are dead and gone forever and yet I have not, in any way, accepted that I will never be able to hold you again, laugh with you again, be silly with you again, seek your wisdom, ask you questions, share my tri-

umphs, earn your pride; that we will never again two-step in the living room, carve pumpkins, short-sheet Jason's bed, call Uncle Willis with a joke, make popcorn in a paper bag, steal watermelons from the neighbor's garden, go to a Neil Diamond concert together, talk about sex, discuss love — my love, your love — drive to the mountains, sob over that Wynonna Judd song, walk among the Aspen, fight over the TV volume, agonize over Jason, make polenta, sing Alabama's Christmas carols near the fire, tease each other, comfort each other, cry together, share a moment.

I hate you for it, Mom. I never imagined I could be angry at you for dying and here I am furious at you with the same intensity I felt at God when you were sick. I want you back here. When you left, you took part of my life and I will never be able to regain that aspect of myself again. You stole part of my life! How could you? How dare you? You — who protected me, loved me, inspired me, and punished me — you have betrayed me. I trusted you with the love only earned by parents, with the love only granted by children. How can I ever trust anyone again? How can I ever live like that again? I probably never will — and for that I am angry, too. I have been damaged, and my ability to love has been damaged, and my willingness to love has been damaged.

Mom, I've tried to start relationships in the past year and, though I yearn for someone to understand me and all I need, it is impossible. I feel like a hollow shell — somebody who may look whole and complete and happy on the outside, but someone who is echoing on the inside like an empty room made of tin. I'm trying to discover what it's like to love myself again without your influence, without your guidance … and I miss you.

I miss you so much, Mommy. I don't go through a day without thinking about you or wishing I could tell you something. It leads me many times to believe that you aren't really gone, that last year was just a nightmare and one day you will reappear on my doorstep, tan and fit from this extended vaca-

tion you are taking. But no. Never will I see you again. Never will I hear you again. Never will I touch you again. never never never never never never never never never never

That doesn't work. No matter how much I tell myself that you are gone, I cannot rationally figure out what that means. What is forever?

I also feel like you suffered very little in comparison to what I am feeling right now. You had seven months of misery, but I will feel your absence for the rest of my life. It's just not fair! We were so happy, Mom! We had the kind of relationship that other people envied. We were friends, dammit! Best friends! And you are gone. Such happiness cannot be common in this life and I resent the fact that I may now not ever experience that again. Why now? Why did you have to go now? Why not when I was older, when you were older, when Jason was older? We had it so good. So very good. I am proud of that, and yet I am paying for all of that love now.

So, what would I share with you if I could get you in front of the fire for one evening? I'd ask you questions, Mom, until you cried from the revelations we shared and I knew more about myself — all the things I may now never know: Who do you think Janalee is? What did you want Janalee to be? What was I like when I was 5? 6? 7? Who was your mentor in life? What did you want to do when you retired? What should I do about my job? How can I best help Jason get through things that scare him? What scared you? What should scare me? How do I attain my dreams? What were your dreams? Did you plan on fulfilling them?

And I'd tell you things:

I'm a published fiction writer! I want to fall in love. I want a new job. Chris is in Chile. I want to buy a house. I have a Jeep! I have a new friend named Ann. I turned 26 and Ann threw me a surprise party. I won two more national marketing awards this year. Robin got married! Brooke got married! Stacy got married! (They all missed you at the wed-

dings.) Aunt Margie and I are friends. Jason has a girlfriend named Melinda and they are really in love. Chelsea is happy with Earlene and Charlie. Pat and Teri are starting their own business. I need you. I miss you.

My life is confusing, Mom, and you are not here to help me. I see you in the sunsets and I think of moments we shared, but you are not here, and your wise words are not here, and your warm arms are not here, and your blue eyes are not here, and your strength is not here. Like your ashes, they have scattered in the wind.

How dare you leave me, Mommy. How dare you.

ONCE I TRUSTED myself enough to express anger, like a filly trusting its new legs, I trotted and then galloped through feelings I hadn't even known existed inside me. I realized that I wasn't allowing myself to grow beyond her death because I truly didn't believe I could. From the day I was born, my role model, consciously and unconsciously, was Mom. Everything from my physical identity to my personal, professional, and emotional growth had been organically grounded in her influence. That's the innate nature of parenthood. Denied her physical presence, her hug of approval, her voice saying, "I'm proud of you," I lost my footing. The tangible benchmarks of inspiration were gone. The rug was pulled out from beneath me — a rug on which I normally flew.

My anger helped me to realize that I still sought Mom's approval and that I had to learn to approve of myself and empower myself. I struggled, though, to find a source of strength purely my own. I feared that I might push Mom out entirely. I thought that relying on myself meant abandoning Mom's influence, as though 25 years of growth would suddenly disappear. I couldn't conceive of a balance between the two sources, but I longed for it. This required a lot of solitude; I needed to discover my own source of strength.

THURSDAY, JANUARY 19, 1995

I have no idea what time it is, but it's somewhere around noon. I'm up at a friend's cabin in Conifer and I'm searching for myself.

I got up here about 10:30 a.m. and promptly built a fire — never my greatest talent. But I did it! The wood-burning stove is in the middle of the little living room and I can already picture my toes perched in front of it tonight as I continue this self-journey on into the evening. It is cold in the cabin still despite the fire and a little space heater, so I am sitting in the sun on the side deck. A squirrel is chatting to me demandingly from a nearby tree. I've already put corn and nuts out for him and the birds. What does he want?!

There is no running water here. A kettle of frozen water sits atop the stove for tea or soup later. And, unfortunately, I am also alone with a pile of Hershey's Kisses. Great.

For a little over a month, I have been missing Mom terribly. Much of it has to do with the season and time of year, I'm sure. Her birthday, Christmas, New Year's, the two-year anniversary of her diagnosis — they have all contributed to make this a time which I've struggled through. But there's more to it, I think. I have felt, until this moment, very out-of-touch with her. I don't even think I recognized how much I've been missing her until a few days ago. When the pain taps on my door, I ignore it. Then, after time, it becomes a knock, a pound, and suddenly a battering ram crashing into my life. This has happened before. Apparently, I didn't learn from it last time. Why do I ignore my own emotions?

One of my theories is that I long to share them with someone. I can't seem to experience my emotions alone. I block them. I'm afraid of them. When I cry and I'm alone, I feel lonely — making me long for someone to listen, question, hold me, rock me, cry with me. I've realized that I cry when I talk to Aunt Margie or Ann, but when I'm alone I can't/won't do it. There's nothing necessarily wrong with that except that I don't reach out to them until I'm almost over the edge — like now. "I'm fine." I'm doing well." "My life is good." I say these things when at my core I need a good cry.

I've got to learn to take Jana time — regularly — not when I'm getting ready to crack, when my job is suffering, when my temper is shorter than a paper match. It doesn't have to be a whole weekend and it doesn't have to be a "Mom vigil" but it does have to happen. And it probably should involve being in the mountains. My soul finds peace here. I've known that since I left for college and I must accept it as my body accepts nourishment.

I've gotten so caught up in being productive all the time that I get antsy watching one-half hour of news at night! I should be "doing," "accomplishing," "producing." I think this has stripped me of some of my capacity to relax and, hence, feel. I need to take breaks and breathe, see, feel, experience — I don't always have to do do do!

I believe I have spent the last 18 months just coping and I've done a damned good job of it! I never imagined that I would live after her death, yet here I am. But I think there is a difference between living and coping and I have reached a point when I must begin living again. It has been two years since Mom's diagnosis when I immediately put my life aside to assure that the rest of her life could be as good as possible. I stopped going to school, put the bare minimum into work, drove thousands of miles and researched food, cancer, treatments, doctors, etc. Much of me has not abandoned that role or mode to re-focus on my life, my needs. During Mom's illness, I was busier and more focused than at any other point in my life. I tried to go to school, I worked from Mom's home, and on weekends, I cared for Mom and I tried to get help for myself via therapists, books, friends. I was a machine.

I have become a machine, but not a very efficient one based on what I really need. I need to nurture myself. I need to relax. But I sit here wondering how. I can't tell myself,

"You need to relax and feel." That's like saying, "produce a feeling." If I learn to relax, the feeling will naturally follow.

(The water is thawing inside!)

What do I miss about Mom and how can I learn to live with that? I must learn to live with it, not under it, not despite it, not above it, not detached from it, not within it, not against it. Much of my frustration probably stems from the fact that I want to be fine so I tell myself I will be fine and I go on. I must be able to live (not cope), work, create and experience joy with that pain as a secondary part of my life.

I miss Mom's wisdom and I miss Mom's touch. Those two things have become so apparently absent from my life. And my response has been to search for them in others. (Do you know who I am? Do you understand me? Do you have advice for me? Will you hug me?) It has been almost two years since I was able to talk completely unguarded to anyone. I am achieving something resembling that with Ann and Aunt Margie but it is not quite the same. Should I even expect such a relationship to enter my life again? Is that realistic? As long as I look for it, my relationships — male or female — may be doomed to mediocrity, as I define it. Only if I am willing to accept that there may never be another in my life to fulfill that specific "Mommy role" of unconditional love, can I open the possibility of a different — no less rewarding — kind of relationship in my life.

(It is now warmer inside the cabin than outside! There is hope!)

So, how else have Mom's death and absence affected my life?

I am questioning everything. That's one of the main things that has lead to this "crisis escape." Nothing seems to make sense. All the things that are supposed to matter and provide meaning seem like bullshit to me. I do not feel that my life is pointed in any direction. I do some of this, a little of that, a dab of this, a whack of that, and I do them all well, but it's like someone on four assembly lines. I keep maintaining the same position and pace, applying the same widgets but I am great at nothing.

I must pause here to describe what I've just done. I've turned this cabin into a smoky crypt. My talents as a fire starter/Girl Scout have always been sorely lacking. I decided to build a fire in the second stove for additional heat and have so far succeeded brilliantly in cloaking the cabin and much of the nearby forest in gray clouds. I sure hope the fire department is asleep. Then, as I fought and struggled over that fire, I let the other die down to nothing. So, now I have both doors open to let this creepy gray cat escape and I am rapidly losing all the heat I had so jealously stockpiled. I still have no fire. Mom is laughing her ass off right now.

FRIDAY, JANUARY 20, 1995 — 9 A.M.

What a morning! I got up with the sun at seven and promptly built a fire. Give me another week and I may get that down. I was toasty warm all night and the squirrel cheerily greeted me on my first chilly trek to the toilette (two-seater out-house!). I ate raisin bran and an orange as the cabin warmed up and watched the Today show on TV! TV! I sat and watched TV!

I can feel relaxation setting in today and I'm somewhat puzzled by it. I had a fleeting urge this morning to go home. Kind of like, "Well, you watched TV! You must be a changed woman!" Yeah, right. Stay put, Chmel. Lots to do.

My mother is gone. Mom is dead. Mom is gone forever. (Remarkably, I'm not crying.) Forever. I don't think I have yet adjusted the way I look at my life or the way I live my life to incorporate that fact. Probably normal. But it may be time to begin the adjustment because the alternative is now becoming a detriment to my life. Part of my identity for the past 18 months has been "woman whose mother died too soon." It will always be a part of me, but it doesn't have to be something I wear like glasses. It can be less essential — more like earrings — an accessory to my life. A little less apparent, and yet still part of who I am and who I choose to share with people.

I think that within the last six months I have begun the adjustment. I've been writing more creative stuff. I've gone through entire conversations without thinking of her. These are big steps, very big. I think I am also beginning to pity myself less and am learning to be proud of myself, instead. Yes, I am becoming more convinced of my own capabilities. I was very proud of myself during Mom's illness because I discovered an inner strength unmatched by many my age. It was a strength given to me, taught to me by Mom.

But how do I begin to live like a woman and not like a woman who just survived her mother's death? I must somehow accept the finality of her death. Tall order, Chmel. But I do somehow continue to live as though I'm working toward the day when I can have her back again. It's like I'm trying to earn her back from God: work like hell, accept nothing about her absence, search for her in every soul I meet and the light at the end of the tunnel will be Mom. I'll be able to have her back. This helps me to realize that I have taken her death very personally. As though she was taken away from me personally.

"IF YOU COULD paint your world right now, what colors would you use?" I asked Ann over coffee one Saturday morning.

"Grays," she said. "Like a winter morning when you know it's going to snow and all you want to do is put on a sweater and sit under a blanket."

"Is it cozy?" I asked.

"I guess I can choose to make it cozy," she said. "That's why I put on the sweater. Otherwise, it's cold."

I nodded. Ann was still struggling to incorporate her creative life into her daily life. She sought a way to give her life meaning in ways that only she could provide herself, and it required breaking free from roles she'd been taught to value.

Our struggles were similar. I was trying to discover a passion or creativity, that would provide my life with meaning within the realities of the day-to-day tasks of earning a salary and holding a job.

"I'm reading a book right now by Clarissa Pinkola Estes called 'Women Who Run With the Wolves,' " I said.

"I've heard of that," Ann said. "Dreams and myths, right?"

"Much of what I'm reading reminds me of Mom's wisdom," I said. "It talks about listening to your gut and how important it is to hear yourself."

"It's so hard to do!" Ann exclaimed. And, as though she'd already read the book, she was expressing the difficulties I was having with it, as well. "I get so many other messages. I find my hands drawn to my brushes and I think, 'I'd better finish the laundry,' as though that is more important than this feeling that overtook me when I thought of my canvas! How do I learn to listen to my gut and not my guilt?"

"The wolf analogy in the book is really good," I said. "It's helping me to separate those. It talks about women's instincts, our gut, in terms of wolves. Like uncanny, wild, raw, sniffing, and hungry. I think the other stuff, the guilt stuff, feels less natural, like weights or sadness. Like a gerbil! Not wild and raw."

"I bet you separate the two better than I do, though," Ann said. "I was always taught to listen to the guilt."

I nodded, smiling.

"I think Mom always taught me to listen to myself," I said. "She tried, anyway. She had guilt motives, too, of course. But she knew how to listen when she chose to, and I think she taught me. I never felt that she thought I was too young to make a decision for myself. She asked, 'What do you want to do?' and then she'd ask me, 'Why?' which was always tougher. But as I grew up and faced dilemmas, she didn't set in, roll up her sleeves and try to make it all better. She guided me through my gut with those same questions."

"So, you're still learning from her," Ann said, smiling.

I nodded, and took a deep, thankful breath.

"Me, too," she said. "I think next time I get pulled toward the laundry, I'll ask myself, 'What do I really want to do?' If I discover that it really is the laundry, due to some freakish nesting thing, then I'll do it. Otherwise, it can go to hell."

"You must have listened to your gut when you decided to be an artist," I said. "And look at the way you see the world now because of it! I think I long for your gift. Or at least the freedom to allow myself to pursue a creative passion. When I ask you the colors of your world, it's because I love how your creativity shapes your world. I want that newness in my world all the time."

"I think you have it," Ann said. "You just have to choose it."

"Choose it?"

"As opposed to hiding it, from others and yourself," Ann said, pausing. "You're a writer."

Instantly, I knew she spoke truth, but I'd not allowed myself to approach it as a need. I treated writing more as a hobby. Suddenly, I wondered if I could pursue it as a vocation, and to paint the world in colors for others to see just like I longed to see the colors of Ann's world.

Serenity

CHAPTER 4

"Daddy, I've decided to pursue a master's degree in creative writing," I said over the phone one Saturday morning. Our friendship had deepened since Mom's death. Daddy called religiously every weekend and I'd gotten to where I squealed "Daddy!" when the phone rang at 8 a.m. on Saturday morning.

"Marvelous!" he said loudly. "Janalee, that's wonderful!"

"Really?" I said. "Why?"

I was still testing this goal out and his immediate enthusiasm for it felt great, but I wanted to know the reason behind it. If it felt so good to him, maybe he'd seen this path a long time ago. That felt reassuring — like the vision most parents had and that I'd feared I'd lost with Mom.

"Why?" he said. "Because it's a natural choice for you, darling. "I never understood the management degree you were doing. You've always been creative. This is fantastic. I'm so happy for you."

"You think I can write?" I asked, still probing his enthusiasm. It felt great to hear this from someone who knew me so well.

"Can you write?" he said incredulously. "Not only can you write, but you're creative. I think that's why newspaper reporting annoyed you. It was too structured. And you didn't like the reporting end of things, either. But do you know how many journalists became famous writers, honey? Hemingway, Stephen Crane. It's a great foundation and you have a good heart for it."

Daddy gushed and I melted. Here was the parental approval I sought. Here was the unconditional, enthusiastic support. Because he has a fine arts background, I never expected Daddy to say, "You'll never make any money with that," but I honestly had no idea he would think writing was such a great pursuit for me. My decision was made.

But if I'd had any leftover doubts, Daddy nailed the decision when he said, "I'm proud of you, honey. Creative endeavors are never easy. They must be a passion, and I believe that's what you've discovered. You're being honest with yourself."

Then, to add a little humor, he said, "You get that trait from your old man, you know."

We laughed. Suddenly I knew what I wanted, needed, to do with my life.

I registered to begin taking classes in the fall. About the same time, I was recruited by another department on campus — fundraising — to take over their direct mail program. It offered both a welcome change and an opportunity to try a new style of writing. I accepted.

FRIDAY, SEPTEMBER 16, 1995

The more I discover what's important to me, the more I miss Mom. I'm so excited about this degree I'm pursuing, and the classes are fantastic! But when I get excited, I want to tell Mom. Of course, that's not possible.

Aunt Margie says she talks to Mom. She just sits down and talks out loud. I can't even imagine that. I literally cannot bring myself to utter "Mom" out loud. I cannot, will not, sit and talk to her. I'm not really angry at her any more. I just have no idea how to let her be part of my life. When someone is your friend, they grow with you and you learn from them. I feel like my relationship with Mom is stagnant. I can't grow within it; I'm a little girl with her but the questions I'm asking are very adult. I don't get the answers, or exploration from her that I need from a friend right now.

Dammit, she's dead. How can I know her better? How can she help now?

I hate that the instant I feel joy, I want to share it with her … and then I get sad.

Part of me really wishes her memory would fade. It would be easier to welcome happiness if I didn't long to share it with her. Her absence is bigger than my happiness.

A NEW CLIMB began. I'd found strength within to pursue a fulfilling life on my own, but I longed for Mom on a new level. I wanted Mom's friendship and companionship. Yet, I believed that an impossible goal. I defined friendship by conversations, time together, immediate guidance, on-the-spot resources, hugs, shared tears, and shared triumphs. Friendship required a physical presence, if not a good phone call. I always believed Mom's spirit lived on and I imagined her as a guardian angel, but she merely viewed my life from her perch on the mountaintops. She was not a participant. Truly, I wouldn't allow her to be.

It was more comfortable, now that I was making good, true decisions for myself, to assume I didn't need her anyway. Why go through the pain of allowing her into my life as a constant companion when that companionship only served to hurt me? Like a spiteful child, I decided that I wanted all or nothing and I pushed her out completely.

SUNDAY, NOVEMBER 5, 1995

I haven't prayed since Mom died. I realized — remembered — that I used to pray every night before going to sleep. I even used to make myself start every prayer each night by saying, "God, thank you for today." Then, I'd name at least one thing for which I was grateful, even if it had been a hateful day. If I couldn't think of a thing, I'd think of a person. Most of the prayers were more like conversations. I even rambled and then joked about rambling with ... Him, or whoever I saw as my higher power. I was very proud of having what I believed was a real relationship with my God. We joked, worked through things, tackled issues. I actually talked very casually and honestly with my higher power. At the end of each prayer, I'd say, "Thank you for ..." and listed all the important people in my life and made special pleas for needy friends. It felt good. I couldn't go to sleep unless I did it.

Now I can't even do it.

I've tried. I say, "God?" It's always a question. Then I stop. I can't go on. I've lost the ability. The echo in my head of my own unspoken words feels so empty. I don't think I've stopped believing, but I don't think I feel such a relationship with any higher power. I don't have a comfort zone, so I've stopped.

Also, I think I get Mom confused with my higher power. After she died, I no longer wanted to speak to God and I didn't know how to talk to her. But her wisdom is what I've sought through the years.

I'm confused. Only recently, I've missed praying because it felt like such a positive way to wrap up my day. And such a positive way to maintain my own brand of faith.

I still consider myself very spiritual, but I may need a little direction. Perhaps I should study some Eastern philosophies. I want to talk to Mom, but I'm very scared to have a relationship with her again. She's always part of my life, but can she participate? On the few occasions I've said her name in an effort to talk to her — even only in my head — it comes out just like I say God's name. A question.

"Mom?"

AS I PURSUED my master's degree and my new job, I increasingly withdrew into myself. I sought solitude constantly. When I was at work, I thought all day of going home and being alone. Frequently, I spent entire weekends by myself from Friday night to Monday morning, not even speaking to another person. I still didn't answer the phone and I rarely made calls. I wasn't lonely. In fact, I wrote and studied a lot and enjoyed the solitude immensely.

Men asked me on dates and I would go, even enjoyed myself with some. But the instant a guy threatened my alone time, I jettisoned him. Mr. Right could have landed on my doorstep with a dozen roses, and I probably would have wrinkled my nose, responding, "Bad timing, hon," and shut the door. I enjoyed dating; I feared losing my space.

Jason, on the other hand, had fallen madly in love with a bright, gorgeous girl named Melinda. They met in school and she had the academic discipline to not only motivate him, but to help him set his sights much higher than he might have on his own. He possessed the sensitivity and honesty that she was unable to get from her family. They were perfect together.

Jason and I talked about Mom and we both admitted missing her, but he said he just didn't have time for it.

"I want to go to Hermit Lake," he said one day on the phone. "But I want to go when all this bullshit is over."

"School?" I asked.

"Yeah," he said. "I want to go alone for a long weekend. I want to feel it, Jana."

His voice sounded like a plea.

"I want to feel close to her, and I don't now. But I want time. I want to cry and sleep and talk to her, and I just can't do that now."

"The recovery time takes forever, huh?" I said.

"Yes! It's like I'm down for weeks when it gets me. I can't afford that now. But I will. My plan is to do it when I'm out of grad school."

I was impressed that he'd given it so much thought. And he had decided how to let her be part of his life again. The timing seemed so far away from that moment, but I respected his needs. I also intuitively knew Mom would wait. Personally, I tried to keep myself away from those emotions. I had decided that missing her felt stagnant. I longed for growth with her; I wanted her friendship. But without her presence, I believed such a relationship was impossible. Despite my rigid defenses, though, the pain and loss still snuck in, and they shocked and angered me.

SATURDAY, JANUARY 27, 1996

Goddam this fucking pain! It's been two and a half years! I can't keep doing this! I was sweeping my kitchen floor! That's it! Having a great Sunday afternoon. I made Grandma's whole wheat bread and some soup. I'm reading a fun book. It was a good day! Then, as I was sweeping, the Wynnona Judd CD played "All That Love From Here."

It spoke to me. She sang exactly what I felt.

I heard those words and suddenly I knew I was going to cry. I didn't want to. Usually I can stop it. But I just sat down right there with the broom, leaned on the fridge and sobbed, and I couldn't stop. The song ended and some annoying fast song came on. I went to the living room and replayed the song, laid down on my back on the floor spread eagle and kept crying.

Why did it all happen? Why is she gone? It wasn't supposed to be like this! I know it. She wasn't supposed to hurt. I'm not supposed to live without her. Jason should be able to go home to do his laundry like most college kids.

Every injustice I felt stampeded through my mind, great and small. They all hurt. And now I'm pissed at the pain. What good is it? What good is it!

It would be easier to never think of her. To never be with her.

IN THAT FRAME of mind, I lived my life through 1996. Basically, I thought solitude was serenity.

Serenity

CHAPTER 5

Jana?" Jason said on the phone. It was December 1996 and I was at work.

"Hey Bro!"

"I have big news," he said.

"What?" I put my reports down, turned my back to my door and looked out the window.

"I asked Melinda to marry me and she said yes."

His voice was calm and happy.

"Jason! That's so wonderful! Congratulations! I'm so happy for you both!"

"Thanks," he said, sounding so peaceful. "I have something else I'd like to ask you."

"OK," I said.

"Jana, I can't think of anyone I want up there with me but my best friend, and that's you. Would you be my best man?"

He giggled and I cried.

"Jason, that's the most beautiful thing you've ever said to me."

"Don't I know it," he said.

"I would be honored," I said. "Hey! Can I wear a tux?"

"Oh, no, I don't think Melinda would go for that."

"OK, worth a shot, though. When?"

"March. Before we go to school in Philly," he said.

As the date approached, I drove to Colorado Springs for dress fittings. Melinda's Mom made all the dresses. Melinda's sister, Christina, would be Mel's maid of honor. They planned a very small wedding — immediate family and a few friends. Despite that, the stress of school and wedding plans led them to joke about elopement. Both of them hated the idea of fanfare; they just wanted to be married and get on with their lives together.

"Jason?" I asked one day as we shared lunch while Melinda was at work. "How upset are you that Mom can't be here for your wedding?"

"Not at all," he said quickly. "She'll be there. I'm sure of it."

I took a deep breath. In many ways, he was so much more at peace than I.

March 24, 1997 arrived and moved swiftly and gracefully, just as Jason and Melinda hoped. She looked like a tiny angel and Jason looked so grown-up. I was mesmerized by the man he'd become — so responsible, so loving, so loved. I was proud.

The reception was held at Melinda's parents' house, up on a hill with a mountain view. Daddy and his wonderful wife, Nancy, drove from the wedding to the reception with Chuckles and Aunt Margie. My family was together and I was so very happy.

At the reception, I gathered Jason's friends and handed them shaving creme, aluminum cans, string and condoms. They didn't know, though, that Jason and I had already designed a wicked plot. Instead of pointing them to my truck, in which I was going to drive Mel and Jason to the airport, I pointed at Daddy's rental car.

"Jason and Mel are returning it for Daddy, and I'm taking Daddy and Nancy to Denver with me," I lied.

With the gusto of lifelong pals, five of Jason's friends went to work on Daddy's rental. Jason and I had reasoned that we never got to decorate Daddy's car when he married Nancy, so this was only fair. Besides, I didn't want all that crap on my truck.

While they worked on the car, I worked the living room, trying to keep Daddy inside. Inevitably, I was asked the obligatory questions:

"How does it feel to have your baby brother married before you?" "How old are you?" "Well, aren't you dating anyone?"

Admittedly, it made me wonder and I felt lonely. For the first time in a long time, I thought that maybe it would be nice to be in a real relationship. It had been nearly four years since Mom's death. At the same time, I couldn't imagine fitting that into my life. I was so used to being alone that companionship on any level felt like a nuisance at best, an invasion at worst.

When it was time for the newlyweds to leave, they said their goodbyes inside and the three of us raced out the door ahead of everyone else. We moved right to my truck and jumped in. The reactions were hysterical. The guys first acted confused and then, one by one, yelled, "Hey! Wait a minute." But Daddy's reaction was classic. He had forgotten what his rental looked like, so he waved goodbye like a proud father. When he saw that a car had been decorated, he looked at Jason's pals like, "You morons. Wrong car." His hand still waved. Then Nancy said, "Uh, Patrick," and his hand lowered as the realization rose.

"Jason Paul Chmel!"

And we drove off, imagining the guys explaining to Daddy that they had no idea.

IN THE SUMMER of 1997, around my 29th birthday and four years after Mom's death, my life started to change again. Or, better stated, I changed my life again. I began recognizing traits about my life that I wanted to change, namely, my solitary existence.

THURSDAY, JUNE 5, 1997

I'm discovering something about myself that I don't really like. Actually, I've recognized it for a while, but have thought it was an OK "trait." Now, I realize that it's getting worse or I'm taking it to extremes.

I stopped answering the phone when Mom got sick. I

haven't answered the phone now in almost four years! Originally, I stopped because I couldn't handle talking about her illness over and over. It progressed into feeling trapped every time I answered because people wanted to talk no matter what I might be in the middle of. I want to talk when I have the time or when I initiate it. Or, to use the words I've heard from several people lately, "on my own terms." I guess I need to control other people's entrances and exits from my life. Wow! I've never put it that way before! Entrances and exits! I've always thought of it as not wanting to drop everything simply because the phone rings, but controlling other people's comings and goings in my life feels more accurate. (Or am I believing all my recent bad press?)

OK, it's not just the phone. Though, I have gotten to where I'm actually afraid to answer the phone without screening. It makes me nervous. I fear being trapped! I'm a phone-o-phobe! I also control my relationships in other ways.

Climax: Aunt Margie and I had a battle. She made some valid points; things I'd heard from other people, too. I'm a good friend as long as it fits my agenda, whether that be time, space, financial, whatever. I apparently don't even hear that others need me or want me if I'm too wrapped up in what I want. I very readily keep people at arms' length until I carve out a moment when they will "fit."

Where does this come from? I do think I fear closeness. I didn't put 2 and 2 together until recently, but I've acted like this mostly since Mom died. I crave closeness but once it presents itself, I mistrust it, push it away, try to box it up to "fit" at the proper times and to shelve it when I want to be alone — which tends to be more often than not. I mistrust it. I literally feel edgy when others present themselves to me and say, "Here I am!" My first instinct is to respond, "I'm busy." I choose the safety of self over the risk of giving others any chance of impacting my life beyond my control. It's like I set up big boundaries and say, "Up to this point, you can impact my life.

However, you'll never get past there." I have defined areas of acceptance and dark, shadowy nooks, which no one ever explores. I don't even allow myself in there sometimes. Many times. That's all about Mom.

I think much of this is about Mom. It's like I crave someone who understands that huge absence but I won't let them understand the whole parts first. I get impatient very quickly when a person seems ignorant of how huge Mom's illness and death affected me, but I won't display the parts that survived quite nicely. So, they never even think it's worth the effort. I'm like an open wound looking for the next person to be salt. I assume inevitable pain. I assume loss. I assume superficiality. All, self-fulfilling prophecies.

How can I stop this pattern? How do I allow others in? How do I live beyond Mom? How do I accept Mom's death? How do I relinquish control and give new parts of myself?

THESE REVELATIONS HIT like a crisis, but I also understood that the space I had carved out for myself had been necessary. I had required solitude to find an inner source of strength all my own. It seemed the time had come to finally reach out and let others back into my life. Including Mom.

And the timing couldn't have been better. In the span of two months, July and August 1997, I was promoted to director of my department, graduated with my master's degree, and bought a house. My life was a spinning top. However, experiences like this led me to believe that there were no such thing as coincidences.

I felt like I had worked hard to find meaning in my life and it appeared that some things were finally coming to fruition. I felt a giant sense of accomplishment both professionally and spiritually. I'd had faith and trust in my journey and parts of it were panning out. I also had some relationships to heal. I needed to learn how to let others back in.

WEDNESDAY, JULY 30, 1997

Well, my life seems to be really good! Which has me scared shitless. Why can't I just enjoy it? I feel like I should be committed. My job is great, I'm doing some good writing, I'll graduate in a couple of weeks, I bought a great town home, my family is healthy. So why am I continually looking over my shoulder for the Grim Reaper? I feel like all these precious, fragile elements are sitting on a glass table and there's a boulder dangling by a mere thread only feet above. God, it's an unnerving way to live! When I can ignore those premonitions, though, I realize how awesome life is and even if that boulder fell I'd still have pretty sunsets, blue skies, and good friends. When I attempt that balance, I feel a lot better. Maintaining it is another issue.

But look at this list:

1) graduating
2) bought a home
3) moved
4) have a new job
5) working on a book about Mom

There can be no coincidence at work here. All of these things are happening now for a reason. That's why I have to write. What have I done to come to this? What have others done for me? What could possibly be next?

Before I start picking it apart and analyzing it, I need to express how it feels. I have so much gratitude and joy. But the overwhelming feeling is a peaceful, content one. Ohhhh, is it serenity? My book is titled, "Grant Me Serenity." As astounding (and busy busy busy) as these events are, I find that I'm not surprised. In fact, it's like watching a ball moving in slow motion for two years and finally catching it. I knew it was coming, I just needed to be patient (and move up on it a little!) The cool thing is that I threw this ball to myself over two

> *years ago and I've been moving at high speed throughout its trajectory, back and forth, clearing the way like a running back (is that the right position?) and I am now letting it land solidly in my glove.*
>
> *Yes, I'm proud of myself. I worked damn hard for all of these events and accomplishments. I want to share this all with Mom, and I think I'll soon open up to that possibility, too.*

ONE DAY, ALL alone in my new home, I began an endeavor I had dreaded the moment I knew I was buying a home. Upstairs, in my new spare bedroom, I'd piled boxes of things that had been packed the week after Mom's death. I imagined four-year-old newspaper cradling mementos I'd pushed from my memory. I wanted to open the boxes and search the contents, but I feared the memories. Something inside me felt strong, though, and I said aloud in the room, "It's time."

I decided to start easy and opened one of the many boxes titled, "Mom's books." The boxes of pictures would have to wait.

The first book on top of the first box was, "The Joy of Sex!" I laughed right out loud before I even touched it.

"Mom! You wild woman, you!" Later, I discovered that she owned two editions and I mused, briefly, about her relationship with Chuck. I smiled with quiet pride at learning a little about Mom's private life — a life I was sure she would have shared with me.

I also found several books by and about Carl Jung. I hadn't known she studied his work. I held one out of the bookshelf I was filling, thinking it might be interesting to read.

As I pulled out more books and opened more boxes, I discovered all sorts of things about Mom. She enjoyed anything by C.S. Lewis. She owned what appeared to be every AA-related book ever published. I found books on wild flowers, and books on men (Robert Bly's "Iron John," and Sam Keen's "Fire in the Belly"). She read history, biographies, Eastern philosophers, and had apparently read everything by Dr. Bernie Siegal before she ever got sick. I found two editions of "Sonnets from the Portuguese," and "Walden." She owned several Time/Life "Fix-It-Yourself" manuals, books on knitting and gardening ("How to Prune Almost Everything"), and M. Scott Peck's "The Road Less Traveled." She read "The Feminine Face of God," and "Megatrends."

I was astounded by the breadth of her interests. I was surprised and warmed by the fact that many of her interests matched mine.

Then I discovered the insides of the books. Mom wrote all over her books just like I do. Inside "The Road Less Traveled," I found not only notes in the margin, but pages of her handwriting ripped from a note pad. She wrote things like:

Sanity has been oversold — there's a very healthy part of you that wants to be crazy — think of what eccentrics have taught you.

> *Don't postpone happiness 'til you've got it all together; it ain't gonna happen that way.*
>
> *Love is the commitment of my will to your well-being, regardless of how I feel about it.*
>
> *Sin is choosing not to see (denial, etc.)*
>
> *Successful living is forming a partnership with God. It's very important for some of us to remember who the senior partner is — sending God on errands, etc.*
>
> *Embrace the pain, go toward the pain, hug it, suck on it — it's trying to tell you something.*
>
> *Label feelings that overwhelm you. "I'm having a shame attack."*
>
> *Lying to yourself is a form of medication. We live in a make-the-pain-go-away society.*
>
> *Not everything worth doing is worth doing well! Deliberately do a half-assed job of some things! Ah, freedom!*
>
> *We've got to admit that we were lied to. Life is not fair.*

I studied her handwriting. It gripped me like a voice from the past. I could hear her voice through her written words and I soaked it in. I sucked on it. I felt her presence so strongly with me at that moment that I felt hugged. I imagined her on the floor with me, rocking me in her arms. For the first time since her death, I felt her presence, and I loved it.

Then, just when I felt like I might cry, I picked up, "The Four Loves," by C. S. Lewis. I remembered that Mom had given it to me years earlier, but I'd set it aside and left it at her house. In my overwhelmed state, I opened the cover, then burst out laughing as I read, "Dear Janalee, If God had given your mother a chance to go to bed with this author, she'd have taken it," and she signed it, "A loving friend, 2-8-89."

I hugged the two books to me and through smiles, I cried. And I spoke out loud.

"Mom, I feel you. God, you were extraordinary. I bet there has never been a mom like you ever."

I cried and let myself feel her. I gazed over her books and breathed her energy. Suddenly, I realized that I could still confide in her. I could grow with her. I had, still, a life to share with her. In my heart, she had just left that stagnant death and she'd gained depth beyond who I knew her to be when I was 25 years old, when she died.

I looked at the inscription to me again and I felt like she was speaking to me. She wrote that right before I turned 21. She knew I was becoming a woman. She had known it would happen and she had let me grow up. And she was still part of the process. She was still my mother.

Hours later, into darkness, I completed shelving the books. In a relatively short time, Mom had revealed herself to me in more mature ways than I could have imagined only hours earlier. I drew her closer to me as I recognized the value of her proximity, her presence, her companionship.

"And I thought those would be the easy boxes," I said aloud. I said it to Mom, and we shared a laugh.

Serenity

Chapter 6

Slowly, I became aware of how few deep relationships I had in my life. Ann and I were very close and I relied on her for all of my emotional needs. I wanted more interaction in my life, less solitude, less control. Still, I lacked grace. I stumbled and confused people.

My college buddy, Robin, called often and left messages for me. Many times, I never called back, but she called anyway. Finally, I'd pick up the phone and call. I'd get her machine, leave a message, and think, "I made an effort. She knows I tried," and let it go at that, as though our friendship could grow on such empty efforts. I was consistently inconsistent. I still tried to control people's entrances and exits. Gradually, though, I opened up, made surprise phone calls, suggested dinner plans, and tried to release control bit-by-bit.

Not coincidentally, at that time, a friend recommended that I read anything by Natalie Goldberg. I picked up "Wild Mind: Living a Writer's Life."

SATURDAY, JANUARY 3, 1998

This is becoming a very reflective time for me. Not the time of day. This time in my life.

It is 5:30 a.m. and I've showered and am on my bed. I'm so glad to be reading Natalie Goldberg. Her thoughts are hitting me on many levels.

I seem to be trying to let go of this tight grip I maintain on my life while, at the same time, achieving balance. I am a control freak. I want to be in control of my physique, my heart, my image, my career, my space, my time. Natalie Goldberg talks about stepping into the wild mind. Leaving "the dot" in the sky where we live our lives and diving into the big, blue sky and puffy white clouds. Some call the sky our unconscious; the dot is our ego, our conscious. Natalie thinks "unconscious" is too narrow because that sky could be every experience or thing to which we open our lives.

I think I need help opening my life — jumping off the dot.

AT THE END of July 1998, I looked at the calendar. The five-year anniversary of Mom's death was August 5.

I reflected on my life. I felt like I was at a magnificent turning point. I'd turned 30. I was nearing completion on this book. I was slowly re-opening my life to family and friends.

SATURDAY, AUGUST 1, 1998

It seems to me that my healing, my life over the last five years, has been all about trust. I had to learn to trust the journey. I had to learn to trust myself. I had to learn to re-trust God and Mom. I am learning to lose control and trust friendships. I am learning to give and receive love again. All of this requires leaps of faith —faith in myself and my higher power. Close my eyes, reach out my hand for God's or Mom's grasp, and take the step into the unknown.

It reminds me of Natalie Goldberg's dot in the sky. I'm learning to step out of my safety zone, blind-folded. But I no longer feel alone. I am surrounded by love. Mom is with me. Everywhere. Always.

Have I found serenity? I'm smiling at that question. It seems such a simple question for such a complex answer. Basically, for me, serenity's essence lies in a trust and a faith that my courage and wisdom will deliver me through pain, and present me with joy. I no longer expect that life will be completely safe, the way Mom's hugs made me feel, but I trust that its rewards will be magnificent.

I think I need to do something symbolic of this time in my life. I need to mark this moment.

MY FRIENDS WERE shocked at the event I chose to recognize the five-year anniversary and to recognize my feelings of personal accomplishment in that time. I wanted to take a real leap; I wanted to release all control.

I decided to jump out of a plane.

On Saturday, August 15, I collected my closest friends and headed to Mile High Skydiving. I was fitted with a blue jumpsuit, and watched as a guy with as many earrings in his ears as I stored in my jewelry box, packed my chute. But my only feeling was an excited, adrenaline-rushed anticipation. I followed my tandem instructor to the plane, ran quickly back to hug my friends, then boarded the plane.

The flight to 12,000 feet went quickly.

"Why are you doing this?" my instructor, Billy, asked.

I felt proud, so I responded candidly.

"Because my mom died five years ago and I'm finally ready to let go of the pain and let her back into my life. She's jumping with me."

"Good reason," he said.

Before I knew it, the other jumpers on the plane were throwing themselves out the door and we kept scooting closer to the front of the line. Suddenly, I was looking down on the earth, 12,000 feet below. The mountains were far to my right and the brown landscape directly underneath us looked fuzzy with the distance. I could feel the wind whipping past the window and I had a sudden, funny thought of Dorothy looking out her window during the hurricane, wondering if a cow would go flying by.

Billy yelled, "Ready?"

I screamed, "Ready!" and I released my hand from the plane, grabbed Mom's hand, and jumped.

I didn't feel like I was falling. I felt like air was being pushed past me at 120 miles-per-hour. I heard the air and I felt the pressure, and I looked around in awe at the earth below me. The brown earth. The green mountains. Everything looked tiny, fragile, expansive. I felt like a speck of dust, bouncing on breezes, descending to my home. I had never looked at nature from this perspective. Airplane windows I'd gazed through had blocked joy. The joy of participation.

Spread-eagle, lying on the wind, I felt like I was part of nature. Not like a bird. More like a sunbeam breaking through thick clouds, with my energy shining up to the heavens and down to the earth.

Still in free-fall, I looked down to my right and saw a rainbow near the mountains. I pointed at it ecstatically and tried to shout "Rainbow!" but as soon as my mouth opened, my stomach filled up with air. So, I got down to the business of playing in the sky. We pulled the chute after free-falling 7,000 feet, then I hung like a star, twirling in circles. I screamed and laughed in joy. My legs dangled below me right out of my pelvis. I felt like I was in one of those baby carriers that hang on a parent's back. I kicked my legs back and forth while my head spun left and right.

We landed softly just outside the pit, and I ran to my friends. I felt a freedom I'd never felt before in my life and I'd shared it with the most important people in my life — my friends and Mom.

"Did you see it?!" I exclaimed. "Did you see the rainbow?"

None of them had, which made me smile like a little girl with a secret. We went back to my house to watch the video. I sat on the couch eagerly, my hands clasped in my lap tightly. We hit "play" and we heard music from the movie "Top Gun." I watched myself. Suited up in a blue jumpsuit. Marching off to the small plane and waving as I boarded. Listening to my instructor on the plane. Putting a funny rubber beanie and goggles on my head. Scooting toward the door. Standing in the doorway looking down to the earth 12,000 feet below. My mouth moved to the word "Ready!" and we jumped!

On the couch, I couldn't control myself.

"That's me! Look at me!" I shouted as I stood slightly from the couch, pointing. I watched my arms spread out and my head kept looking back and forth. I was smiling! Big!

And then I watched myself as my hand pointed below me, and my mouth moved to the word "Rainbow!"

My friends in the living room said, "There it is! There's the rainbow!"

I sat back on the couch and took a deep, peaceful breath. My own, private rainbow, I thought. Mine and Mom's.

My Mamma taught me how to stand alone.

She let me go but she still holds on,

And I can still feel all of that love from here.

— Wynonna Judd

Janalee Card Chmel earned a master's degree in creative writing from the University of Denver. She and her husband, Dave, live with Frank the Dog in Colorado, where Janalee works as a freelance writer.

When Janalee needs to chat with her mom, she drives into the hills (the Rocky Mountains) and sits on a rock in the sun … and they chat.

For additional copies of this book,
orders@WriterRadar.com

Readers respond ...

"Having lost my mother to cancer in 1998, Janalee Chmel's story tugged relentlessly on painful memories and excavated a reservoir of love and longing I thought I had locked away forever. This book provides a survivor's roadmap to a journey we all must travel sometime during this life. Janalee opens her heart and psyche for all to witness... from this panoramic view, important revelations about truth, love, life and death come into focus in ways you never imagined. This book is a must-read if you love anyone dearly, and for anyone who loves you."

Michael Koenig

"Those who provide care to a loved one with a terminal condition will find much in common with the author's experience, helping them to realize that grief doesn't proceed stepwise in chronological order, but is rather an experience that is unique to each individual and family."

Larry Lewis, MS, RN